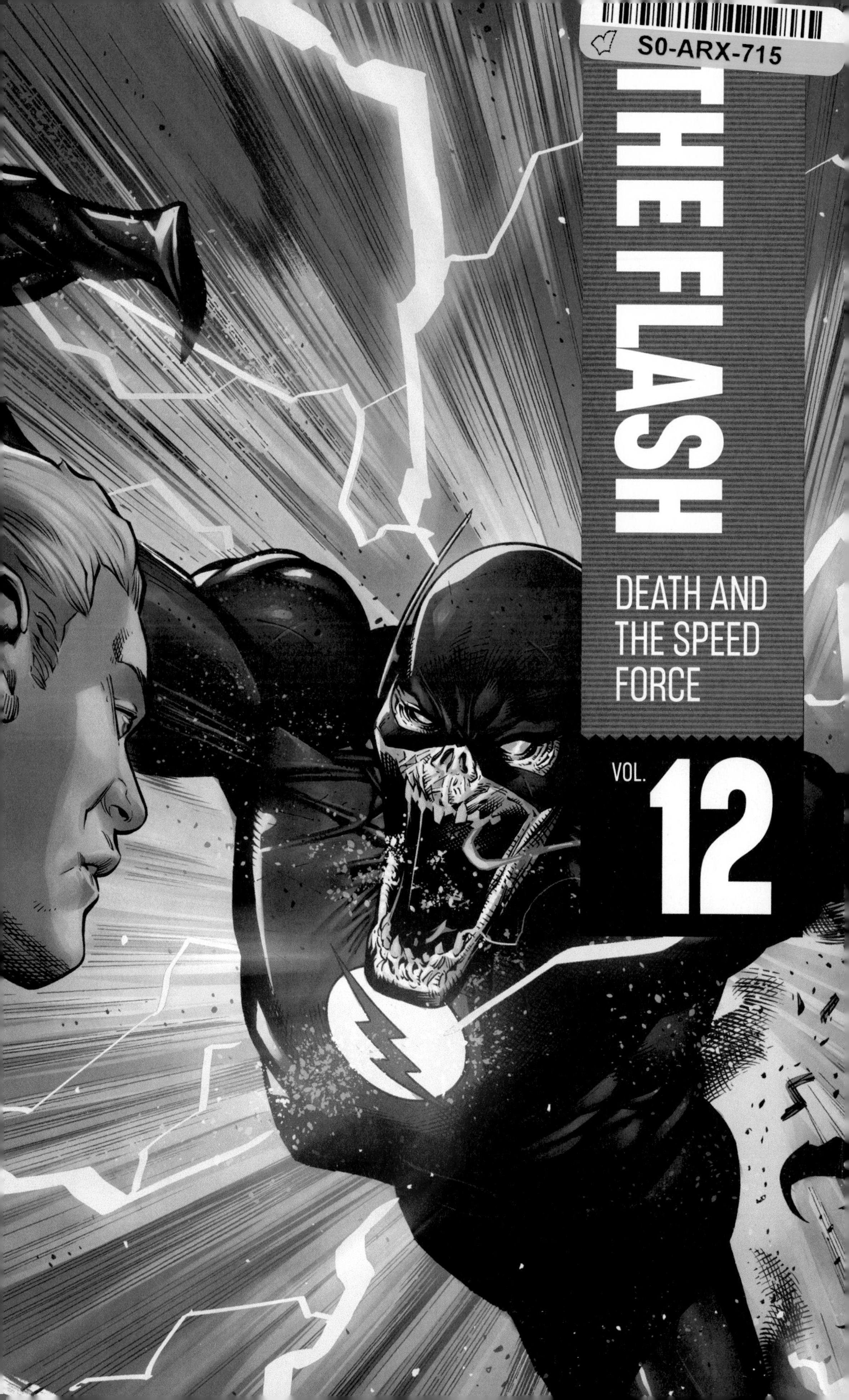
THE FLASH
DEATH AND THE SPEED FORCE
VOL. 12

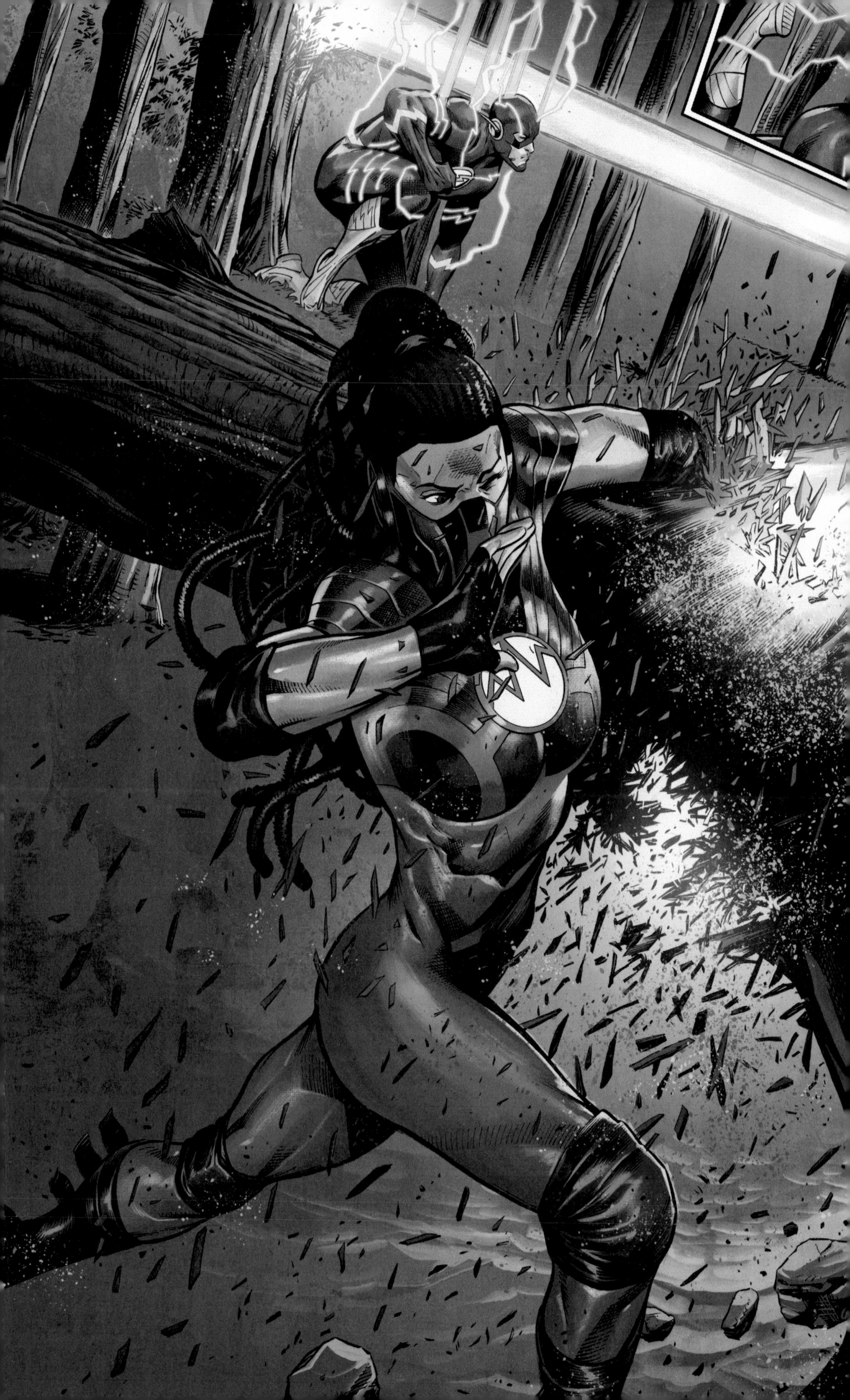

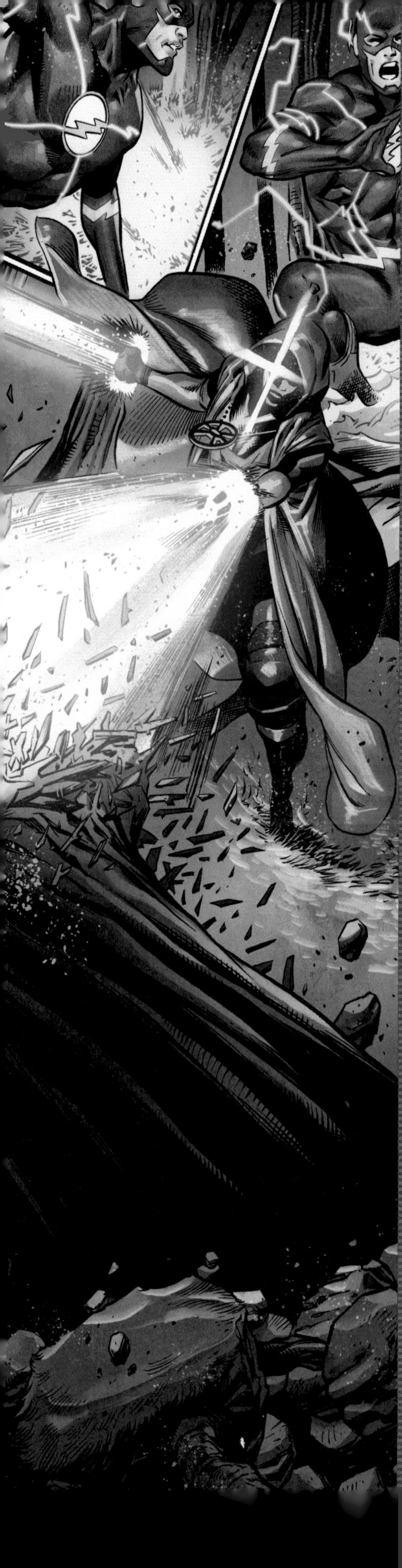

THE FLASH

DEATH AND THE SPEED FORCE

writer

JOSHUA WILLIAMSON

pencillers

RAFA SANDOVAL
SCOTT KOLINS

inkers

JORDI TARRAGONA
SCOTT KOLINS

colorists

TOMEU MOREY
ARIF PRIANTO
LUIS GUERRERO

letterer

STEVE WANDS

collection cover artists

RAFA SANDOVAL,
JORDI TARRAGONA,
and TOMEU MOREY

VOL. **12**

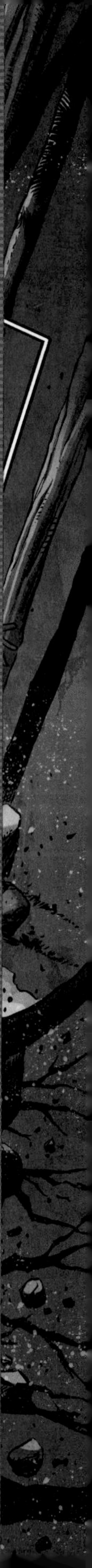

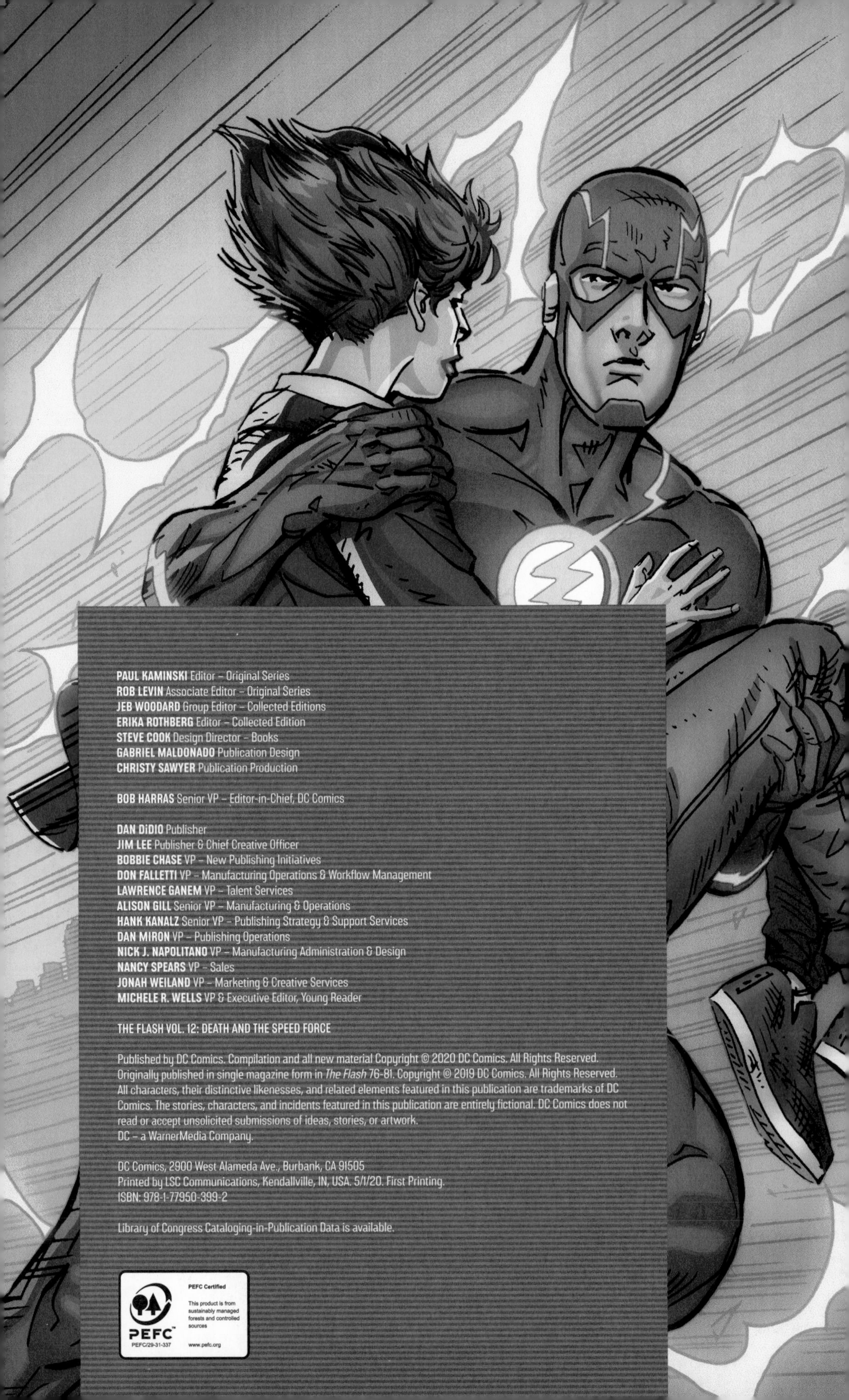

PAUL KAMINSKI Editor – Original Series
ROB LEVIN Associate Editor – Original Series
JEB WOODARD Group Editor – Collected Editions
ERIKA ROTHBERG Editor – Collected Edition
STEVE COOK Design Director – Books
GABRIEL MALDONADO Publication Design
CHRISTY SAWYER Publication Production

BOB HARRAS Senior VP – Editor-in-Chief, DC Comics

DAN DiDIO Publisher
JIM LEE Publisher & Chief Creative Officer
BOBBIE CHASE VP – New Publishing Initiatives
DON FALLETTI VP – Manufacturing Operations & Workflow Management
LAWRENCE GANEM VP – Talent Services
ALISON GILL Senior VP – Manufacturing & Operations
HANK KANALZ Senior VP – Publishing Strategy & Support Services
DAN MIRON VP – Publishing Operations
NICK J. NAPOLITANO VP – Manufacturing Administration & Design
NANCY SPEARS VP – Sales
JONAH WEILAND VP – Marketing & Creative Services
MICHELE R. WELLS VP & Executive Editor, Young Reader

THE FLASH VOL. 12: DEATH AND THE SPEED FORCE

DC Comics, 2900 West Alameda Ave., Burbank, CA 91505
Printed by LSC Communications, Kendallville, IN, USA. 5/1/20. First Printing.
ISBN: 978-1-77950-399-2

Library of Congress Cataloging-in-Publication Data is available.

PEFC Certified
This product is from sustainably managed forests and controlled sources
PEFC/29-31-337
www.pefc.org

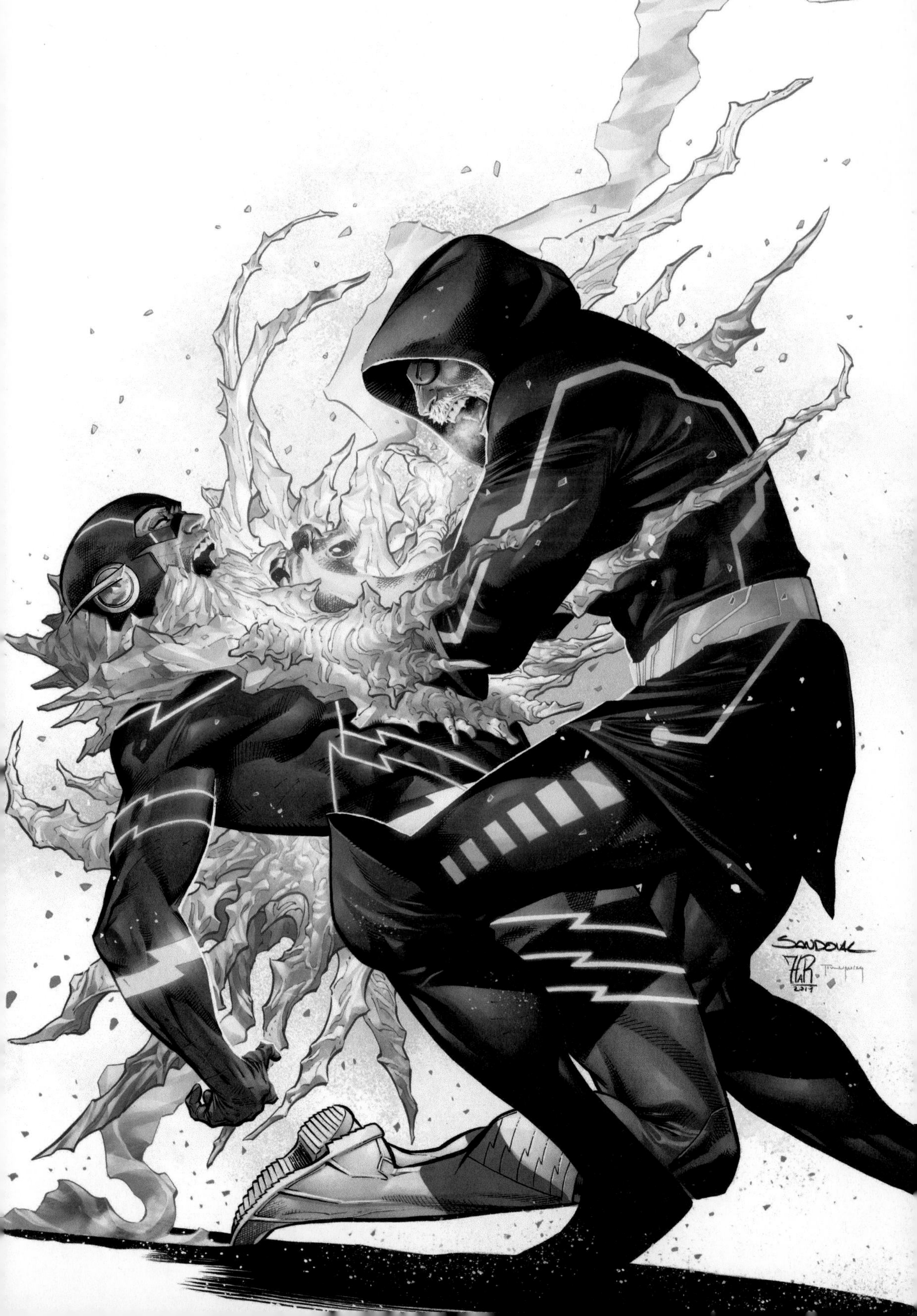
SANDOVAL

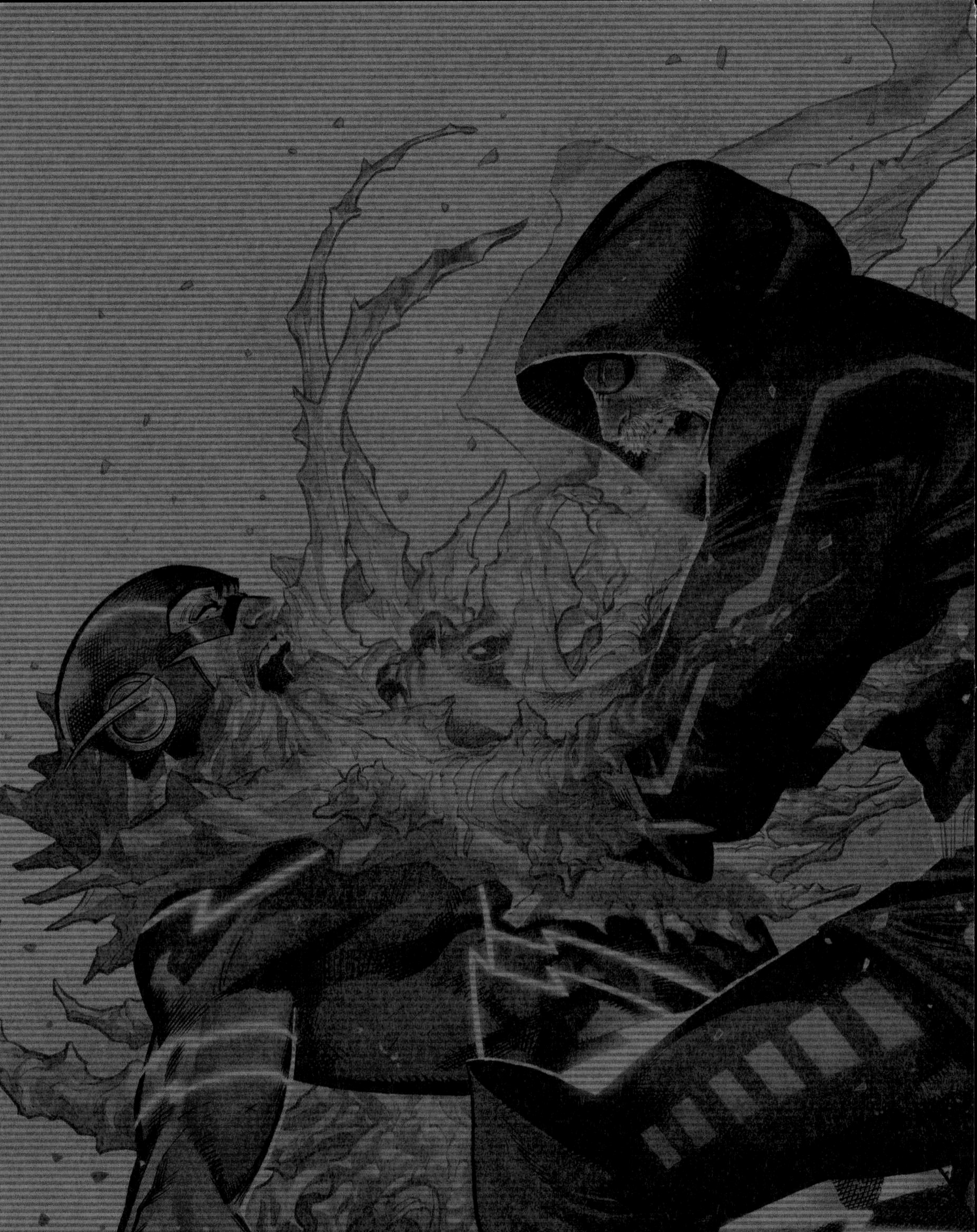

THE FLASH

#76

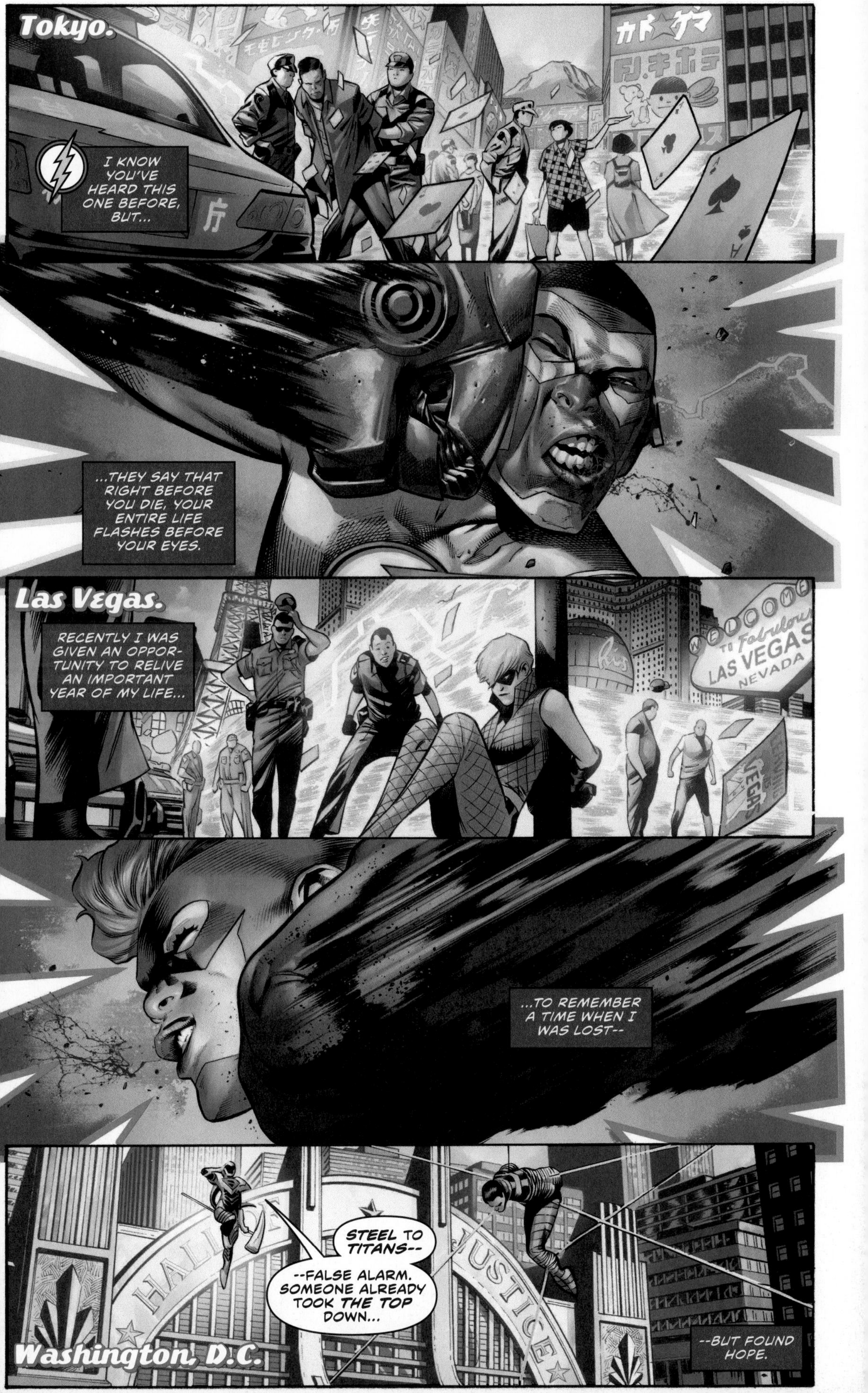
Tokyo.
I KNOW YOU'VE HEARD THIS ONE BEFORE, BUT...
...THEY SAY THAT RIGHT BEFORE YOU DIE, YOUR ENTIRE LIFE FLASHES BEFORE YOUR EYES.
Las Vegas.
RECENTLY I WAS GIVEN AN OPPOR-TUNITY TO RELIVE AN IMPORTANT YEAR OF MY LIFE...
WELCOME to Fabulous LAS VEGAS NEVADA
...TO REMEMBER A TIME WHEN I WAS LOST--
STEEL TO TITANS--
--FALSE ALARM. SOMEONE ALREADY TOOK THE TOP DOWN...
Washington, D.C.
--BUT FOUND HOPE.

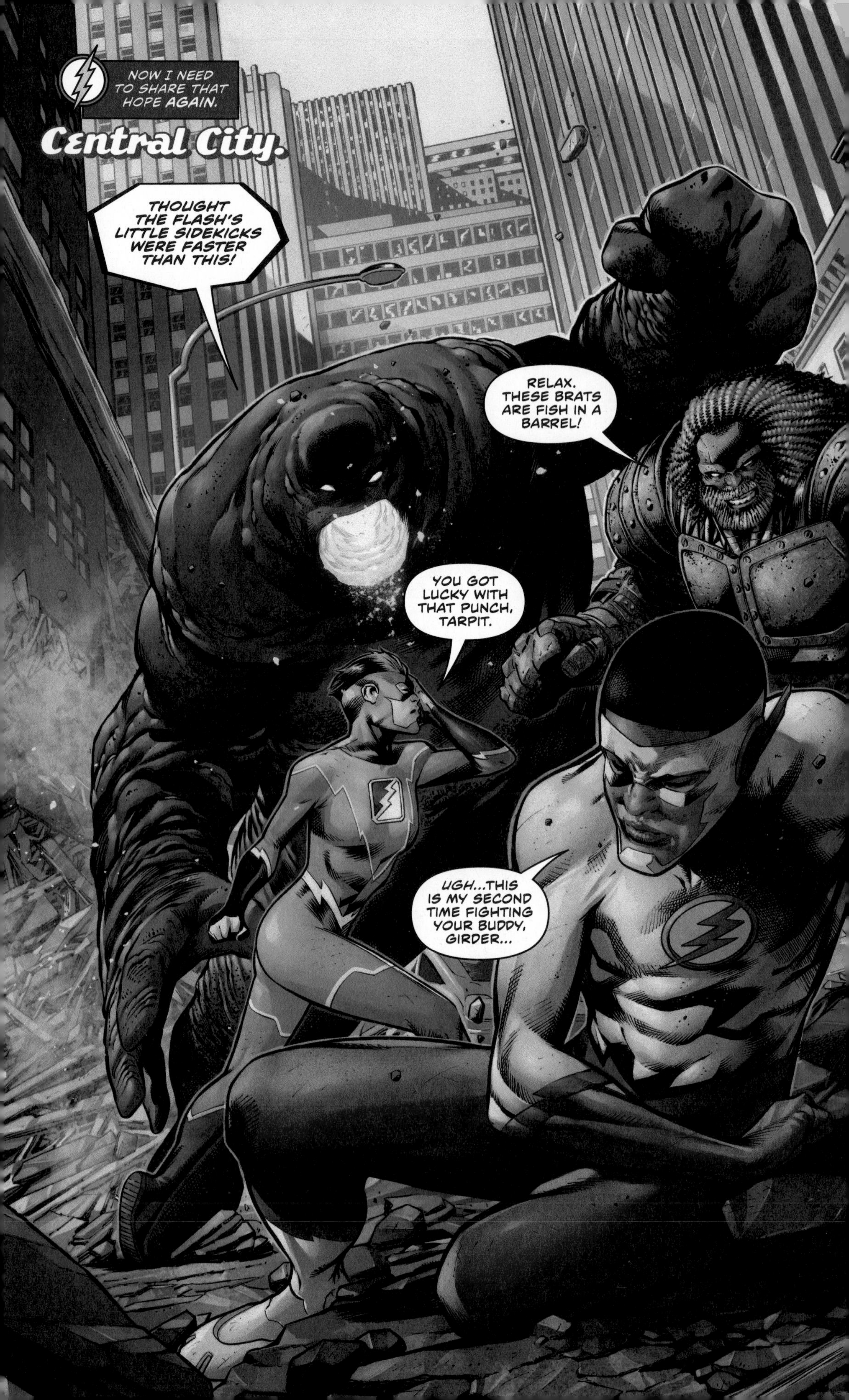
NOW I NEED TO SHARE THAT HOPE AGAIN.
Central City.
THOUGHT THE FLASH'S LITTLE SIDEKICKS WERE FASTER THAN THIS!
RELAX. THESE BRATS ARE FISH IN A BARREL!
YOU GOT LUCKY WITH THAT PUNCH, TARPIT.
UGH...THIS IS MY SECOND TIME FIGHTING YOUR BUDDY, GIRDER...

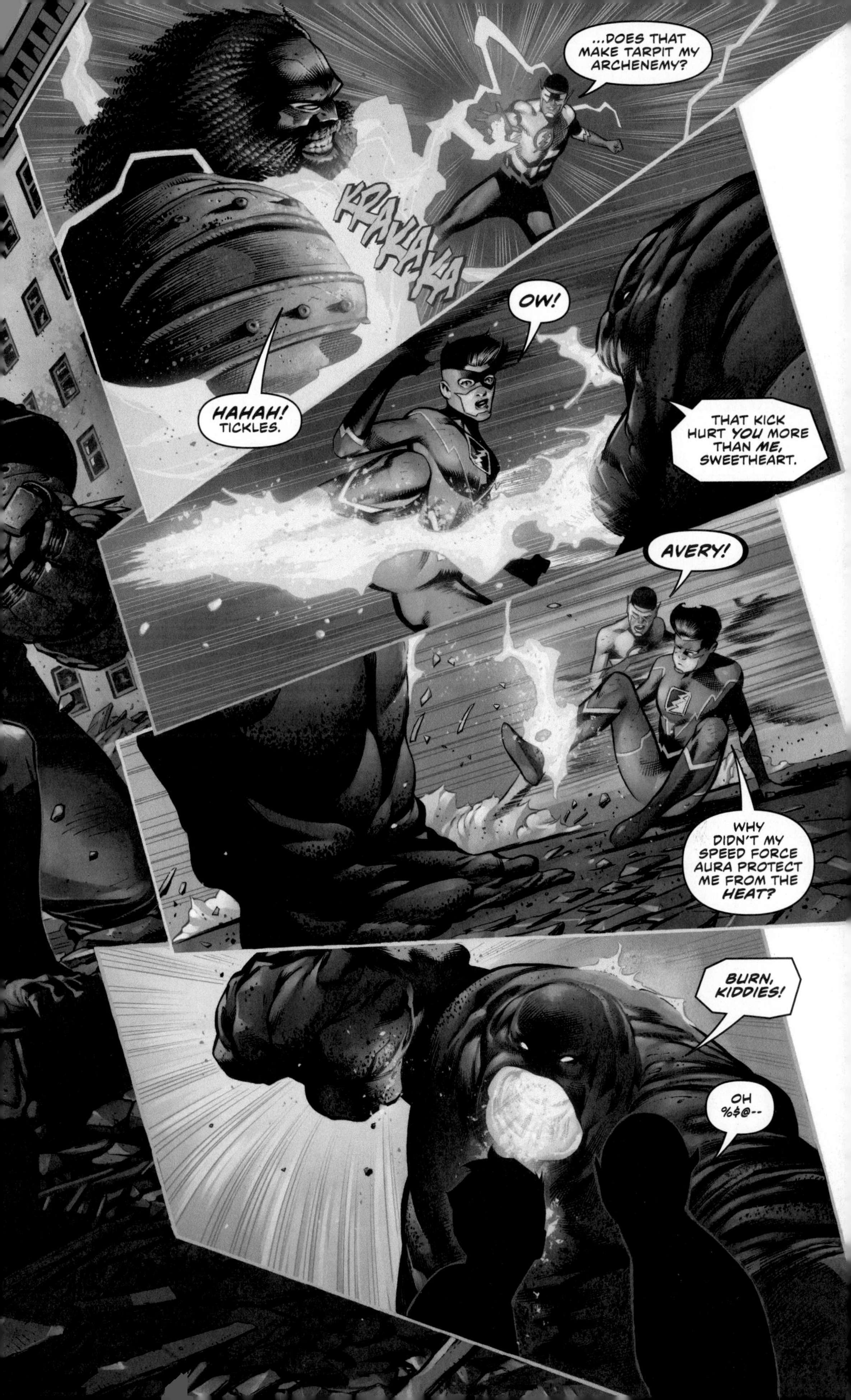
...DOES THAT MAKE TARPIT MY ARCHENEMY?
KRAKAKAKA
HAHAH! TICKLES.
OW!
THAT KICK HURT YOU MORE THAN ME, SWEETHEART.
AVERY!
WHY DIDN'T MY SPEED FORCE AURA PROTECT ME FROM THE HEAT?
BURN, KIDDIES!
OH %$@--

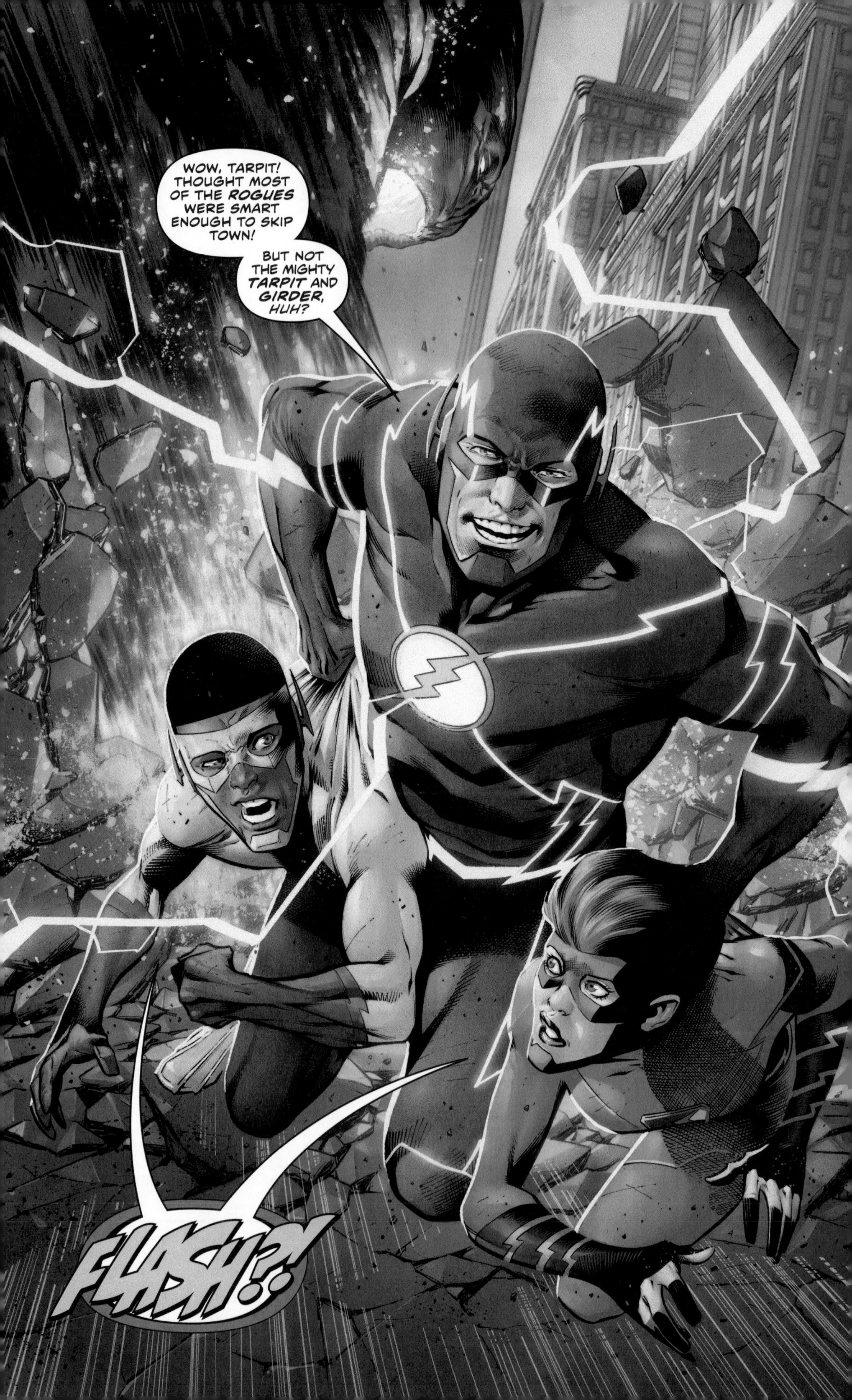
WOW, TARPIT! THOUGHT MOST OF THE ROGUES WERE SMART ENOUGH TO SKIP TOWN!
BUT NOT THE MIGHTY TARPIT AND GIRDER, HUH?
FLASH?!

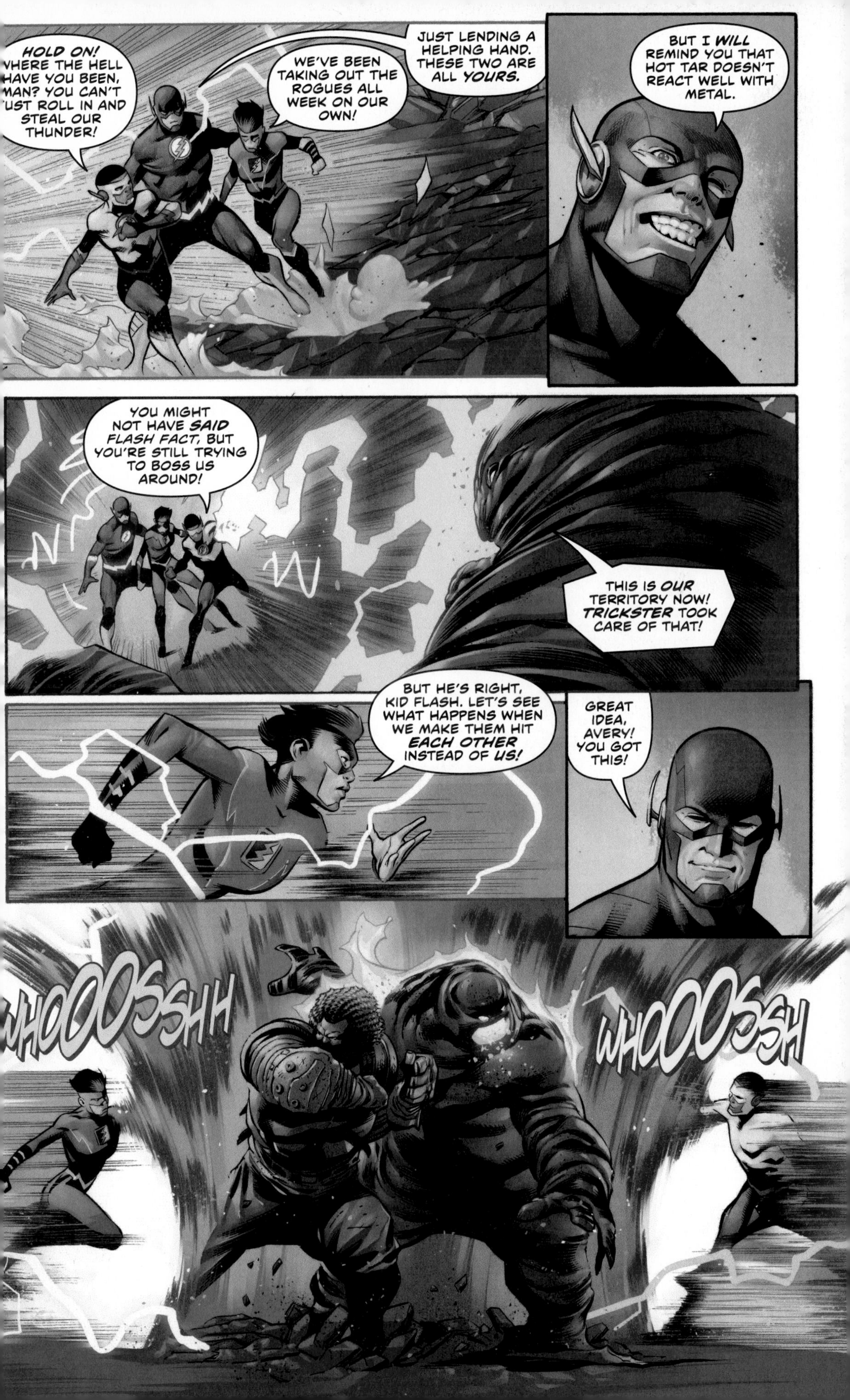

HOLD ON! WHERE THE HELL HAVE YOU BEEN, MAN? YOU CAN'T JUST ROLL IN AND STEAL OUR THUNDER!
WE'VE BEEN TAKING OUT THE ROGUES ALL WEEK ON OUR OWN!
JUST LENDING A HELPING HAND. THESE TWO ARE ALL YOURS.
BUT I WILL REMIND YOU THAT HOT TAR DOESN'T REACT WELL WITH METAL.
YOU MIGHT NOT HAVE SAID FLASH FACT, BUT YOU'RE STILL TRYING TO BOSS US AROUND!
THIS IS OUR TERRITORY NOW! TRICKSTER TOOK CARE OF THAT!
BUT HE'S RIGHT, KID FLASH. LET'S SEE WHAT HAPPENS WHEN WE MAKE THEM HIT EACH OTHER INSTEAD OF US!
GREAT IDEA, AVERY! YOU GOT THIS!
WHOOOSSHH
WHOOOSSH

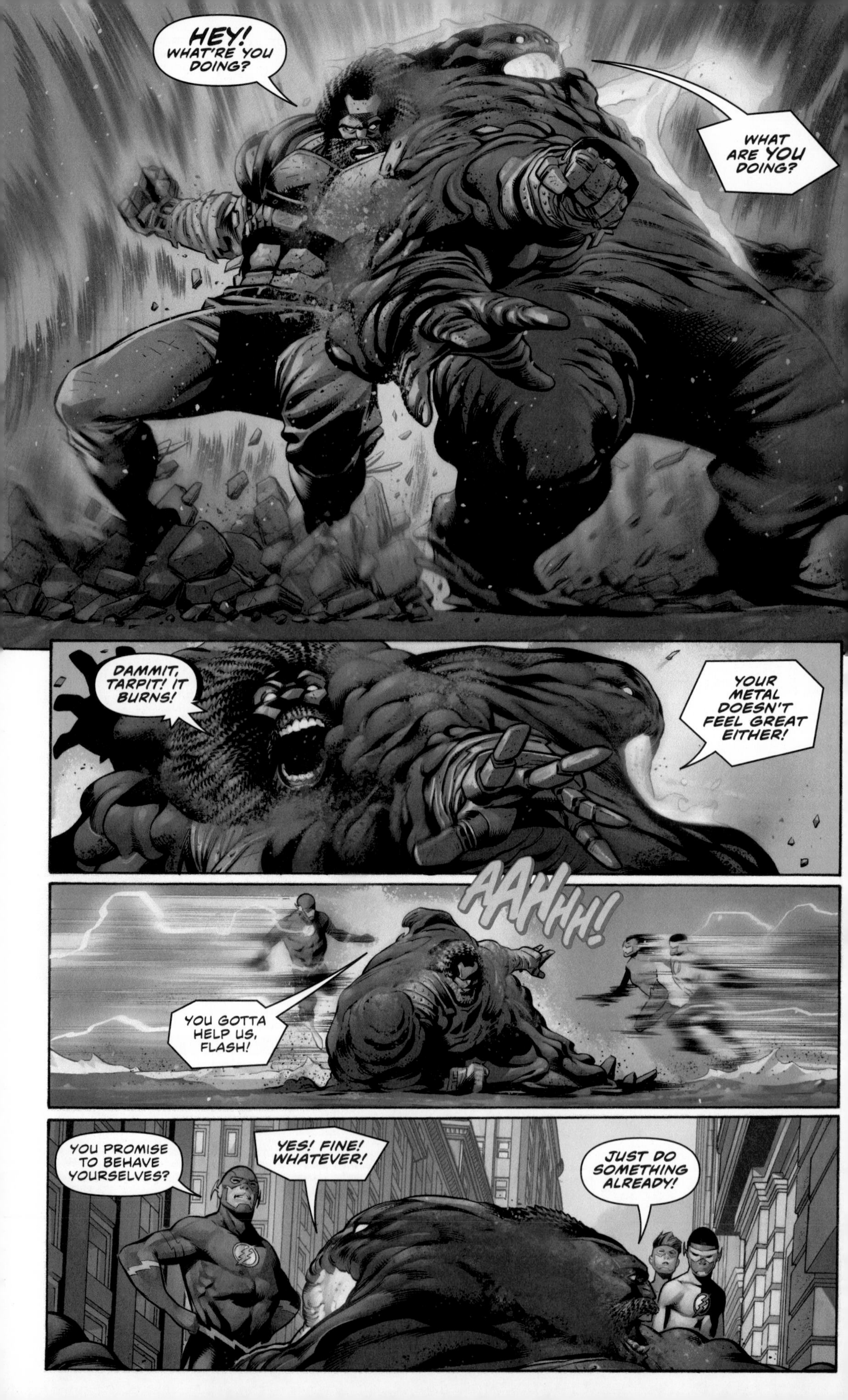
HEY! WHAT'RE YOU DOING?
WHAT ARE YOU DOING?
DAMMIT, TARPIT! IT BURNS!
YOUR METAL DOESN'T FEEL GREAT EITHER!
AAHHH!
YOU GOTTA HELP US, FLASH!
YOU PROMISE TO BEHAVE YOURSELVES?
YES! FINE! WHATEVER!
JUST DO SOMETHING ALREADY!

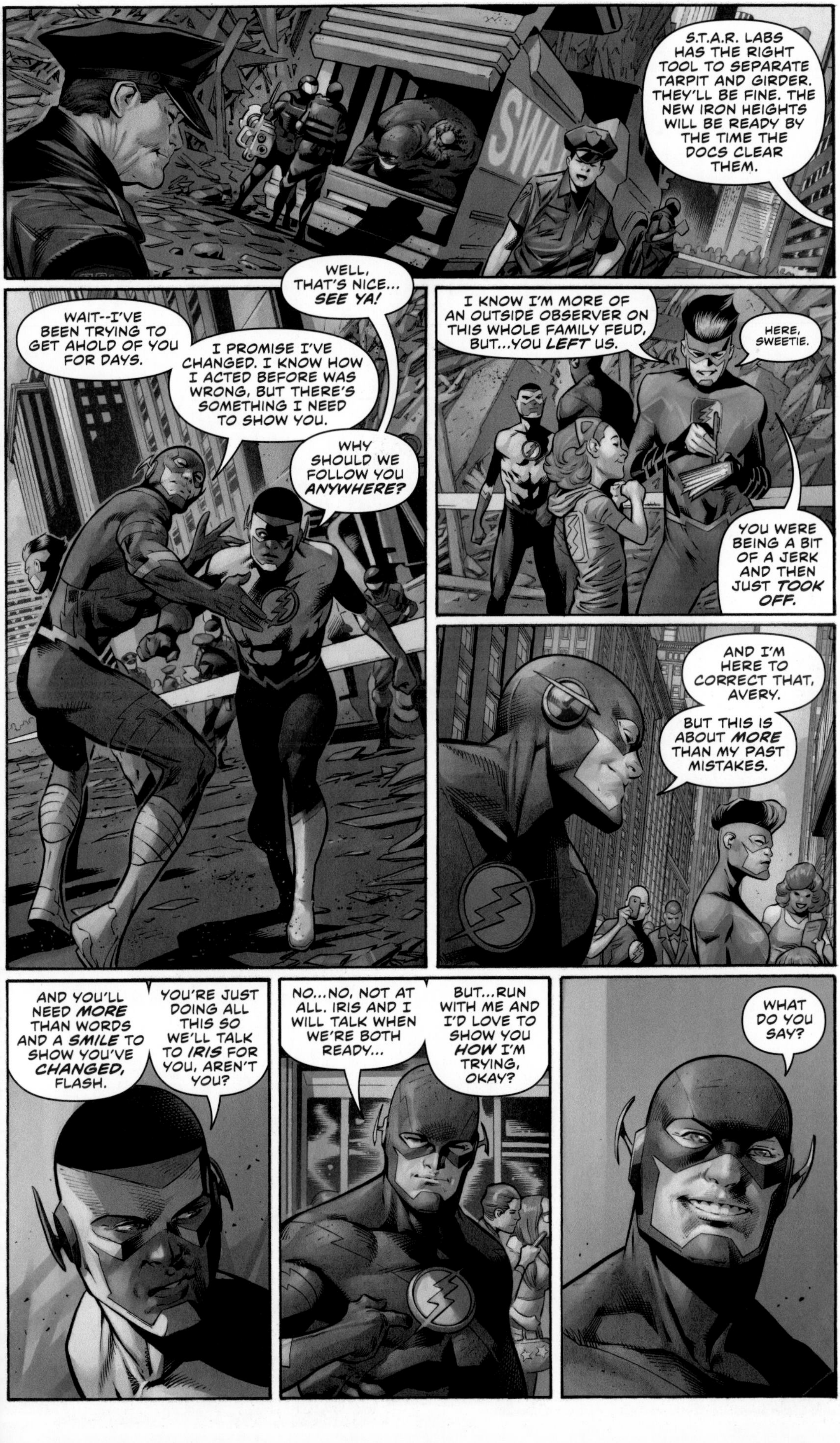
S.T.A.R. LABS HAS THE RIGHT TOOL TO SEPARATE TARPIT AND GIRDER. THEY'LL BE FINE. THE NEW IRON HEIGHTS WILL BE READY BY THE TIME THE DOCS CLEAR THEM.
SWAT
WAIT--I'VE BEEN TRYING TO GET AHOLD OF YOU FOR DAYS.
WELL, THAT'S NICE... *SEE YA!*
I PROMISE I'VE CHANGED. I KNOW HOW I ACTED BEFORE WAS WRONG, BUT THERE'S SOMETHING I NEED TO SHOW YOU.
WHY SHOULD WE FOLLOW YOU *ANYWHERE?*
I KNOW I'M MORE OF AN OUTSIDE OBSERVER ON THIS WHOLE FAMILY FEUD, BUT...YOU *LEFT* US.
HERE, SWEETIE.
YOU WERE BEING A BIT OF A JERK AND THEN JUST *TOOK OFF.*
AND I'M HERE TO CORRECT THAT, AVERY.
BUT THIS IS ABOUT *MORE* THAN MY PAST MISTAKES.
AND YOU'LL NEED *MORE* THAN WORDS AND A *SMILE* TO SHOW YOU'VE *CHANGED,* FLASH.
YOU'RE JUST DOING ALL THIS SO WE'LL TALK TO *IRIS* FOR YOU, AREN'T YOU?
NO...NO, NOT AT ALL. IRIS AND I WILL TALK WHEN WE'RE BOTH READY...
BUT...RUN WITH ME AND I'D LOVE TO SHOW YOU *HOW* I'M TRYING, OKAY?
WHAT DO YOU SAY?

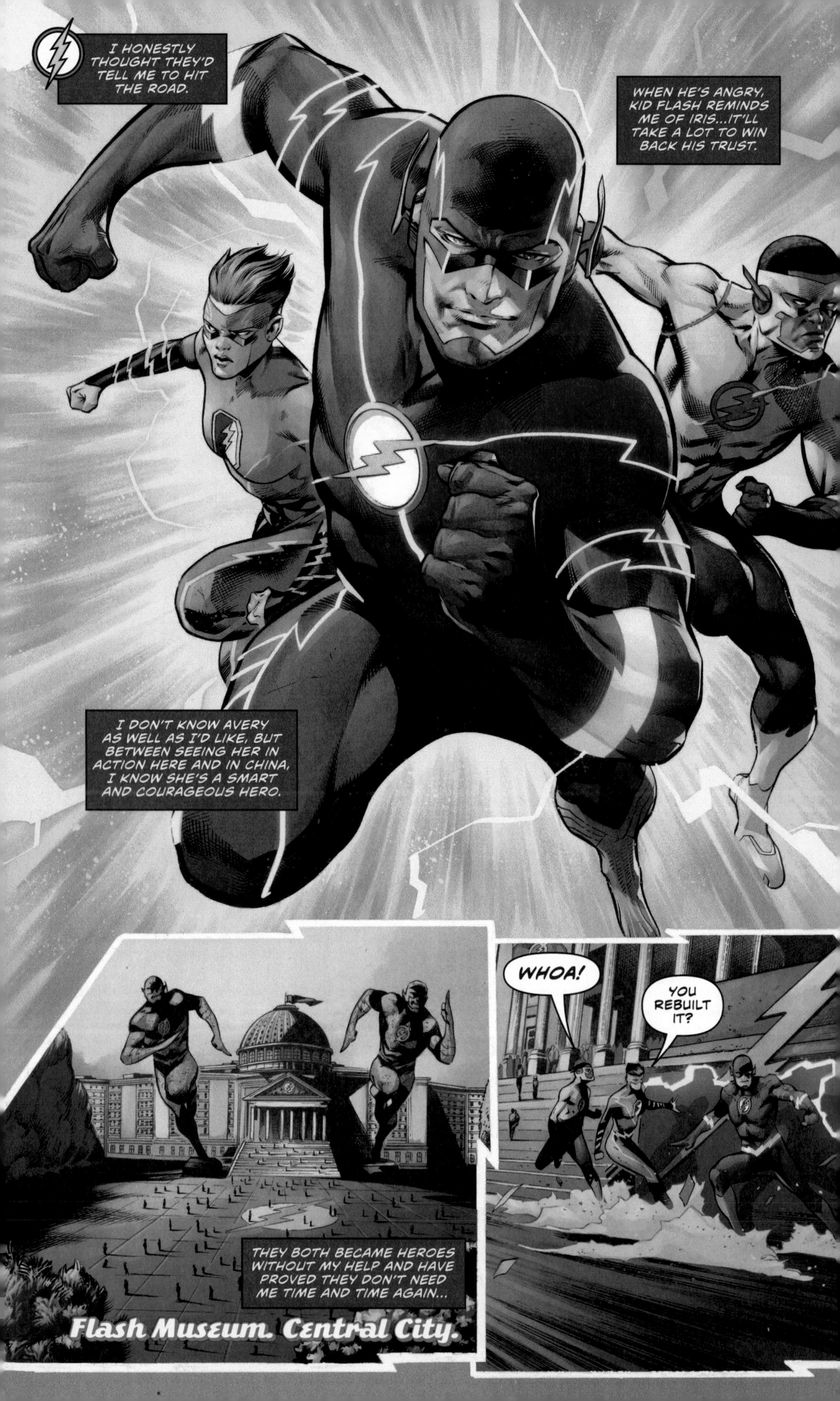
I HONESTLY THOUGHT THEY'D TELL ME TO HIT THE ROAD.
WHEN HE'S ANGRY, KID FLASH REMINDS ME OF IRIS...IT'LL TAKE A LOT TO WIN BACK HIS TRUST.
I DON'T KNOW AVERY AS WELL AS I'D LIKE, BUT BETWEEN SEEING HER IN ACTION HERE AND IN CHINA, I KNOW SHE'S A SMART AND COURAGEOUS HERO.
THEY BOTH BECAME HEROES WITHOUT MY HELP AND HAVE PROVED THEY DON'T NEED ME TIME AND TIME AGAIN...
Flash Museum. Central City.
WHOA!
YOU REBUILT IT?

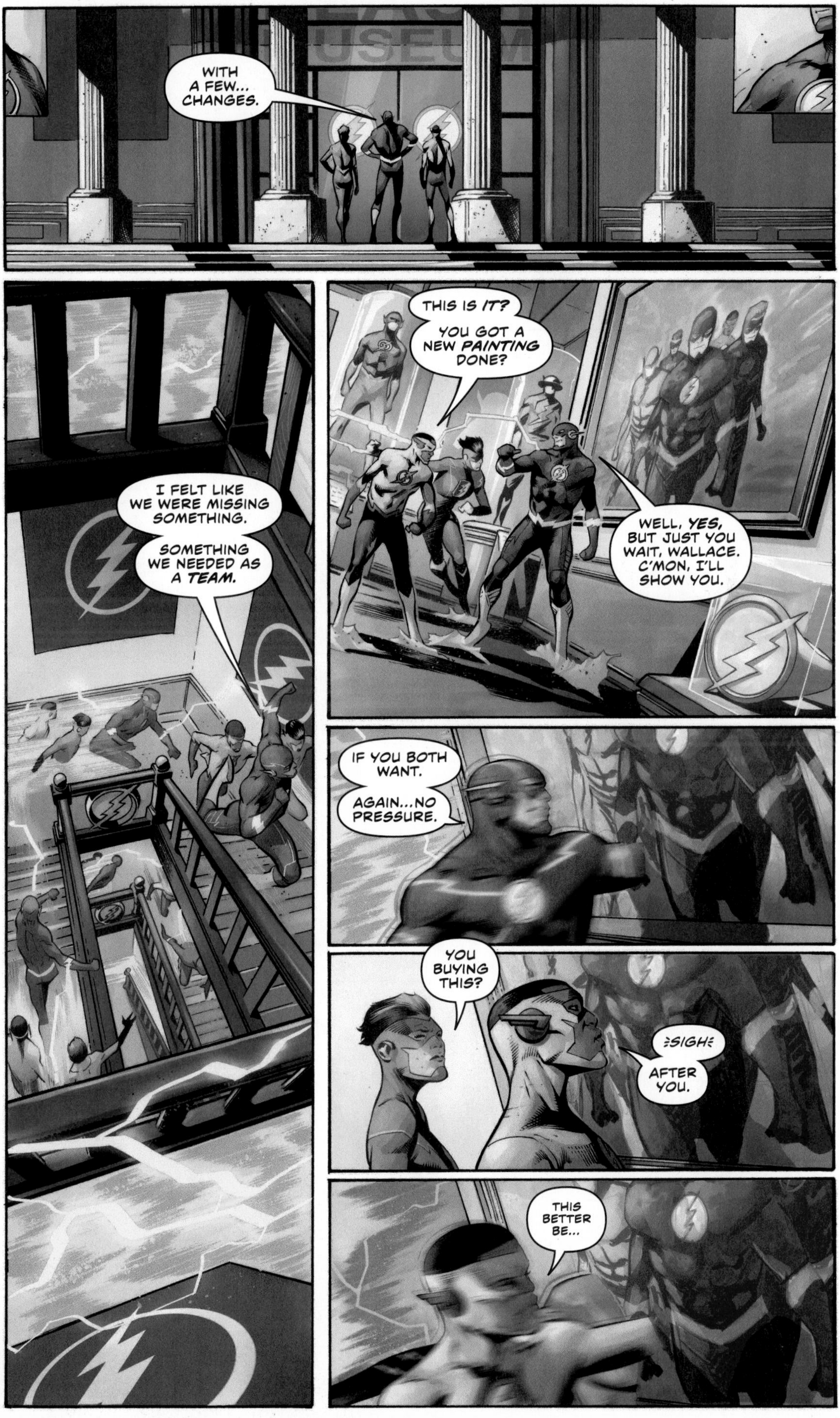
WITH A FEW... CHANGES.
I FELT LIKE WE WERE MISSING SOMETHING.
SOMETHING WE NEEDED AS A TEAM.
THIS IS IT?
YOU GOT A NEW PAINTING DONE?
WELL, YES, BUT JUST YOU WAIT, WALLACE. C'MON, I'LL SHOW YOU.
IF YOU BOTH WANT.
AGAIN...NO PRESSURE.
YOU BUYING THIS?
SIGH
AFTER YOU.
THIS BETTER BE...

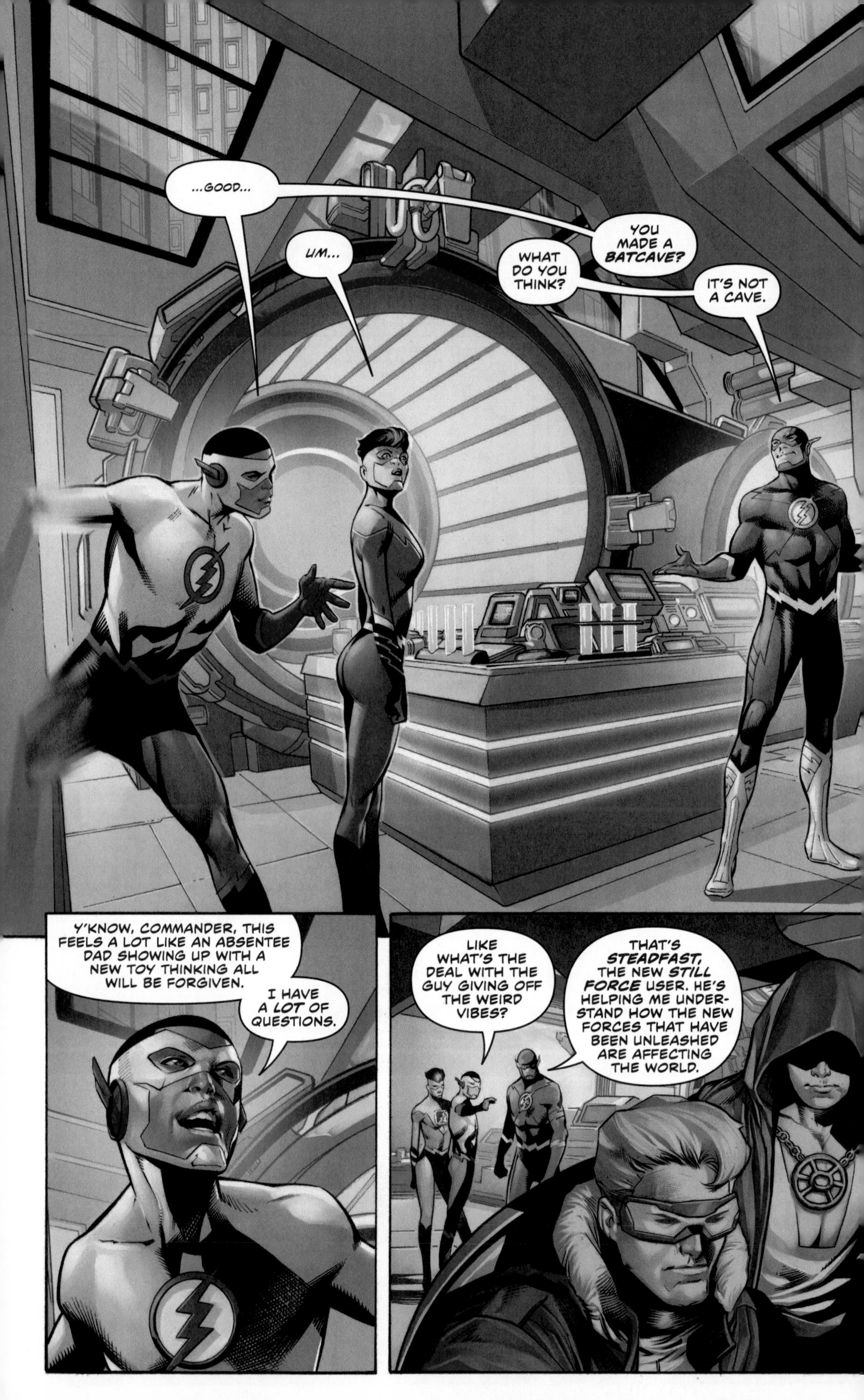

...GOOD...
UM...
YOU MADE A BATCAVE?
WHAT DO YOU THINK?
IT'S NOT A CAVE.
Y'KNOW, COMMANDER, THIS FEELS A LOT LIKE AN ABSENTEE DAD SHOWING UP WITH A NEW TOY THINKING ALL WILL BE FORGIVEN.
I HAVE A LOT OF QUESTIONS.
LIKE WHAT'S THE DEAL WITH THE GUY GIVING OFF THE WEIRD VIBES?
THAT'S STEADFAST, THE NEW STILL FORCE USER. HE'S HELPING ME UNDERSTAND HOW THE NEW FORCES THAT HAVE BEEN UNLEASHED ARE AFFECTING THE WORLD.

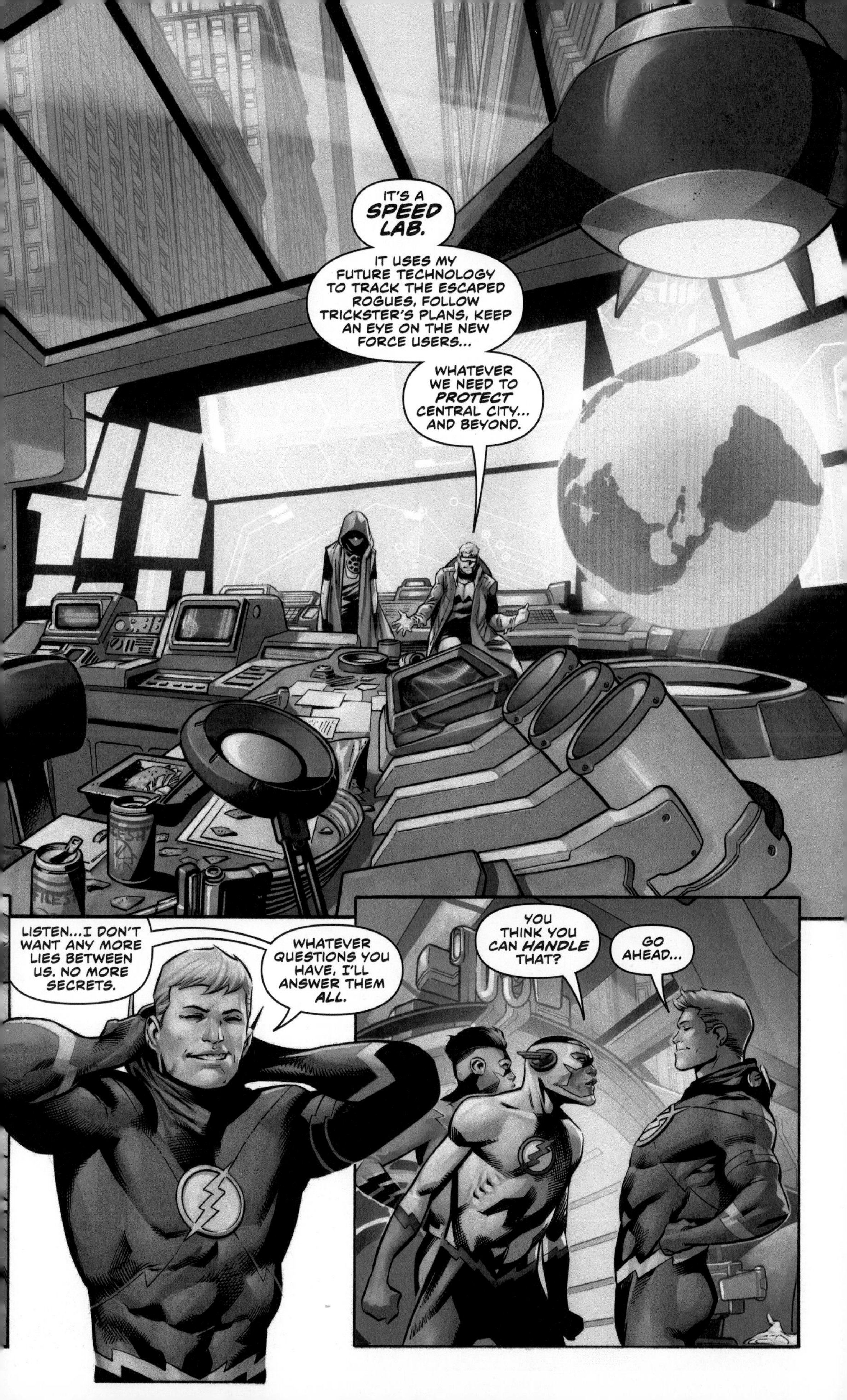
IT'S A SPEED LAB.
IT USES MY FUTURE TECHNOLOGY TO TRACK THE ESCAPED ROGUES, FOLLOW TRICKSTER'S PLANS, KEEP AN EYE ON THE NEW FORCE USERS...
WHATEVER WE NEED TO PROTECT CENTRAL CITY... AND BEYOND.
LISTEN...I DON'T WANT ANY MORE LIES BETWEEN US. NO MORE SECRETS.
WHATEVER QUESTIONS YOU HAVE, I'LL ANSWER THEM ALL.
YOU THINK YOU CAN HANDLE THAT?
GO AHEAD...

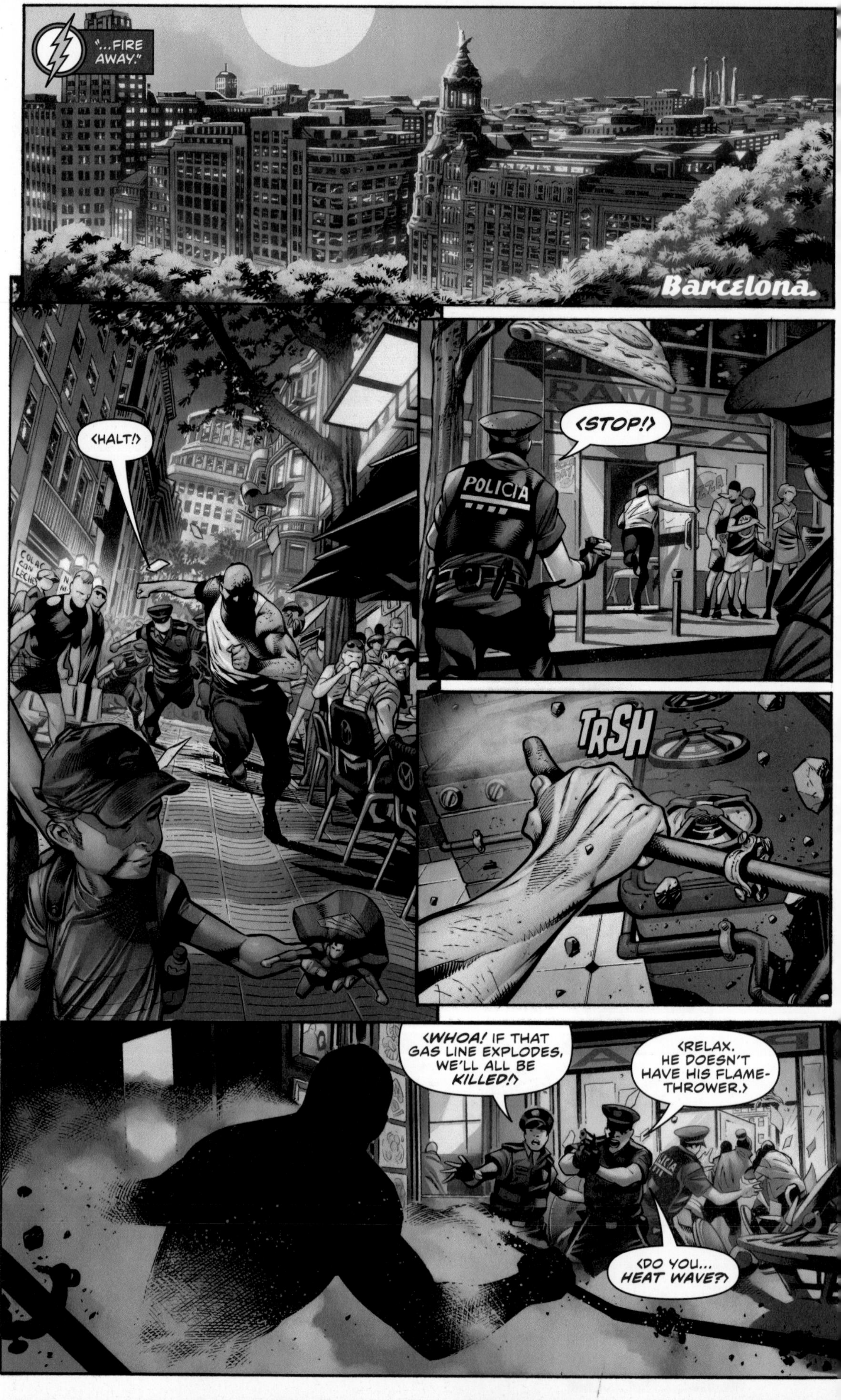
"...FIRE AWAY."
Barcelona.
‹HALT!›
‹STOP!›
POLICIA
TRSH
‹WHOA! IF THAT GAS LINE EXPLODES, WE'LL ALL BE KILLED!›
‹RELAX. HE DOESN'T HAVE HIS FLAME-THROWER.›
‹DO YOU... HEAT WAVE?›

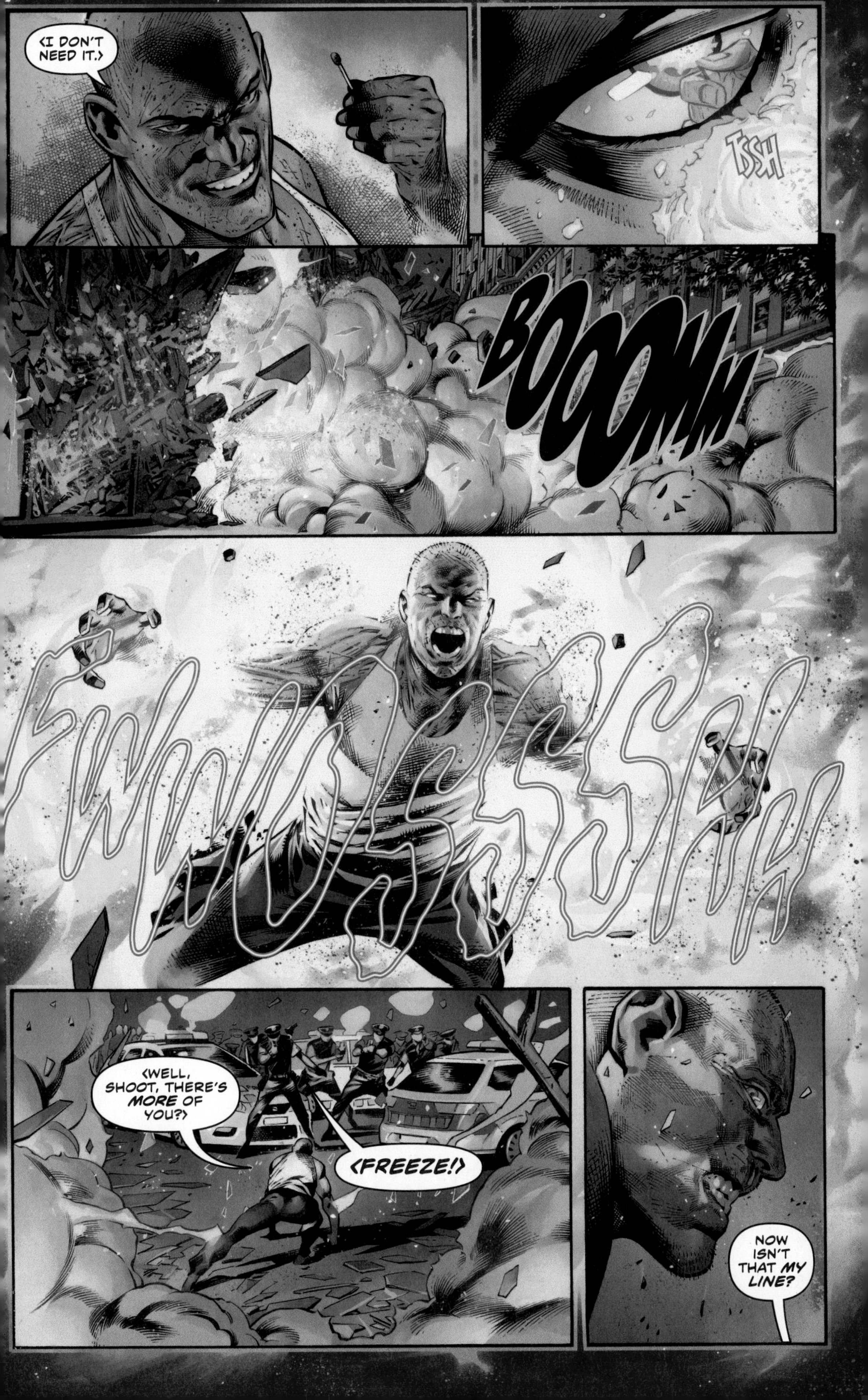

<I DON'T NEED IT.>
TSSH
BOOOMM
FWHOOOSSHH
<WELL, SHOOT, THERE'S MORE OF YOU?>
<FREEZE!>
NOW ISN'T THAT MY LINE?

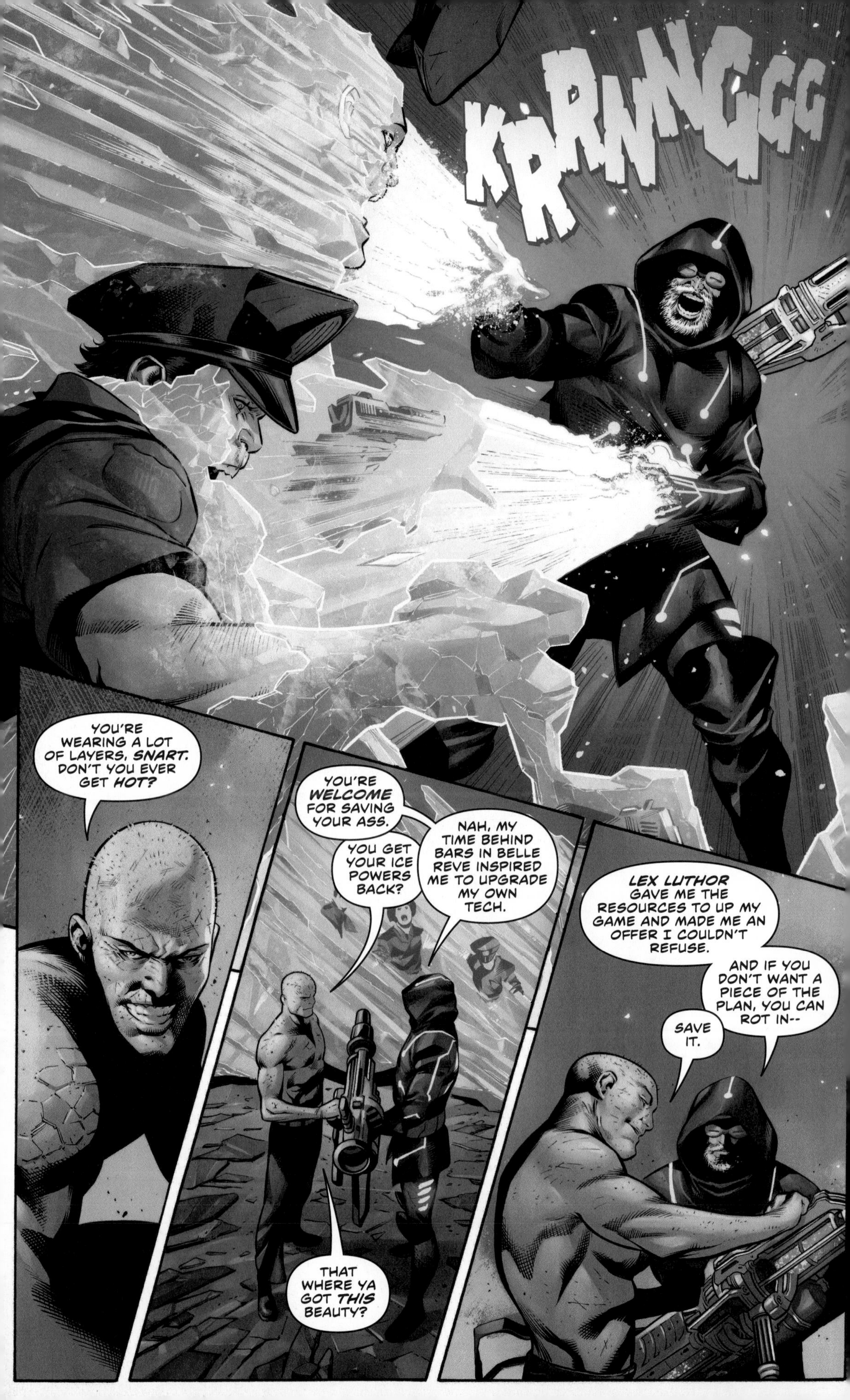
KRRANNGGG
YOU'RE WEARING A LOT OF LAYERS, *SNART.* DON'T YOU EVER GET *HOT?*
YOU'RE *WELCOME* FOR SAVING YOUR ASS.
YOU GET YOUR ICE POWERS BACK?
NAH, MY TIME BEHIND BARS IN BELLE REVE INSPIRED ME TO UPGRADE MY OWN TECH.
THAT WHERE YA GOT *THIS* BEAUTY?
LEX LUTHOR GAVE ME THE RESOURCES TO UP MY GAME AND MADE ME AN OFFER I COULDN'T REFUSE.
AND IF YOU DON'T WANT A PIECE OF THE PLAN, YOU CAN ROT IN--
SAVE IT.

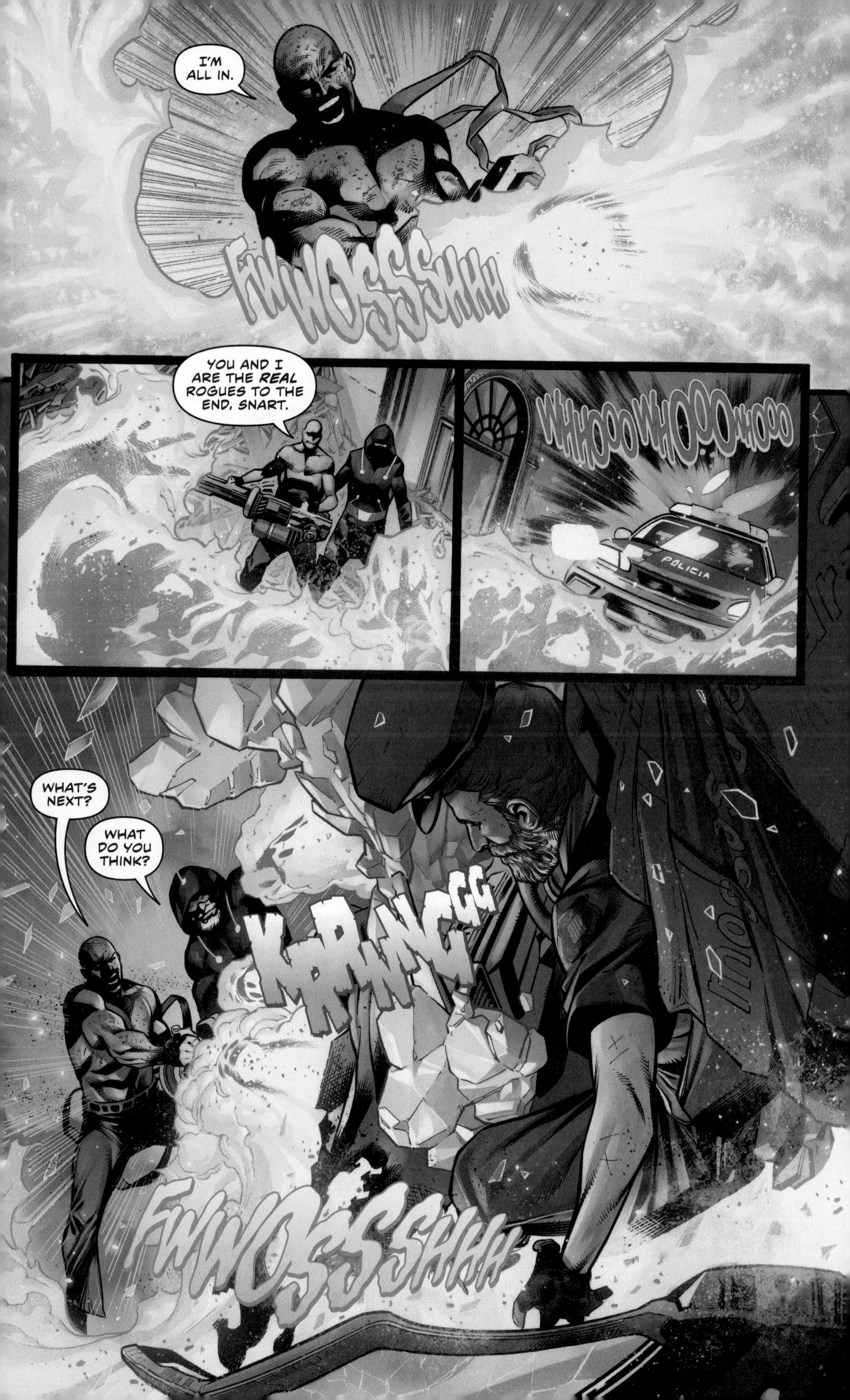
I'M ALL IN.
FWWOSSSHHH
YOU AND I ARE THE *REAL* ROGUES TO THE END, SNART.
WHHOOO WHOOO WHOOO
POLICIA
WHAT'S NEXT?
WHAT DO YOU THINK?
KRRANGGG
FWWOSSSHHH

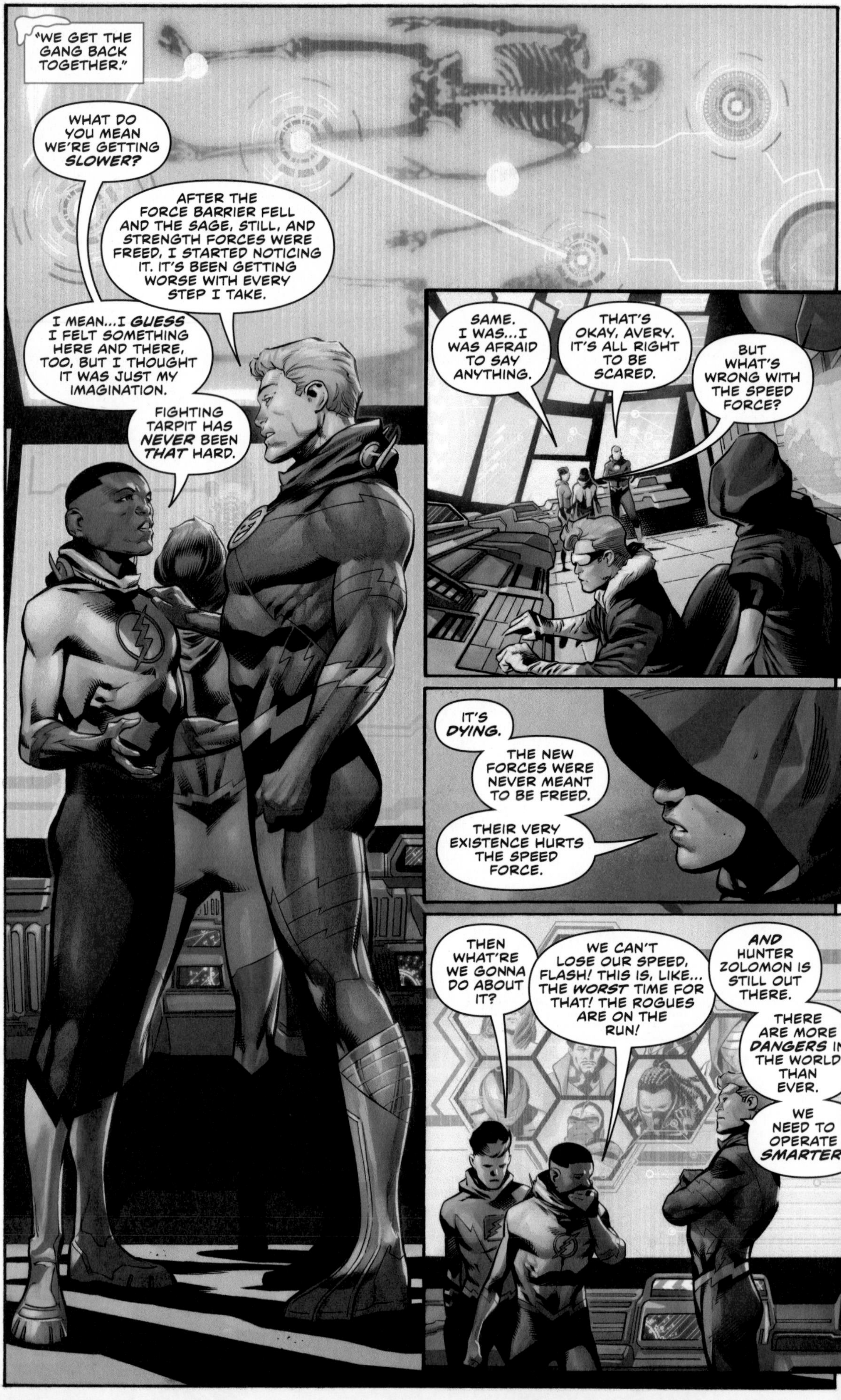
"WE GET THE GANG BACK TOGETHER."
WHAT DO YOU MEAN WE'RE GETTING *SLOWER?*
AFTER THE FORCE BARRIER FELL AND THE SAGE, STILL, AND STRENGTH FORCES WERE FREED, I STARTED NOTICING IT. IT'S BEEN GETTING WORSE WITH EVERY STEP I TAKE.
I MEAN...I *GUESS* I FELT SOMETHING HERE AND THERE, TOO, BUT I THOUGHT IT WAS JUST MY IMAGINATION.
FIGHTING TARPIT HAS *NEVER* BEEN *THAT* HARD.
SAME. I WAS...I WAS AFRAID TO SAY ANYTHING.
THAT'S OKAY, AVERY. IT'S ALL RIGHT TO BE SCARED.
BUT WHAT'S WRONG WITH THE SPEED FORCE?
IT'S *DYING.*
THE NEW FORCES WERE NEVER MEANT TO BE FREED.
THEIR VERY EXISTENCE HURTS THE SPEED FORCE.
THEN WHAT'RE WE GONNA DO ABOUT IT?
WE CAN'T LOSE OUR SPEED, FLASH! THIS IS, LIKE... THE *WORST* TIME FOR THAT! THE ROGUES ARE ON THE RUN!
AND HUNTER ZOLOMON IS STILL OUT THERE.
THERE ARE MORE *DANGERS* IN THE WORLD THAN EVER.
WE NEED TO OPERATE *SMARTER.*

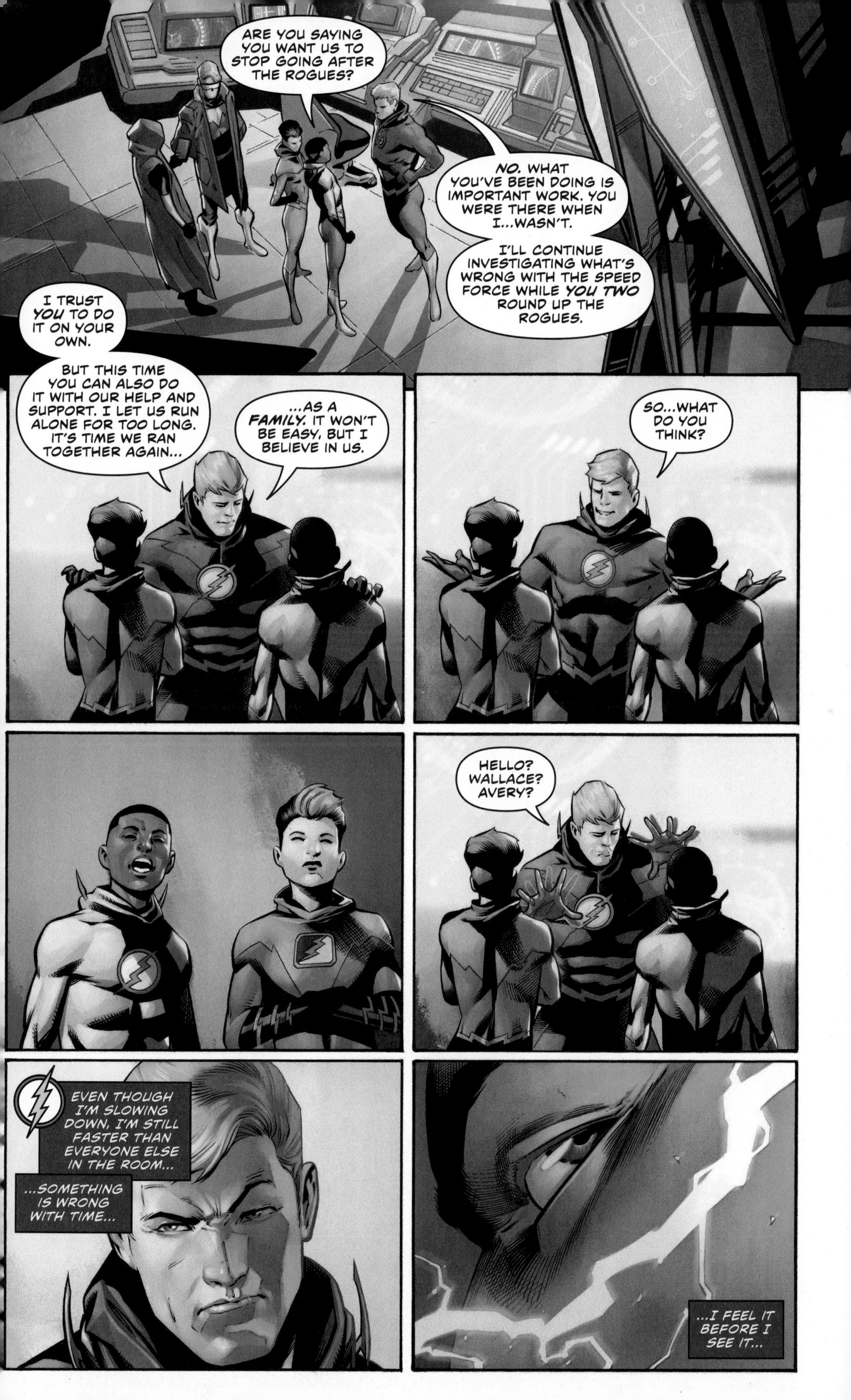
ARE YOU SAYING YOU WANT US TO STOP GOING AFTER THE ROGUES?
NO. WHAT YOU'VE BEEN DOING IS IMPORTANT WORK. YOU WERE THERE WHEN I...WASN'T.
I'LL CONTINUE INVESTIGATING WHAT'S WRONG WITH THE SPEED FORCE WHILE YOU TWO ROUND UP THE ROGUES.
I TRUST YOU TO DO IT ON YOUR OWN.
BUT THIS TIME YOU CAN ALSO DO IT WITH OUR HELP AND SUPPORT. I LET US RUN ALONE FOR TOO LONG. IT'S TIME WE RAN TOGETHER AGAIN...
...AS A FAMILY. IT WON'T BE EASY, BUT I BELIEVE IN US.
SO...WHAT DO YOU THINK?
HELLO? WALLACE? AVERY?
EVEN THOUGH I'M SLOWING DOWN, I'M STILL FASTER THAN EVERYONE ELSE IN THE ROOM...
...SOMETHING IS WRONG WITH TIME...
...I FEEL IT BEFORE I SEE IT...

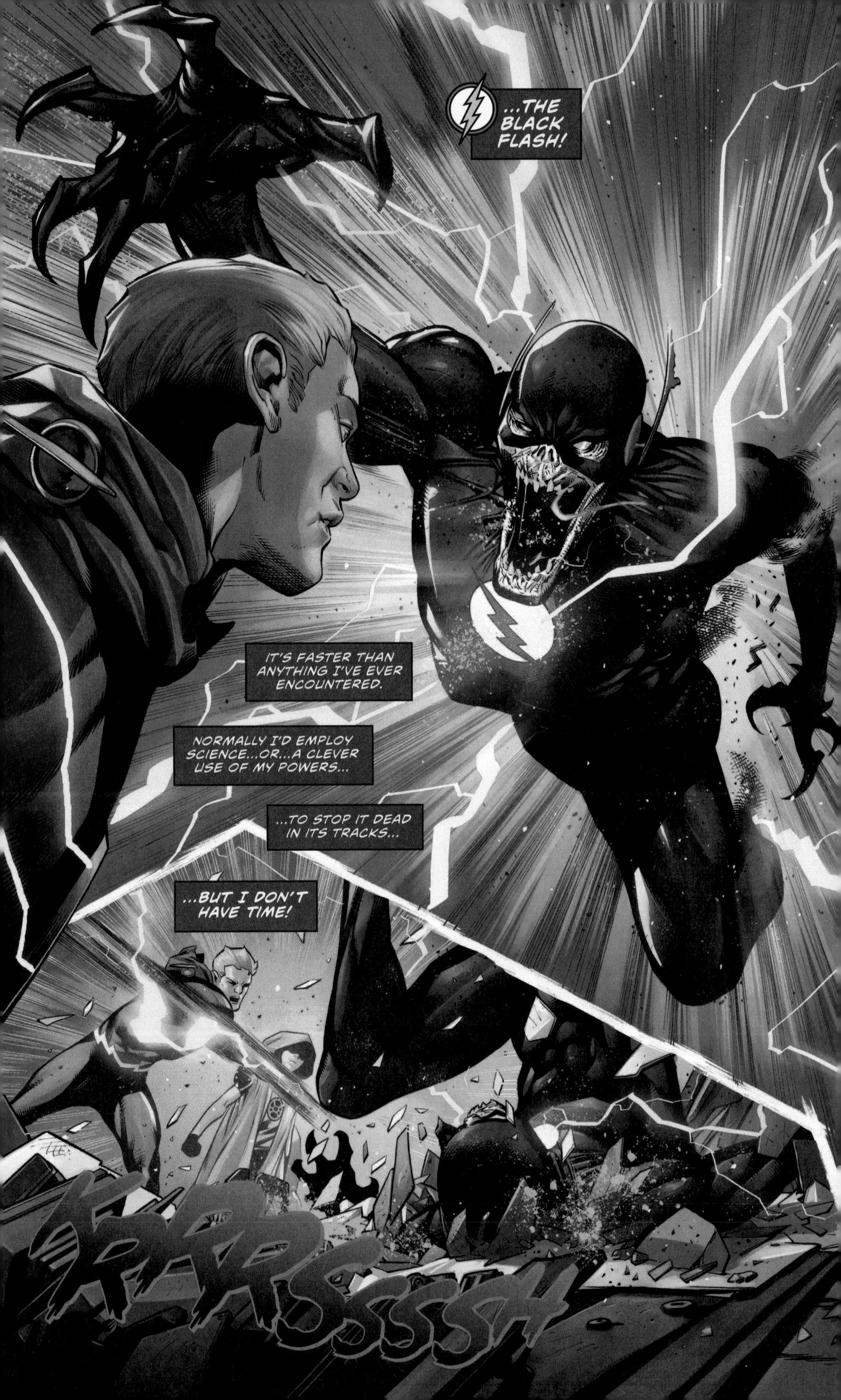
...THE BLACK FLASH!
IT'S FASTER THAN ANYTHING I'VE EVER ENCOUNTERED.
NORMALLY I'D EMPLOY SCIENCE...OR...A CLEVER USE OF MY POWERS...
...TO STOP IT DEAD IN ITS TRACKS...
...BUT I DON'T HAVE TIME!
KRRSSSSH

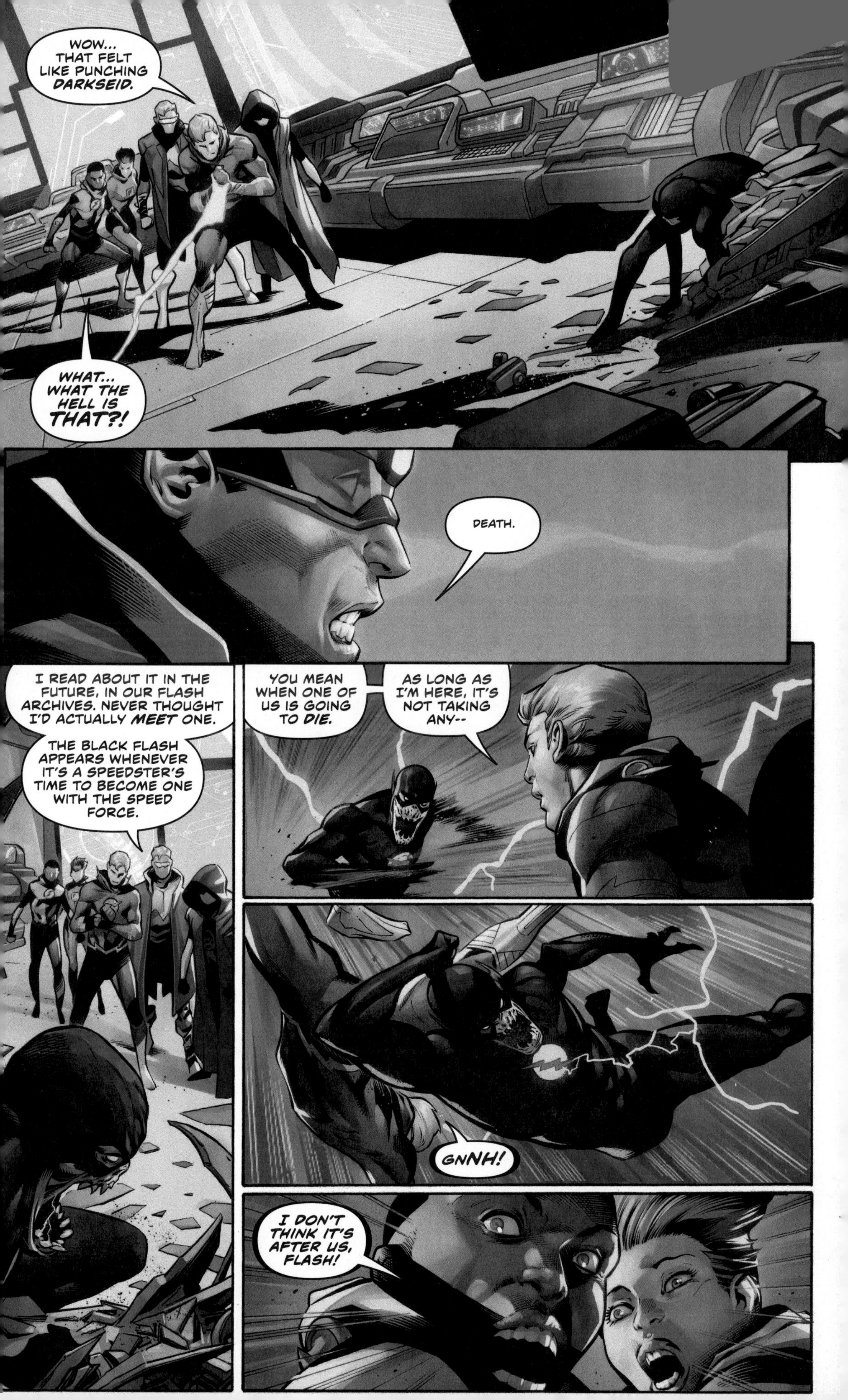
WOW... THAT FELT LIKE PUNCHING DARKSEID.
WHAT... WHAT THE HELL IS THAT?!
DEATH.
I READ ABOUT IT IN THE FUTURE, IN OUR FLASH ARCHIVES. NEVER THOUGHT I'D ACTUALLY MEET ONE.
THE BLACK FLASH APPEARS WHENEVER IT'S A SPEEDSTER'S TIME TO BECOME ONE WITH THE SPEED FORCE.
YOU MEAN WHEN ONE OF US IS GOING TO DIE.
AS LONG AS I'M HERE, IT'S NOT TAKING ANY--
GNNH!
I DON'T THINK IT'S AFTER US, FLASH!

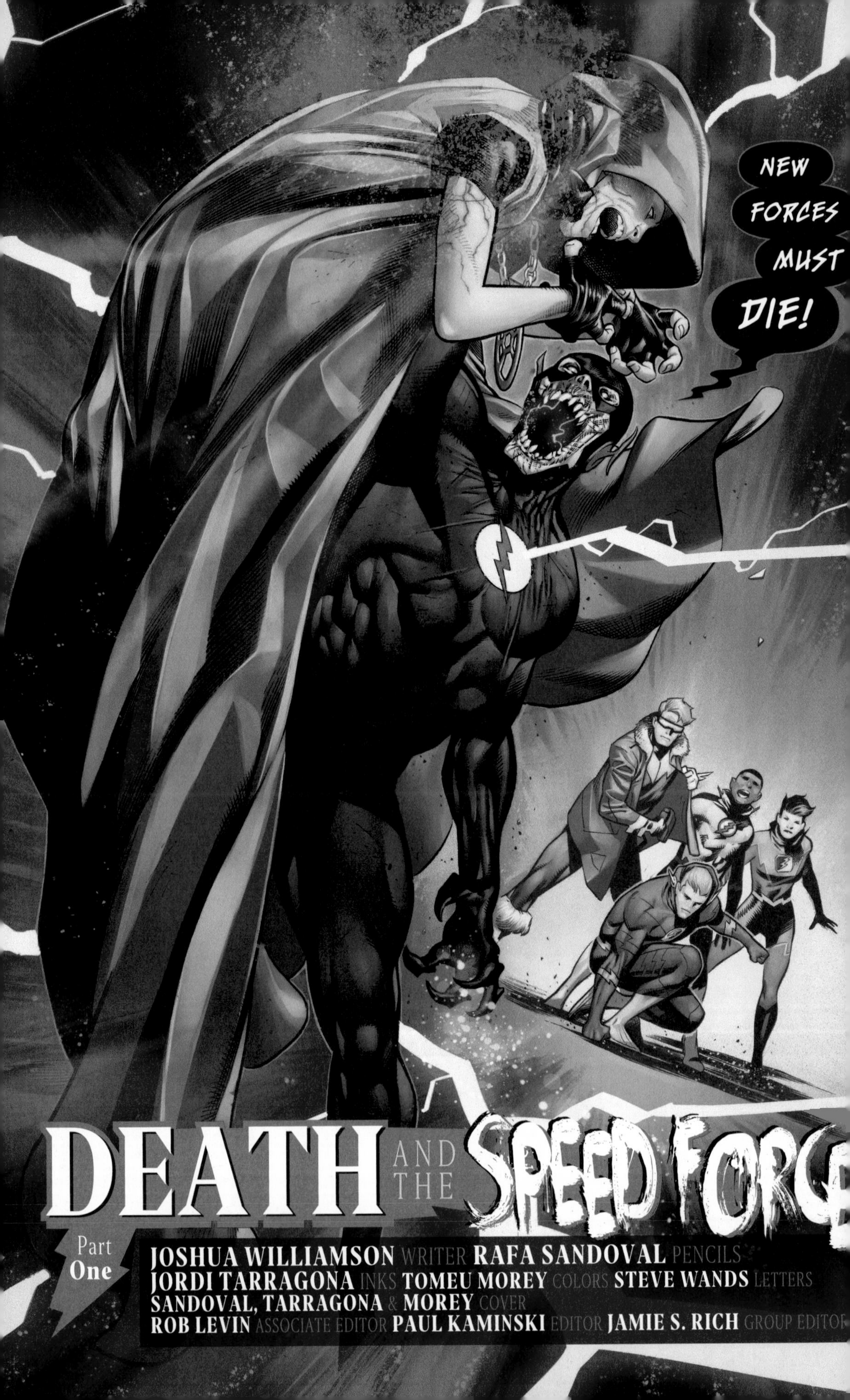
NEW FORCES MUST DIE!
DEATH AND THE SPEED FORCE
Part One
JOSHUA WILLIAMSON WRITER RAFA SANDOVAL PENCILS
JORDI TARRAGONA INKS TOMEU MOREY COLORS STEVE WANDS LETTERS
SANDOVAL, TARRAGONA & MOREY COVER
ROB LEVIN ASSOCIATE EDITOR PAUL KAMINSKI EDITOR JAMIE S. RICH GROUP EDITOR

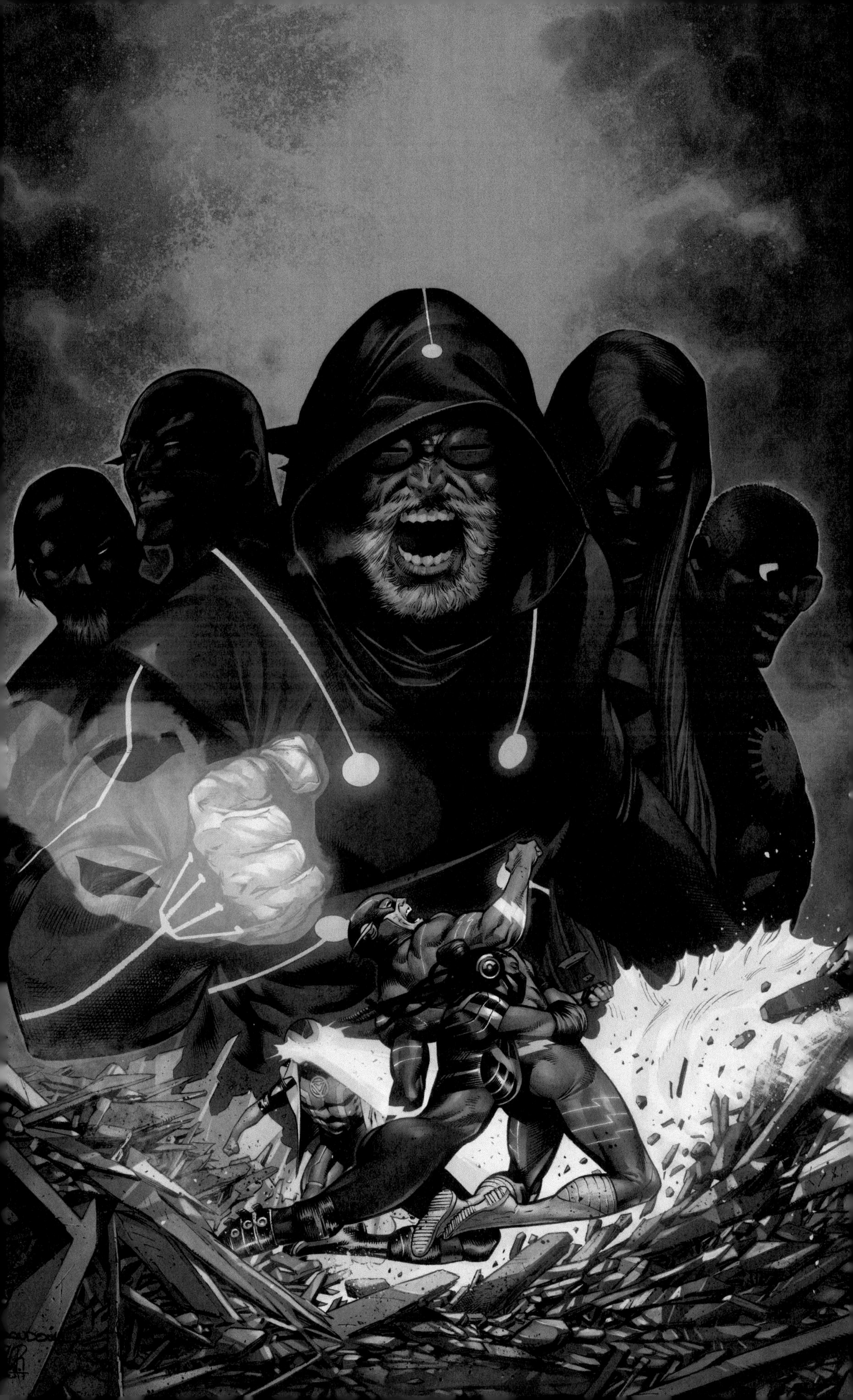

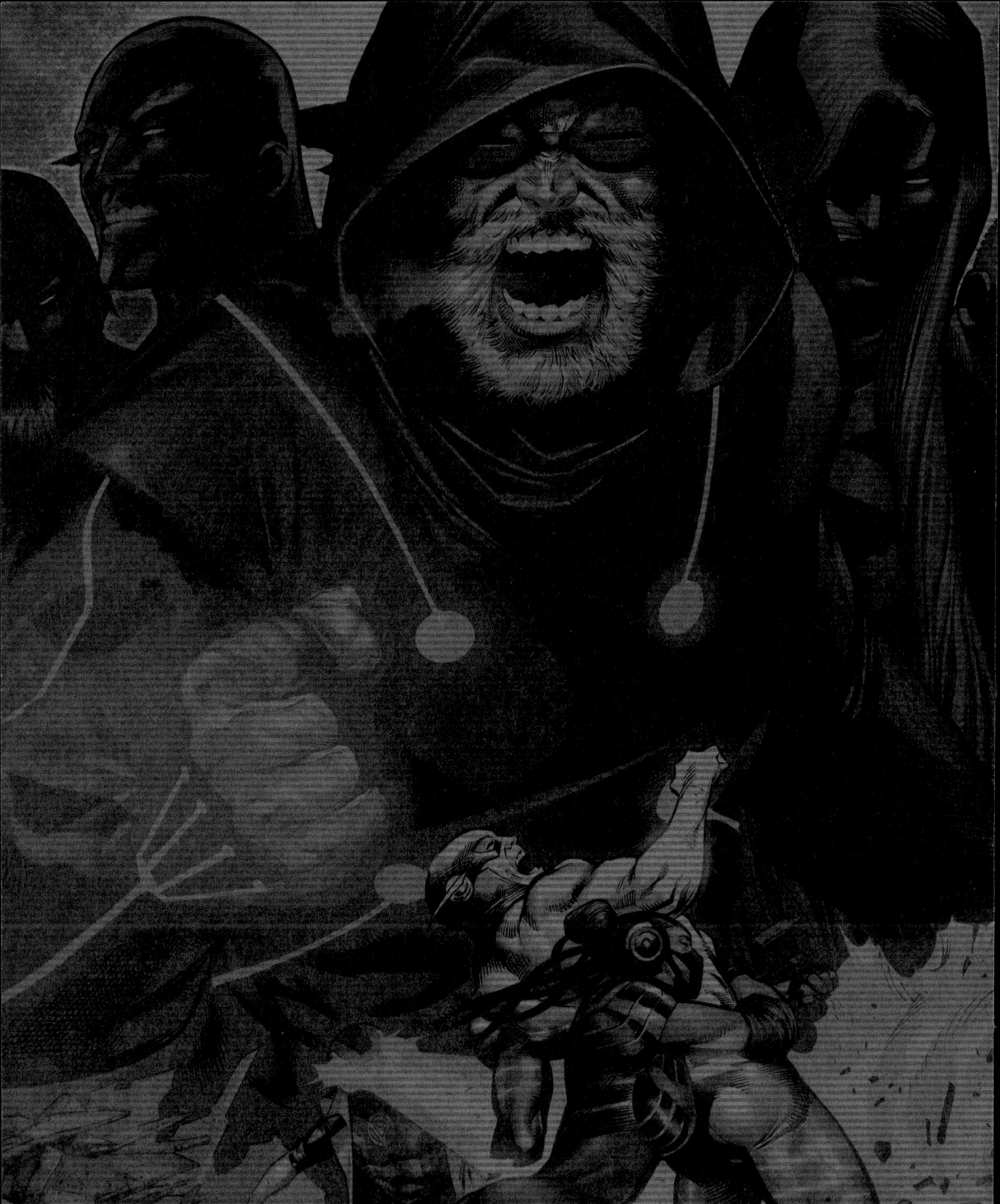

THE FLASH

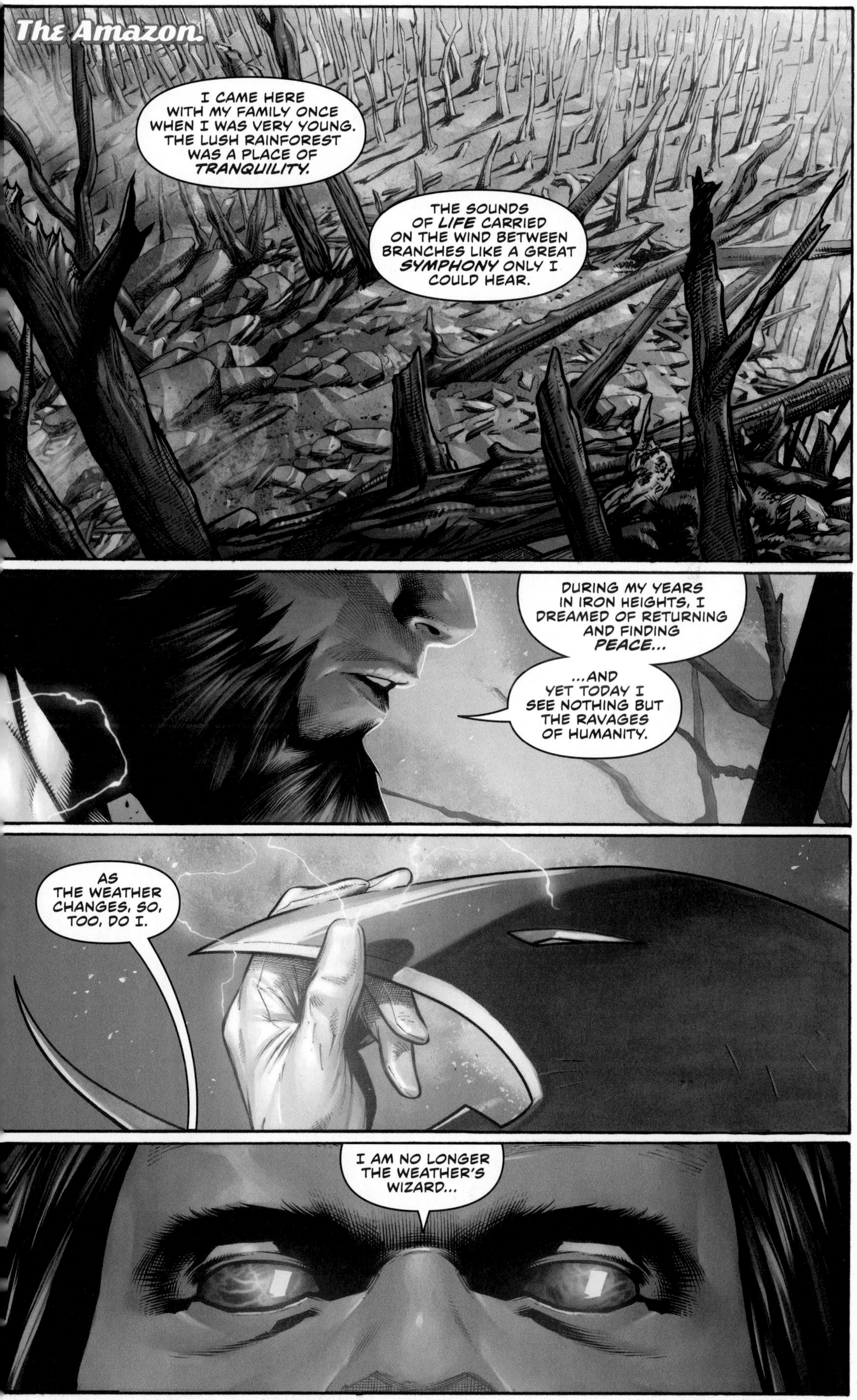
The Amazon.
I CAME HERE WITH MY FAMILY ONCE WHEN I WAS VERY YOUNG. THE LUSH RAINFOREST WAS A PLACE OF TRANQUILITY.
THE SOUNDS OF LIFE CARRIED ON THE WIND BETWEEN BRANCHES LIKE A GREAT SYMPHONY ONLY I COULD HEAR.
DURING MY YEARS IN IRON HEIGHTS, I DREAMED OF RETURNING AND FINDING PEACE...
...AND YET TODAY I SEE NOTHING BUT THE RAVAGES OF HUMANITY.
AS THE WEATHER CHANGES, SO, TOO, DO I.
I AM NO LONGER THE WEATHER'S WIZARD...

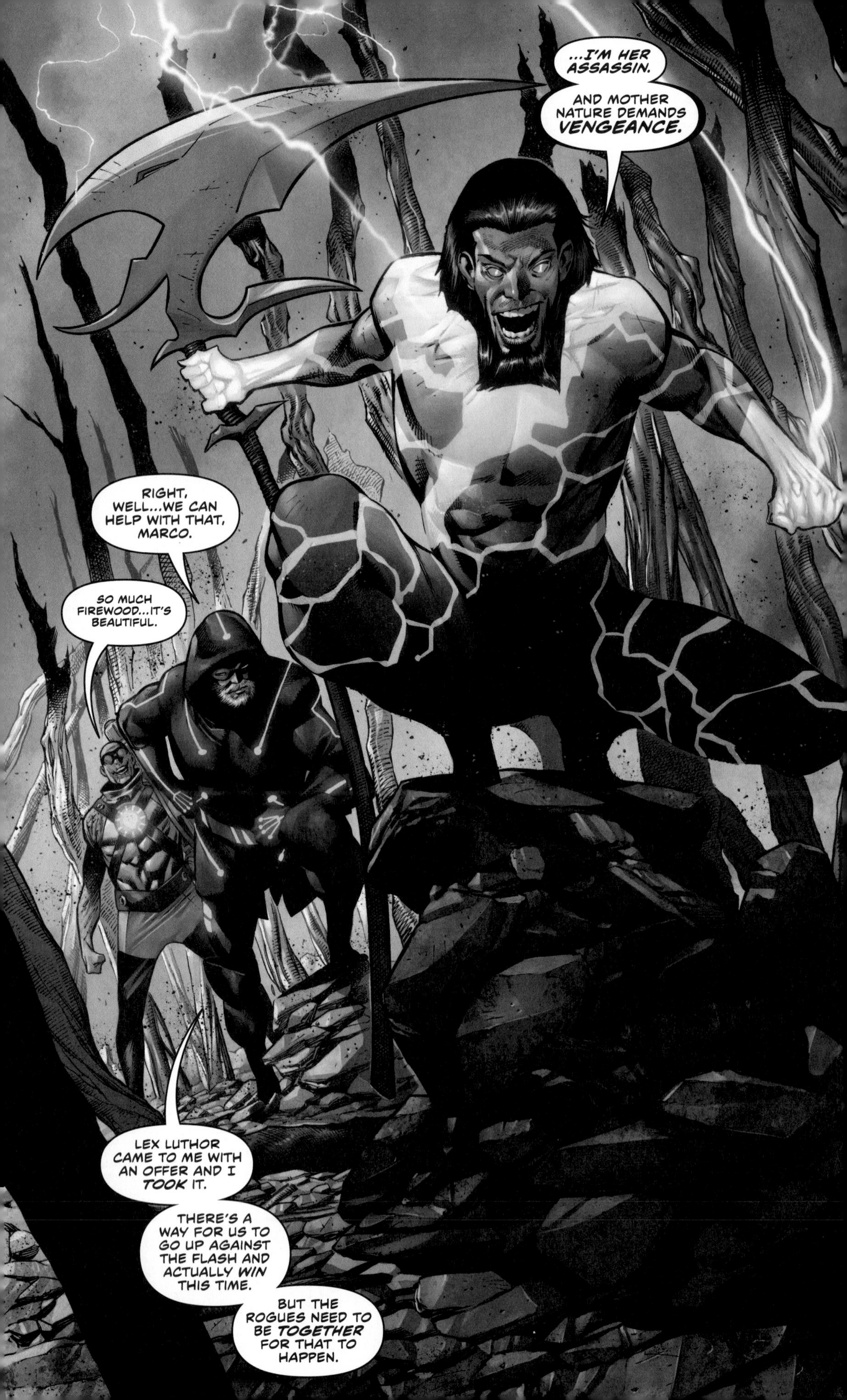
...I'M HER ASSASSIN.
AND MOTHER NATURE DEMANDS VENGEANCE.
RIGHT, WELL...WE CAN HELP WITH THAT, MARCO.
SO MUCH FIREWOOD...IT'S BEAUTIFUL.
LEX LUTHOR CAME TO ME WITH AN OFFER AND I TOOK IT.
THERE'S A WAY FOR US TO GO UP AGAINST THE FLASH AND ACTUALLY WIN THIS TIME.
BUT THE ROGUES NEED TO BE TOGETHER FOR THAT TO HAPPEN.

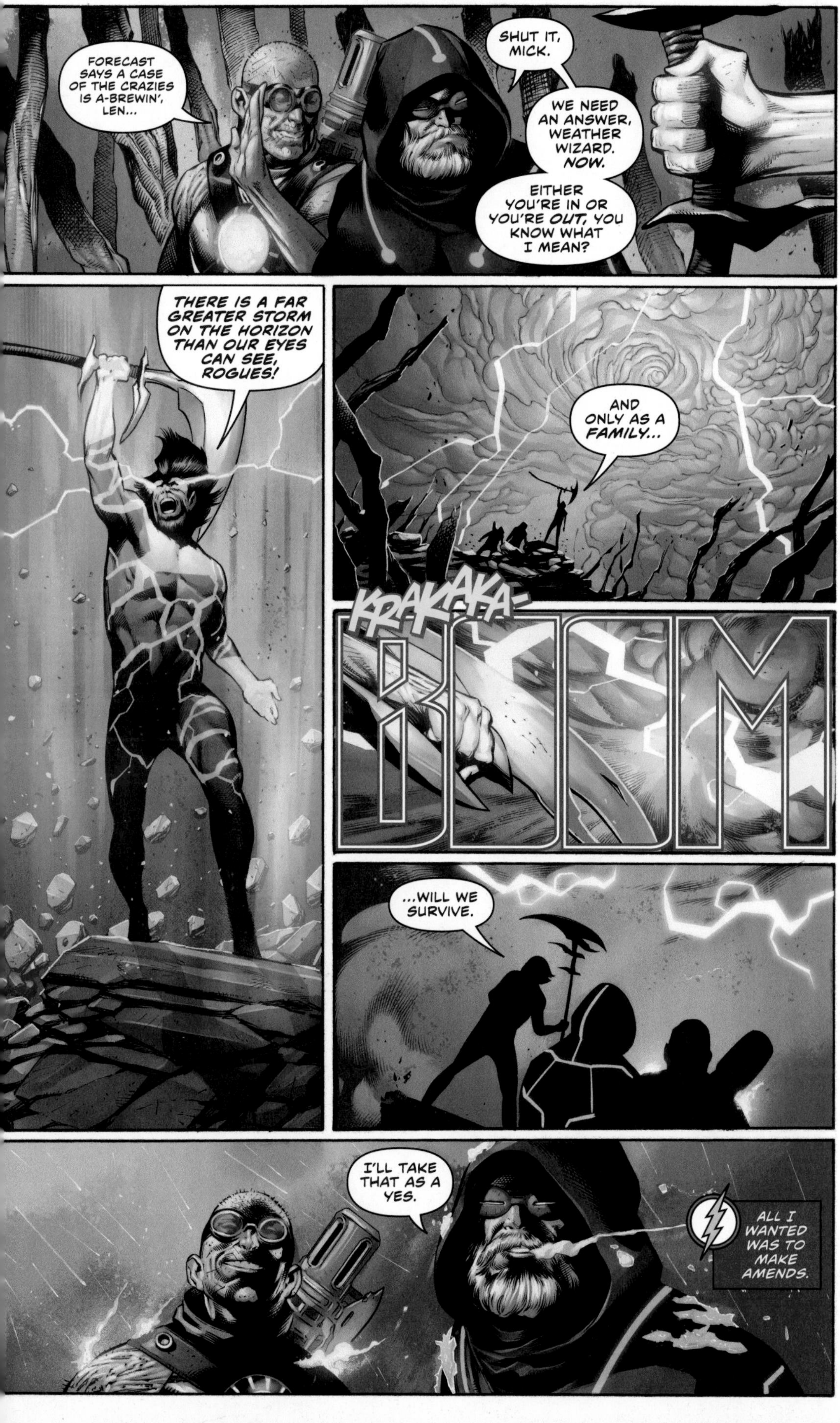

FORECAST SAYS A CASE OF THE CRAZIES IS A-BREWIN', LEN...
SHUT IT, MICK.
WE NEED AN ANSWER, WEATHER WIZARD. NOW.
EITHER YOU'RE IN OR YOU'RE OUT, YOU KNOW WHAT I MEAN?
THERE IS A FAR GREATER STORM ON THE HORIZON THAN OUR EYES CAN SEE, ROGUES!
AND ONLY AS A FAMILY...
KRAKAKA-BOOM
...WILL WE SURVIVE.
I'LL TAKE THAT AS A YES.
ALL I WANTED WAS TO MAKE AMENDS.

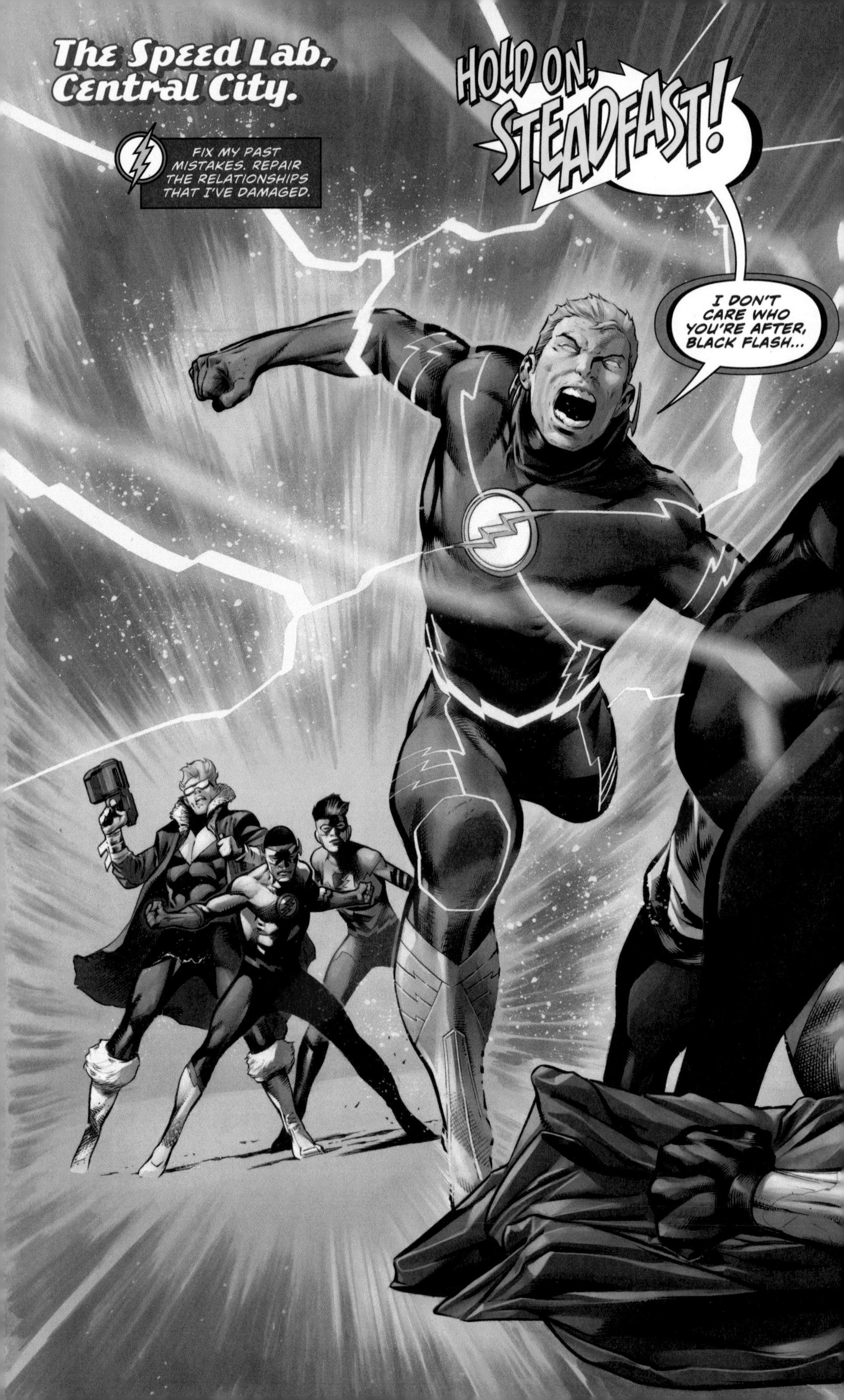
The Speed Lab, Central City.
FIX MY PAST MISTAKES. REPAIR THE RELATIONSHIPS THAT I'VE DAMAGED.
HOLD ON, STEADFAST!
I DON'T CARE WHO YOU'RE AFTER, BLACK FLASH...

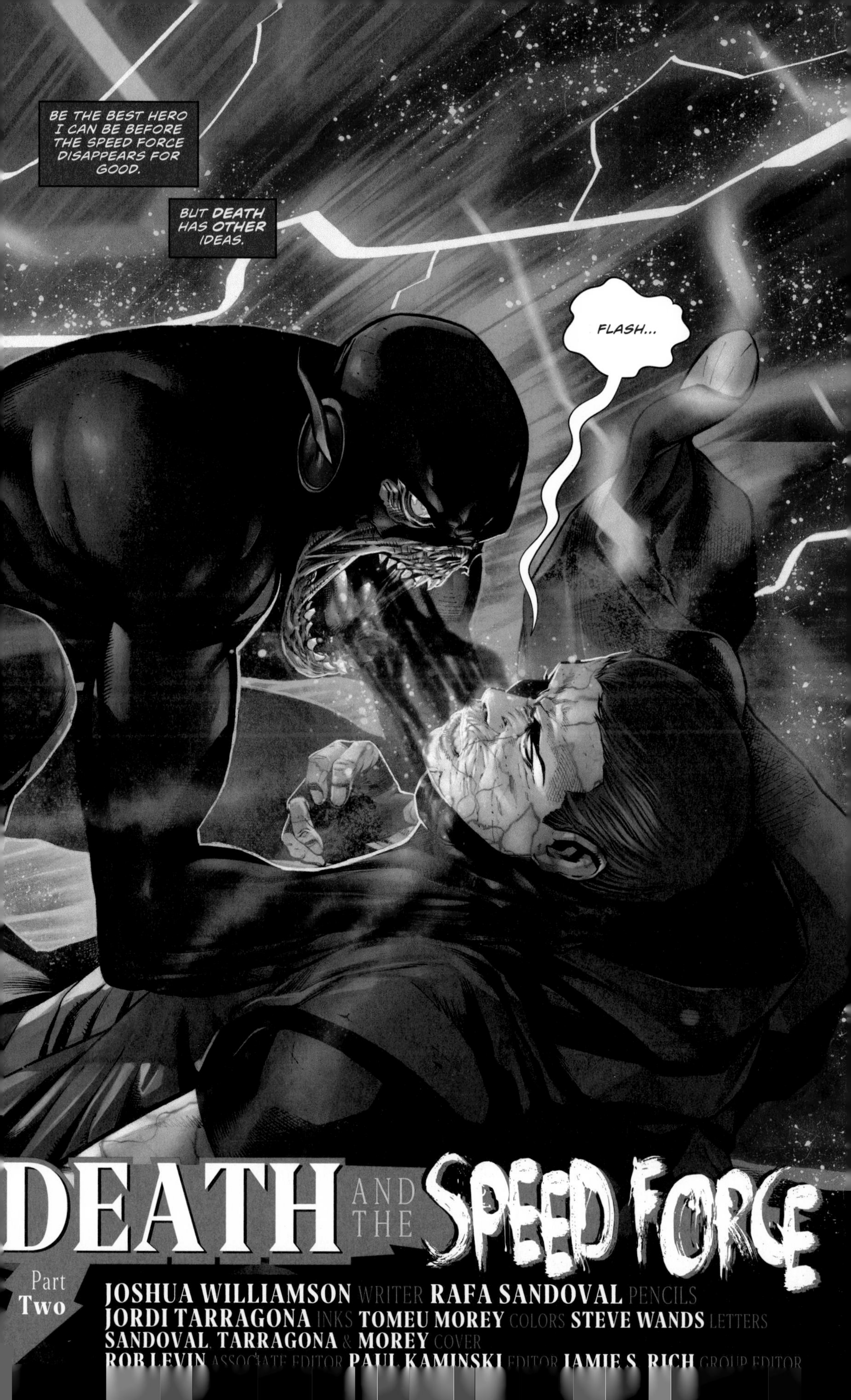
BE THE BEST HERO I CAN BE BEFORE THE SPEED FORCE DISAPPEARS FOR GOOD.
BUT DEATH HAS OTHER IDEAS.
FLASH...
DEATH AND THE SPEED FORCE
Part Two
JOSHUA WILLIAMSON WRITER RAFA SANDOVAL PENCILS
JORDI TARRAGONA INKS TOMEU MOREY COLORS STEVE WANDS LETTERS
SANDOVAL, TARRAGONA & MOREY COVER
ROB LEVIN ASSOCIATE EDITOR PAUL KAMINSKI EDITOR JAMIE S. RICH GROUP EDITOR

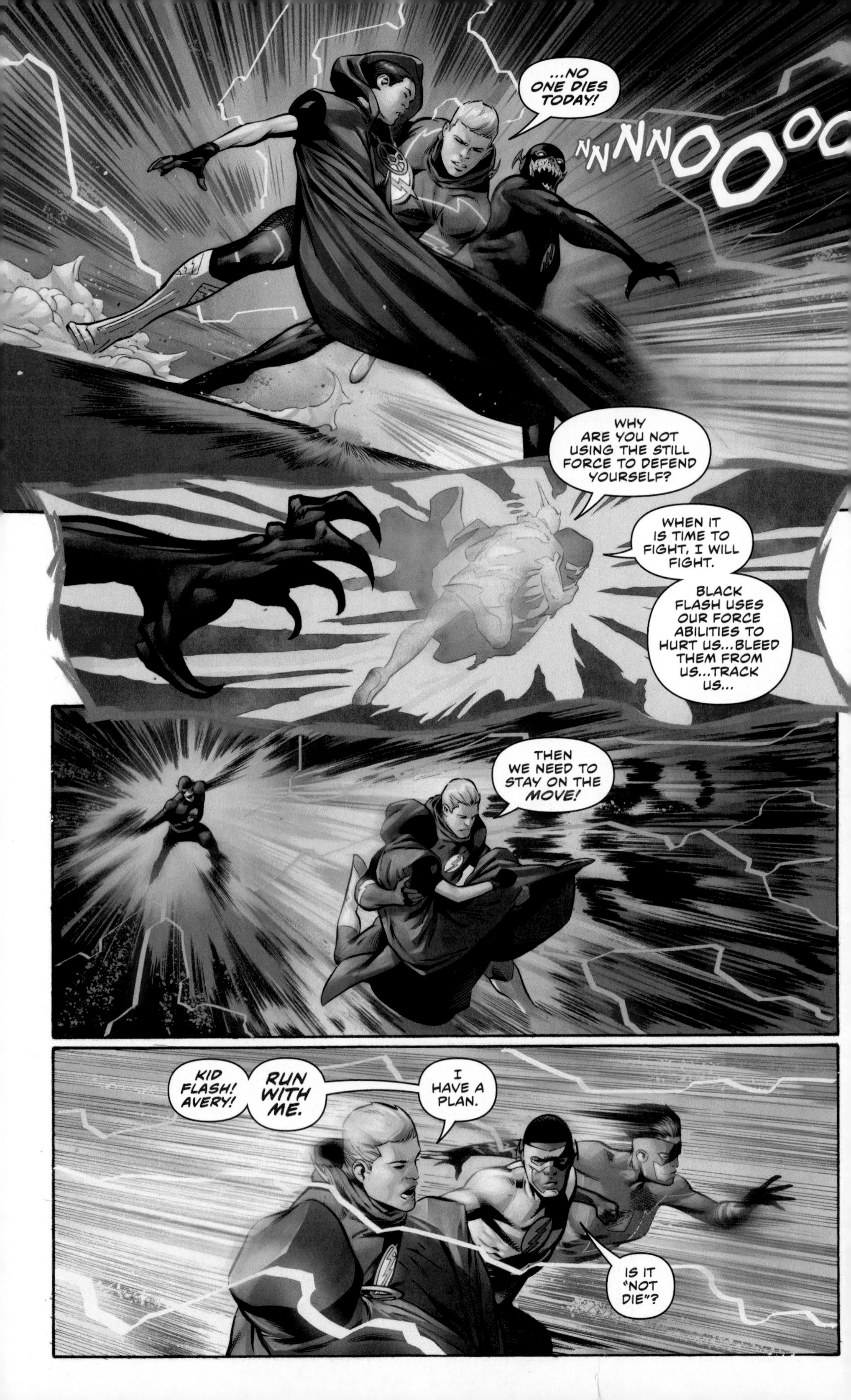
...NO ONE DIES TODAY!
NNNNOOOO
WHY ARE YOU NOT USING THE STILL FORCE TO DEFEND YOURSELF?
WHEN IT IS TIME TO FIGHT, I WILL FIGHT.
BLACK FLASH USES OUR FORCE ABILITIES TO HURT US...BLEED THEM FROM US...TRACK US...
THEN WE NEED TO STAY ON THE MOVE!
KID FLASH! AVERY!
RUN WITH ME.
I HAVE A PLAN.
IS IT "NOT DIE"?

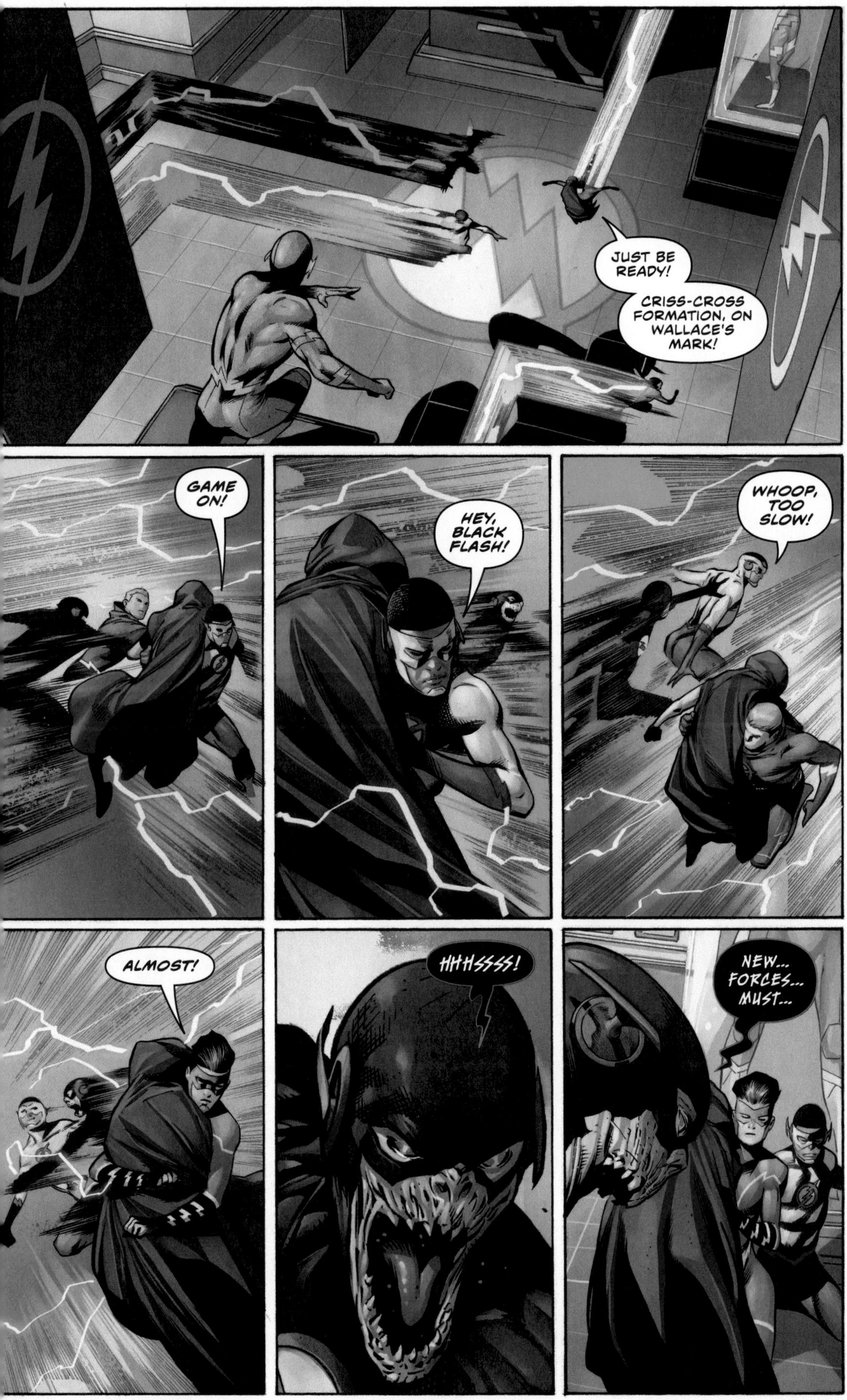
JUST BE READY!
CRISS-CROSS FORMATION, ON WALLACE'S MARK!
GAME ON!
HEY, BLACK FLASH!
WHOOP, TOO SLOW!
ALMOST!
HHHSSSS!
NEW... FORCES... MUST...

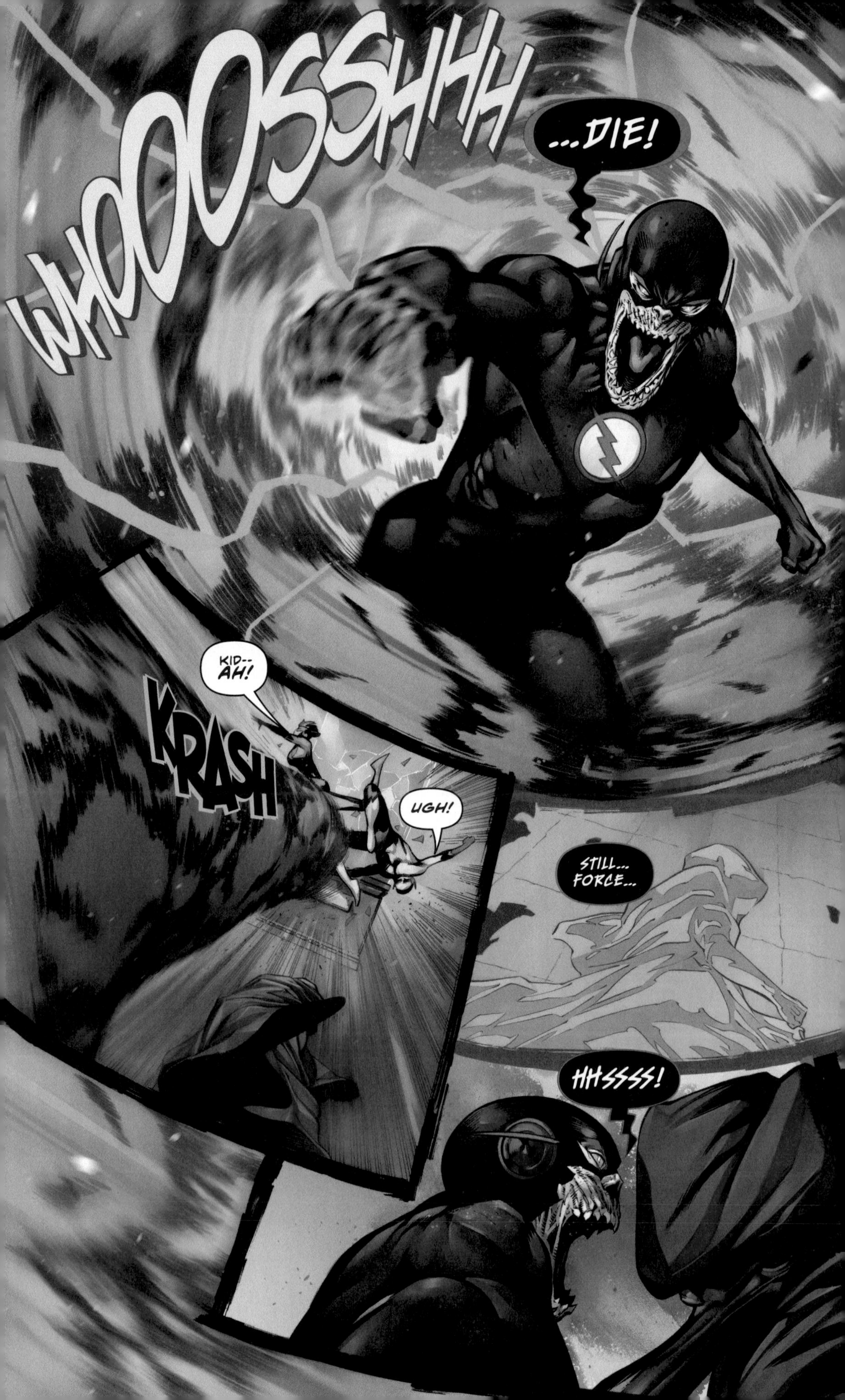
WHOOOSSHHH
...DIE!
KID--
AH!
KRASH
UGH!
STILL...
FORCE...
HHSSSS!

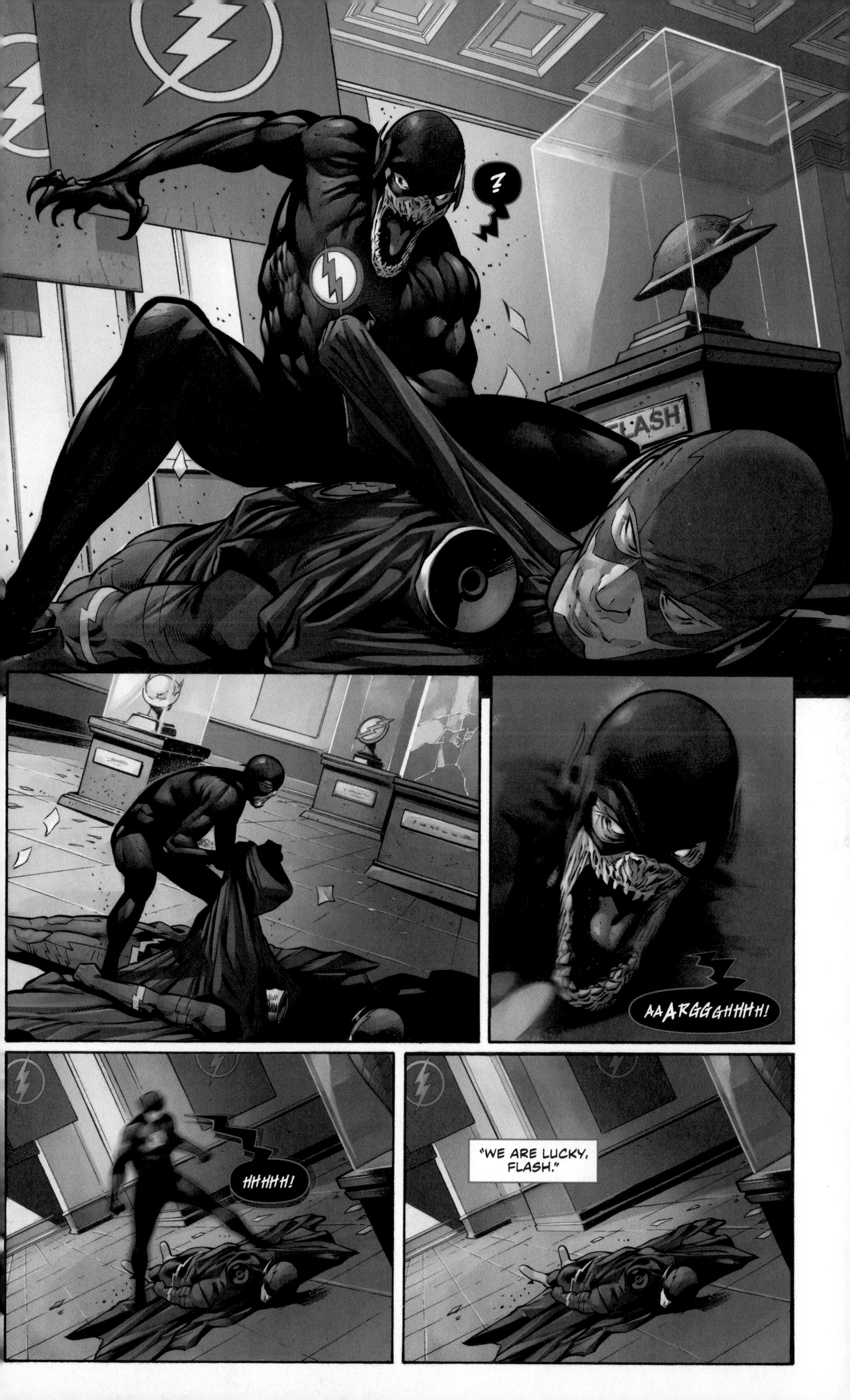

?
FLASH
AAARGGGHHHH!
HHHHH!
"WE ARE LUCKY, FLASH."

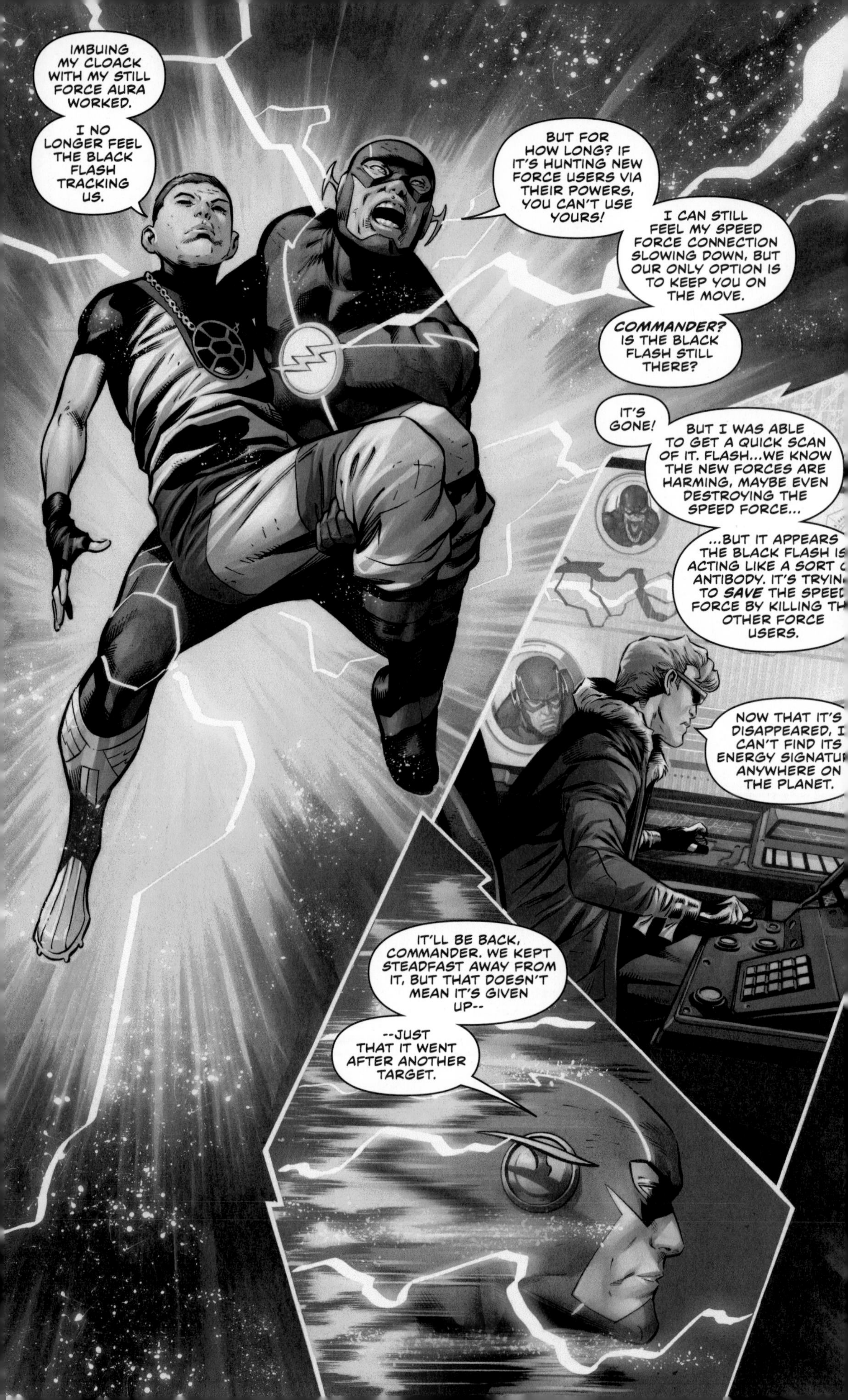
IMBUING MY CLOACK WITH MY STILL FORCE AURA WORKED.
I NO LONGER FEEL THE BLACK FLASH TRACKING US.
BUT FOR HOW LONG? IF IT'S HUNTING NEW FORCE USERS VIA THEIR POWERS, YOU CAN'T USE YOURS!
I CAN STILL FEEL MY SPEED FORCE CONNECTION SLOWING DOWN, BUT OUR ONLY OPTION IS TO KEEP YOU ON THE MOVE.
COMMANDER? IS THE BLACK FLASH STILL THERE?
IT'S GONE!
BUT I WAS ABLE TO GET A QUICK SCAN OF IT. FLASH...WE KNOW THE NEW FORCES ARE HARMING, MAYBE EVEN DESTROYING THE SPEED FORCE...
...BUT IT APPEARS THE BLACK FLASH IS ACTING LIKE A SORT ANTIBODY. IT'S TRYIN TO SAVE THE SPEE FORCE BY KILLING T OTHER FORCE USERS.
NOW THAT IT'S DISAPPEARED, I CAN'T FIND ITS ENERGY SIGNATU ANYWHERE ON THE PLANET.
IT'LL BE BACK, COMMANDER. WE KEPT STEADFAST AWAY FROM IT, BUT THAT DOESN'T MEAN IT'S GIVEN UP--
--JUST THAT IT WENT AFTER ANOTHER TARGET.

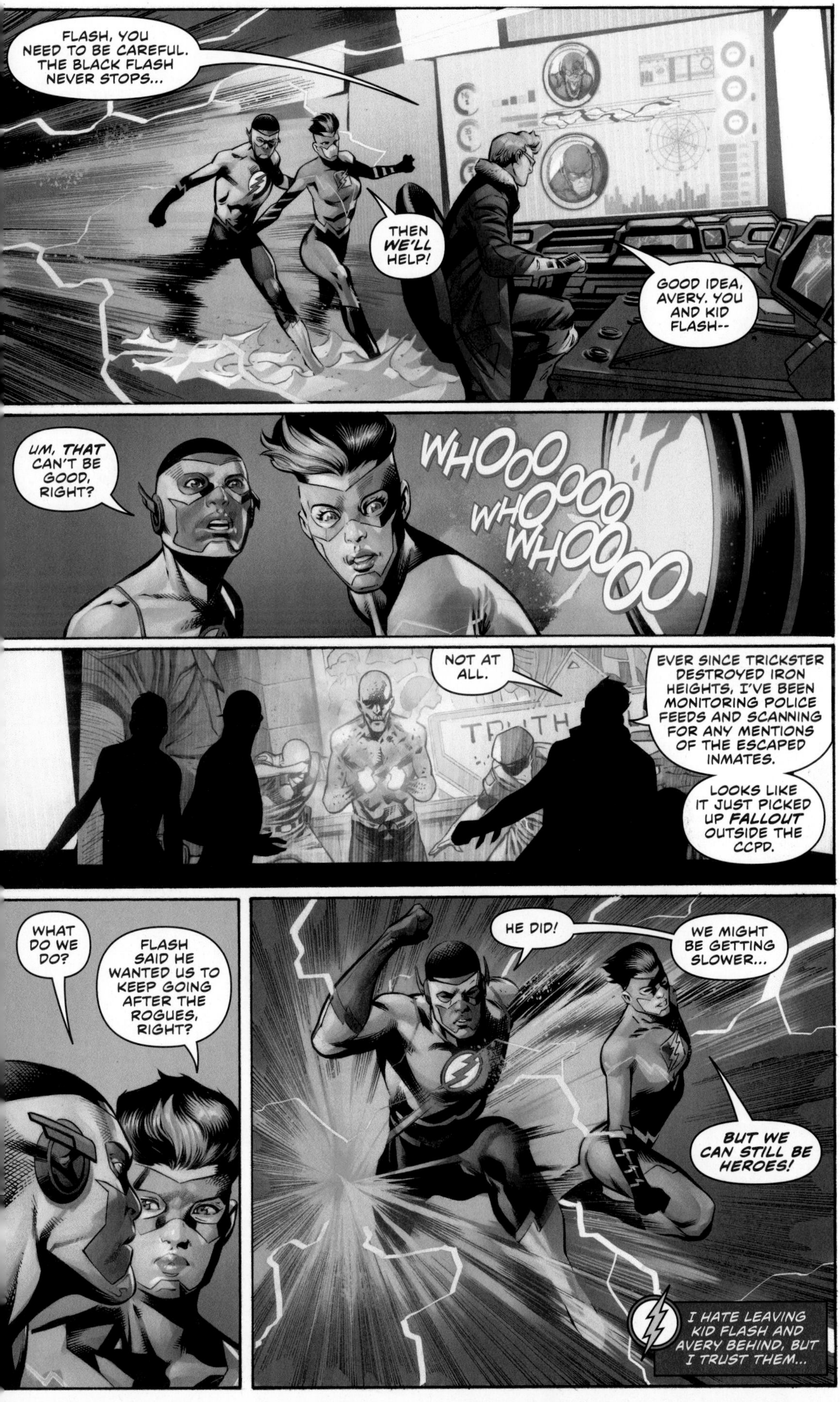

FLASH, YOU NEED TO BE CAREFUL. THE BLACK FLASH NEVER STOPS...
THEN *WE'LL* HELP!
GOOD IDEA, AVERY. YOU AND KID FLASH--
UM, *THAT* CAN'T BE GOOD, RIGHT?
WHOOOO WHOOOOO WHOOOOO
NOT AT ALL.
EVER SINCE TRICKSTER DESTROYED IRON HEIGHTS, I'VE BEEN MONITORING POLICE FEEDS AND SCANNING FOR ANY MENTIONS OF THE ESCAPED INMATES.
LOOKS LIKE IT JUST PICKED UP *FALLOUT* OUTSIDE THE CCPD.
TRUTH
WHAT DO WE DO?
FLASH SAID HE WANTED US TO KEEP GOING AFTER THE ROGUES, RIGHT?
HE DID!
WE MIGHT BE GETTING SLOWER...
BUT WE CAN STILL BE HEROES!
I HATE LEAVING KID FLASH AND AVERY BEHIND, BUT I TRUST THEM...

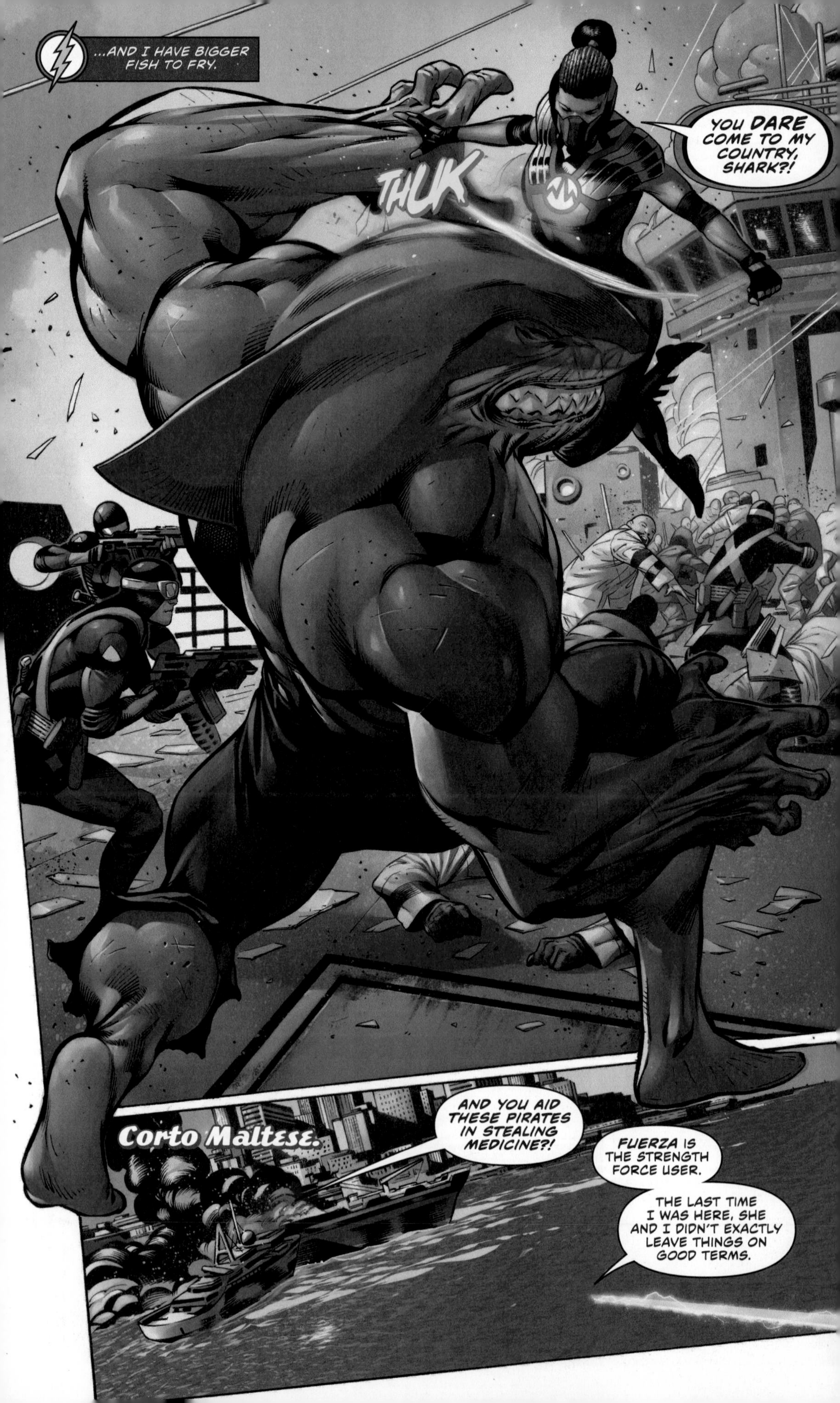
...AND I HAVE BIGGER FISH TO FRY.
YOU DARE COME TO MY COUNTRY, SHARK?!
THUK
Corto Maltese.
AND YOU AID THESE PIRATES IN STEALING MEDICINE?!
FUERZA IS THE STRENGTH FORCE USER.
THE LAST TIME I WAS HERE, SHE AND I DIDN'T EXACTLY LEAVE THINGS ON GOOD TERMS.

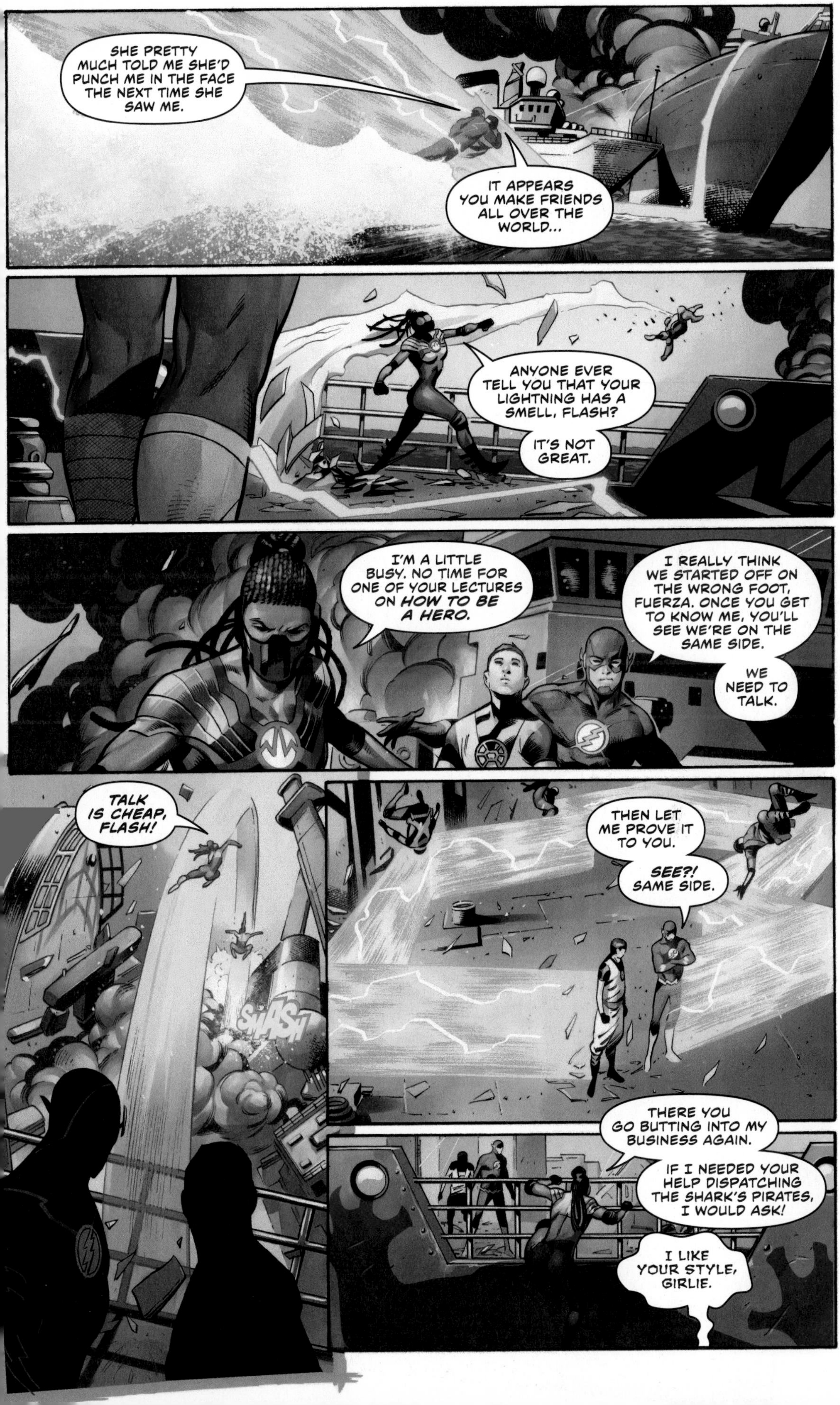
SHE PRETTY MUCH TOLD ME SHE'D PUNCH ME IN THE FACE THE NEXT TIME SHE SAW ME.
IT APPEARS YOU MAKE FRIENDS ALL OVER THE WORLD...
ANYONE EVER TELL YOU THAT YOUR LIGHTNING HAS A SMELL, FLASH?
IT'S NOT GREAT.
I'M A LITTLE BUSY. NO TIME FOR ONE OF YOUR LECTURES ON *HOW TO BE A HERO.*
I REALLY THINK WE STARTED OFF ON THE WRONG FOOT, FUERZA. ONCE YOU GET TO KNOW ME, YOU'LL SEE WE'RE ON THE SAME SIDE.
WE NEED TO TALK.
TALK IS CHEAP, FLASH!
SMASH
THEN LET ME PROVE IT TO YOU.
SEE?! SAME SIDE.
THERE YOU GO BUTTING INTO MY BUSINESS AGAIN.
IF I NEEDED YOUR HELP DISPATCHING THE SHARK'S PIRATES, I WOULD ASK!
I LIKE YOUR STYLE, GIRLIE.

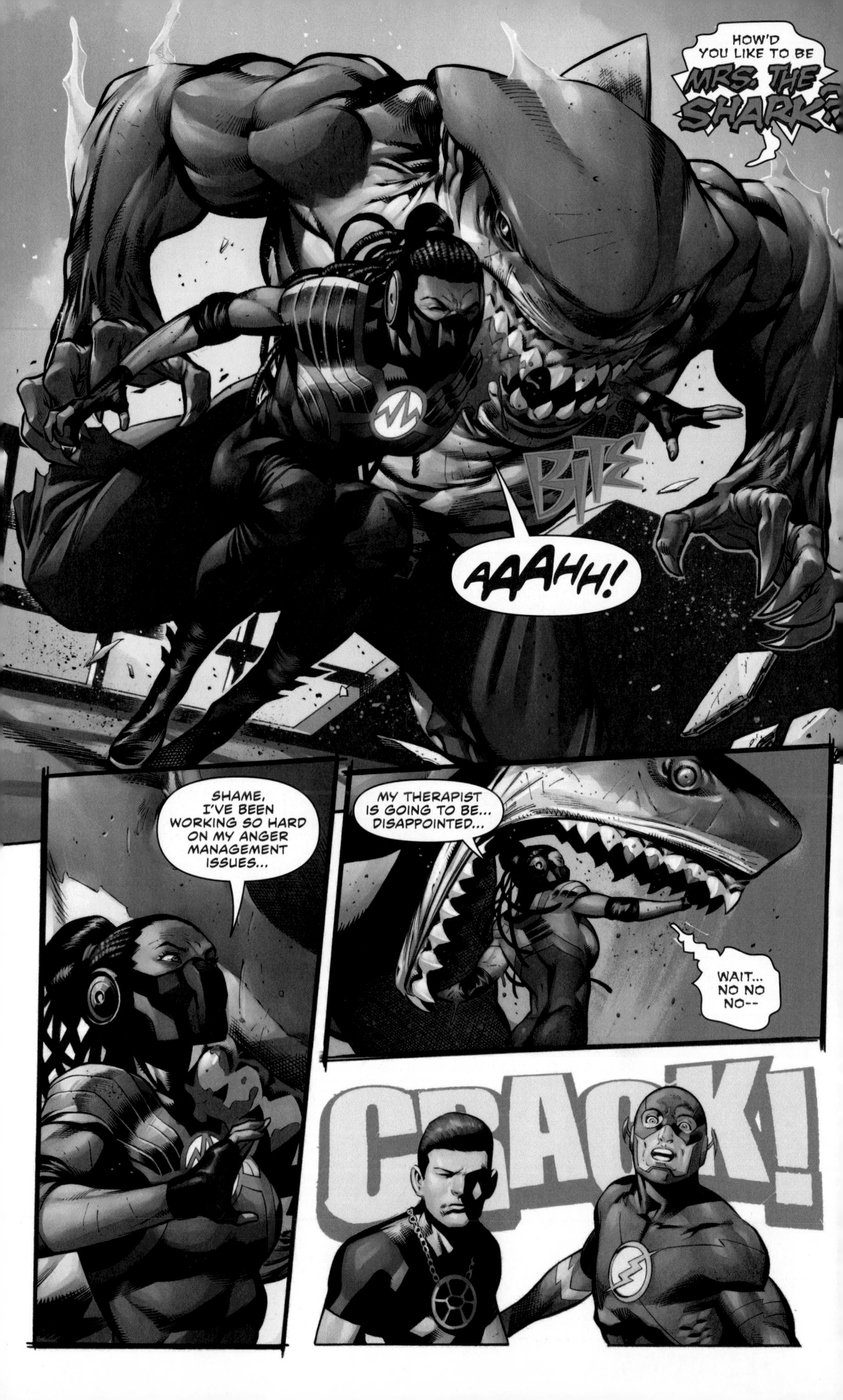
HOW'D YOU LIKE TO BE MRS. THE SHARK?
BITE
AAAHH!
SHAME, I'VE BEEN WORKING SO HARD ON MY ANGER MANAGEMENT ISSUES...
MY THERAPIST IS GOING TO BE... DISAPPOINTED...
WAIT... NO NO NO--
CRACK!

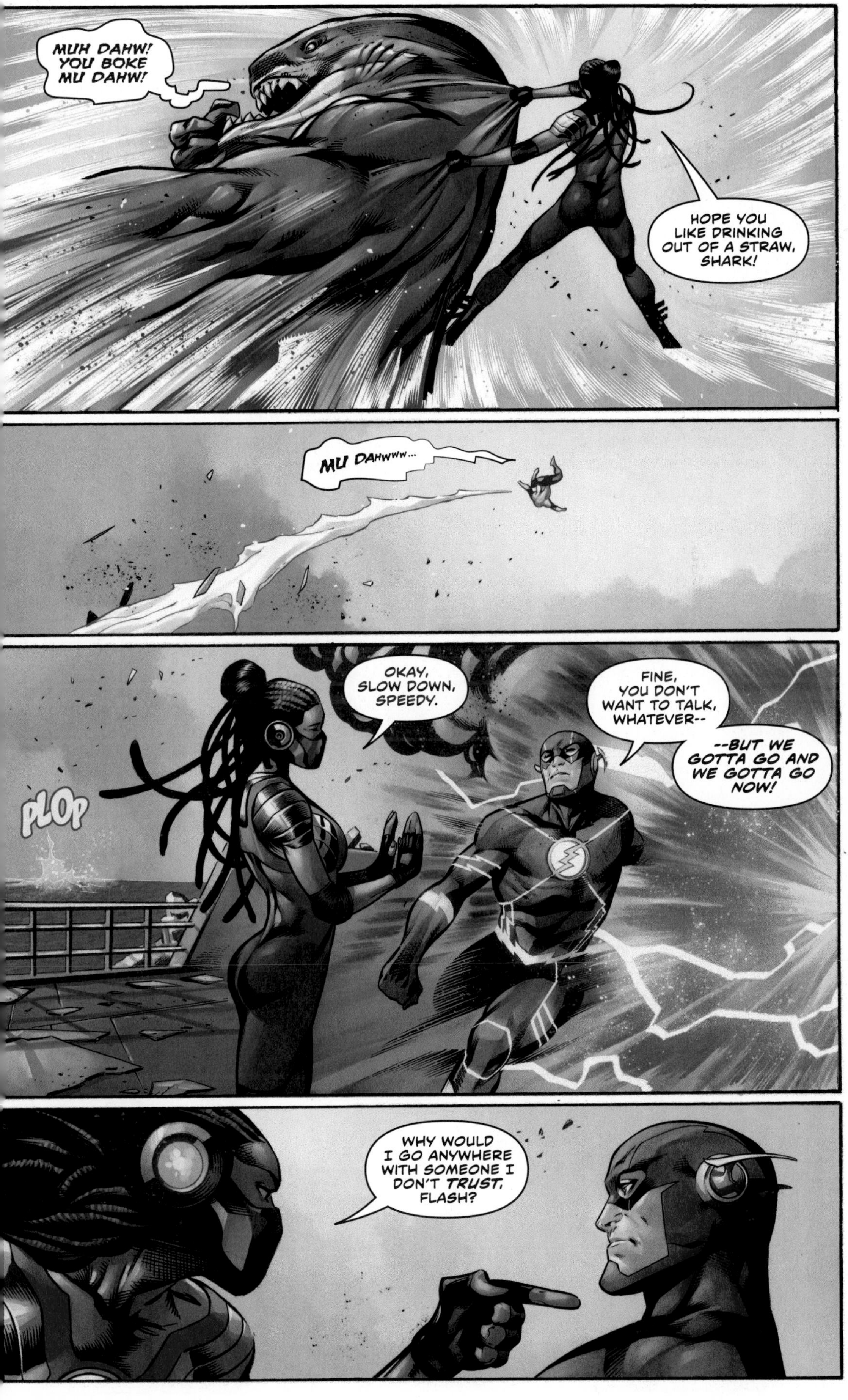
MUH DAHW! YOU BOKE MU DAHW!
HOPE YOU LIKE DRINKING OUT OF A STRAW, SHARK!
MU DAHWWW...
PLOP
OKAY, SLOW DOWN, SPEEDY.
FINE, YOU DON'T WANT TO TALK, WHATEVER--
--BUT WE GOTTA GO AND WE GOTTA GO NOW!
WHY WOULD I GO ANYWHERE WITH SOMEONE I DON'T TRUST, FLASH?

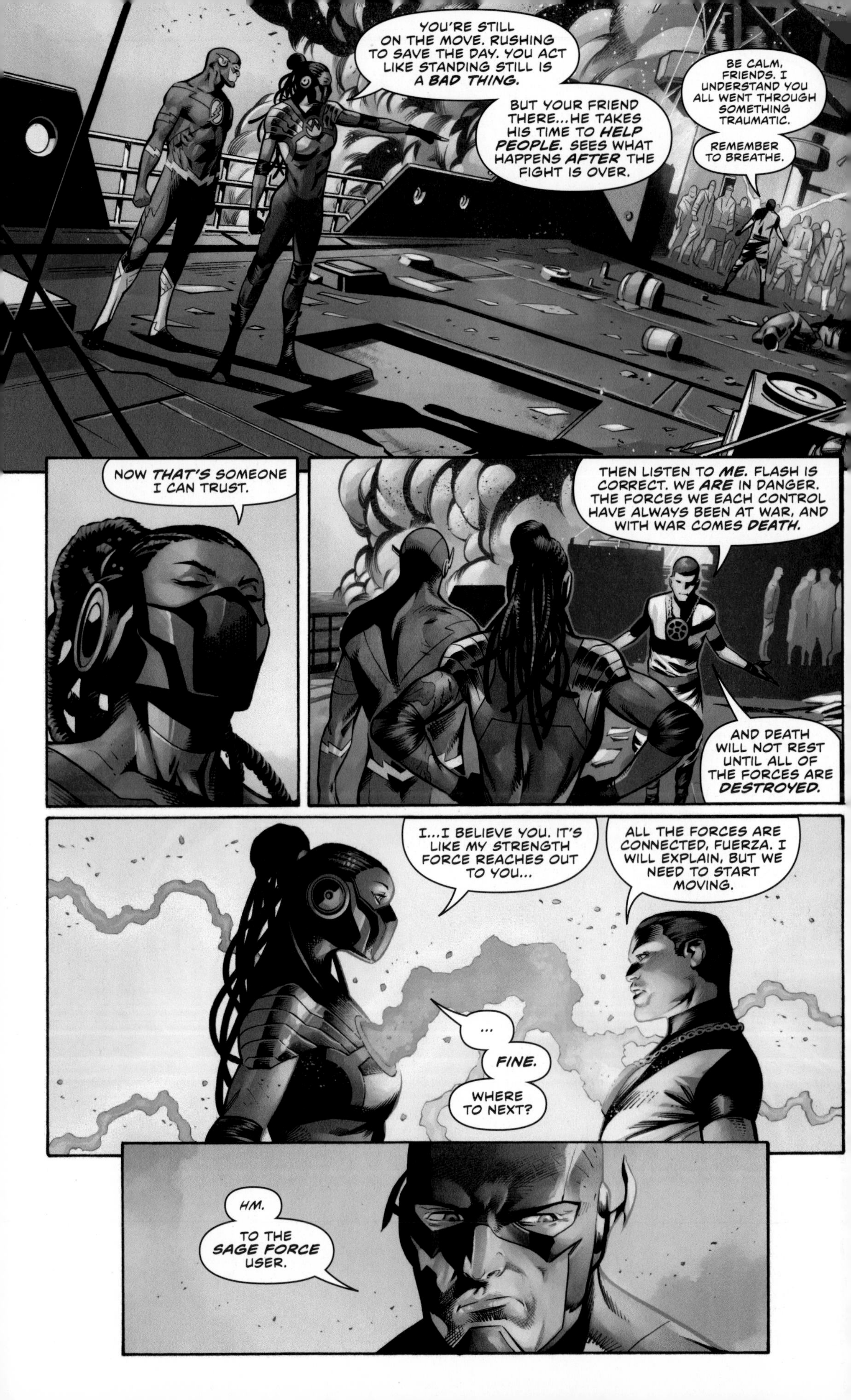
YOU'RE STILL ON THE MOVE. RUSHING TO SAVE THE DAY. YOU ACT LIKE STANDING STILL IS A *BAD THING.*
BUT YOUR FRIEND THERE...HE TAKES HIS TIME TO *HELP PEOPLE.* SEES WHAT HAPPENS *AFTER* THE FIGHT IS OVER.
BE CALM, FRIENDS. I UNDERSTAND YOU ALL WENT THROUGH SOMETHING TRAUMATIC.
REMEMBER TO BREATHE.
NOW *THAT'S* SOMEONE I CAN TRUST.
THEN LISTEN TO *ME.* FLASH IS CORRECT. WE *ARE* IN DANGER. THE FORCES WE EACH CONTROL HAVE ALWAYS BEEN AT WAR, AND WITH WAR COMES *DEATH.*
AND DEATH WILL NOT REST UNTIL ALL OF THE FORCES ARE *DESTROYED.*
I...I BELIEVE YOU. IT'S LIKE MY STRENGTH FORCE REACHES OUT TO YOU...
ALL THE FORCES ARE CONNECTED, FUERZA. I WILL EXPLAIN, BUT WE NEED TO START MOVING.
...
FINE.
WHERE TO NEXT?
HM.
TO THE *SAGE FORCE* USER.

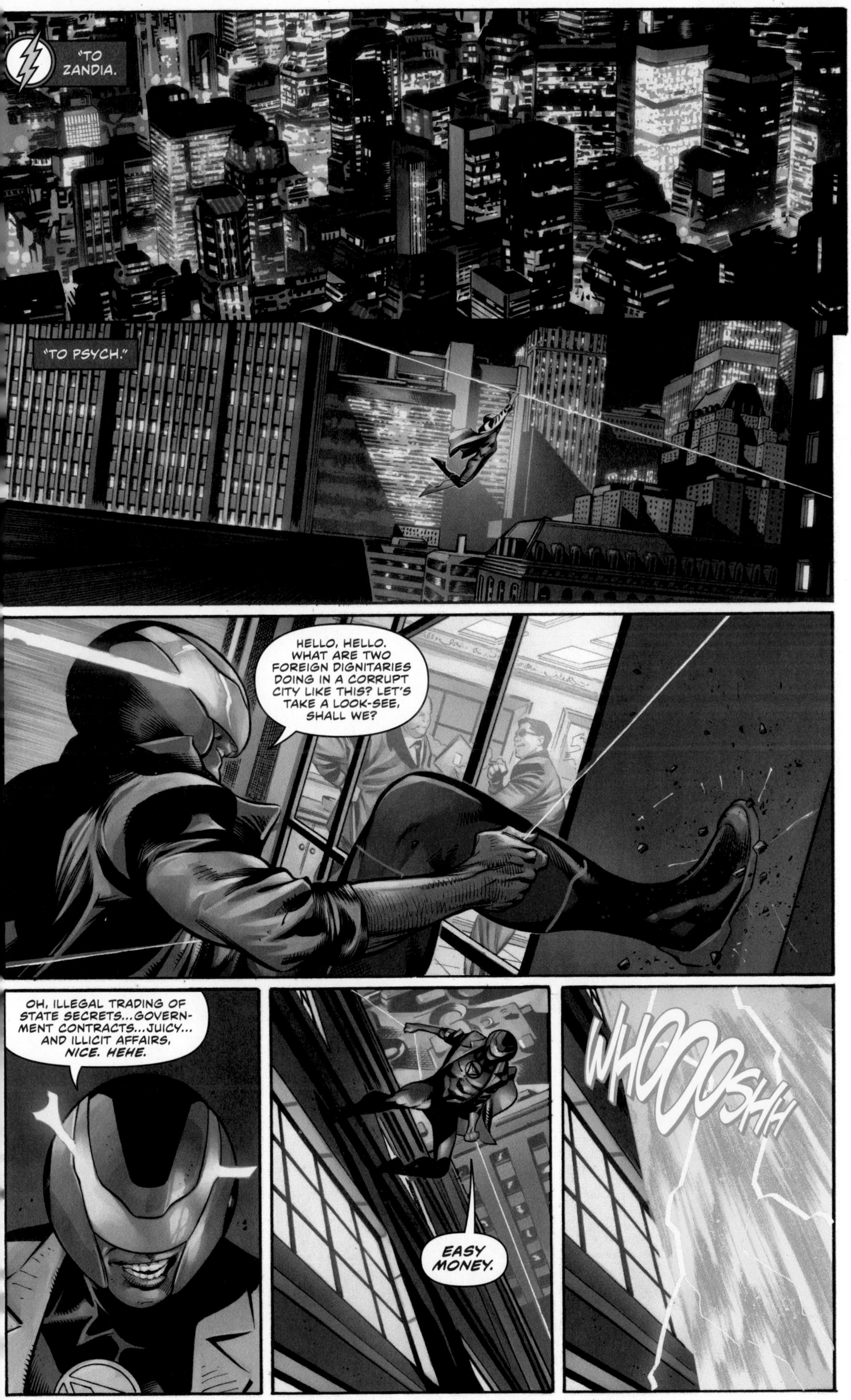
"TO
ZANDIA.
"TO PSYCH."
HELLO, HELLO. WHAT ARE TWO FOREIGN DIGNITARIES DOING IN A CORRUPT CITY LIKE THIS? LET'S TAKE A LOOK-SEE, SHALL WE?
OH, ILLEGAL TRADING OF STATE SECRETS...GOVERNMENT CONTRACTS...JUICY... AND ILLICIT AFFAIRS, NICE. HEHE.
EASY MONEY.
WHOOOOSHH

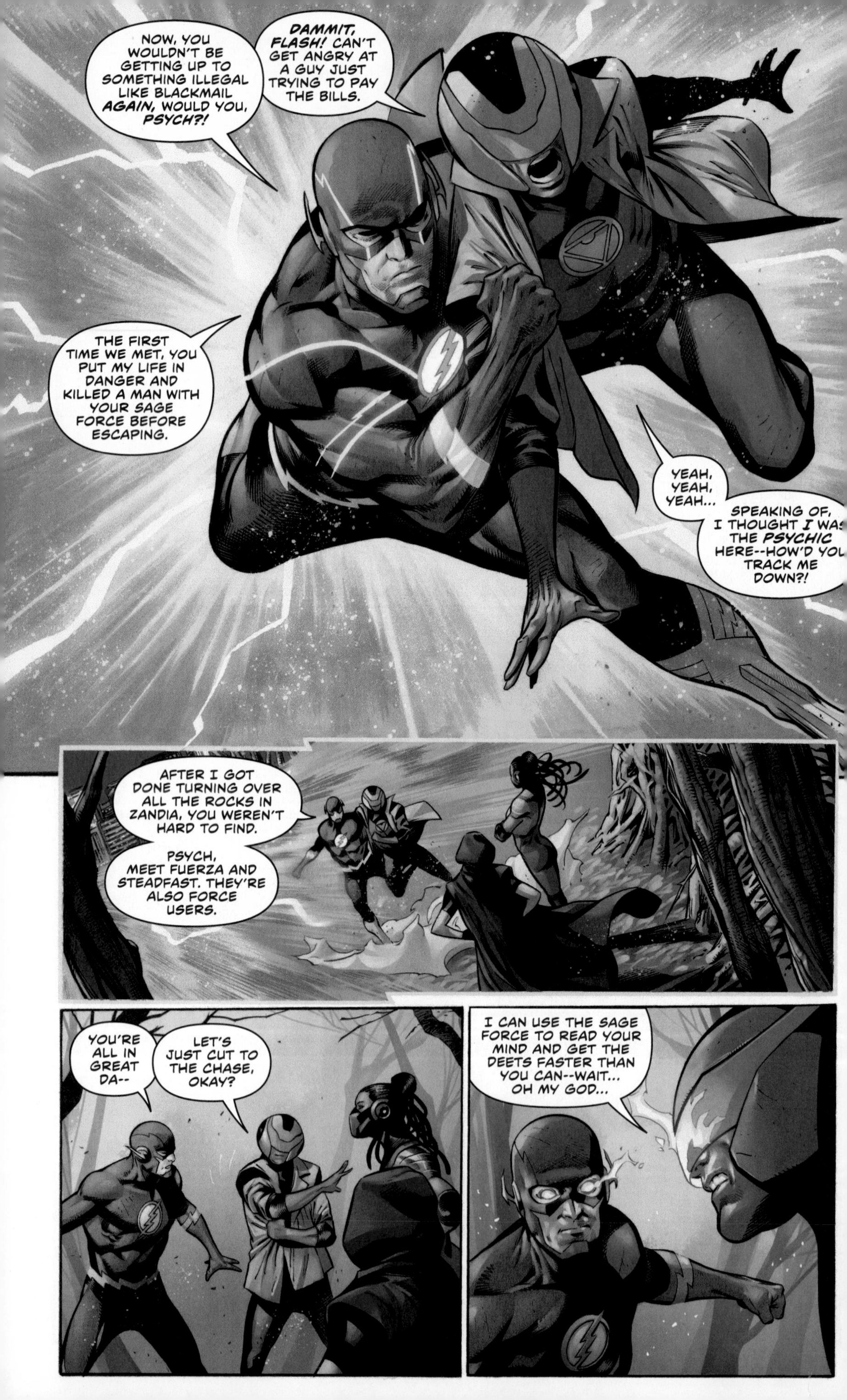
NOW, YOU WOULDN'T BE GETTING UP TO SOMETHING ILLEGAL LIKE BLACKMAIL AGAIN, WOULD YOU, PSYCH?!
DAMMIT, FLASH! CAN'T GET ANGRY AT A GUY JUST TRYING TO PAY THE BILLS.
THE FIRST TIME WE MET, YOU PUT MY LIFE IN DANGER AND KILLED A MAN WITH YOUR SAGE FORCE BEFORE ESCAPING.
YEAH, YEAH, YEAH...
SPEAKING OF, I THOUGHT I WAS THE PSYCHIC HERE--HOW'D YOU TRACK ME DOWN?!
AFTER I GOT DONE TURNING OVER ALL THE ROCKS IN ZANDIA, YOU WEREN'T HARD TO FIND.
PSYCH, MEET FUERZA AND STEADFAST. THEY'RE ALSO FORCE USERS.
YOU'RE ALL IN GREAT DA--
LET'S JUST CUT TO THE CHASE, OKAY?
I CAN USE THE SAGE FORCE TO READ YOUR MIND AND GET THE DEETS FASTER THAN YOU CAN--WAIT... OH MY GOD...

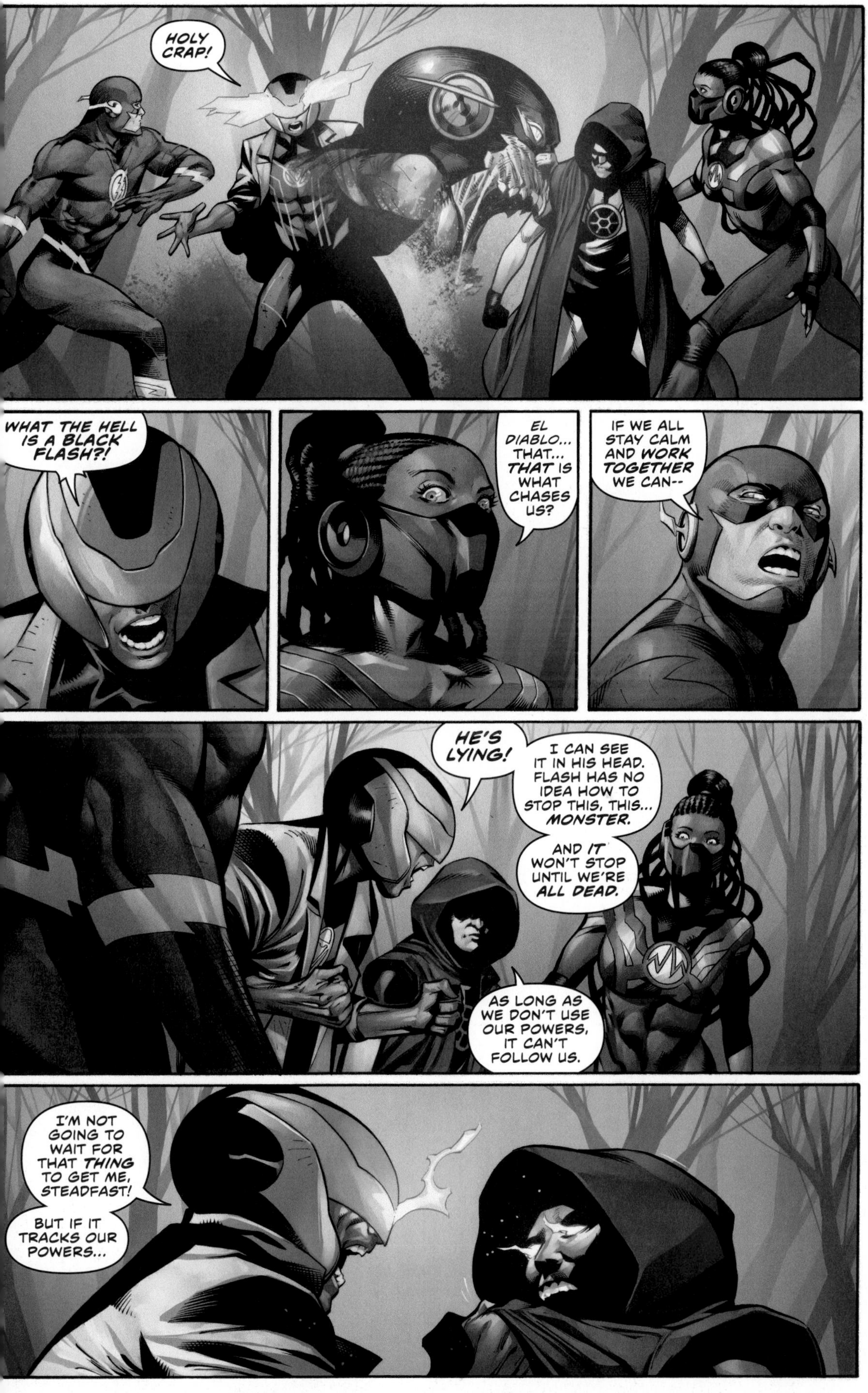
HOLY CRAP!
WHAT THE HELL IS A BLACK FLASH?!
EL DIABLO... THAT... THAT IS WHAT CHASES US?
IF WE ALL STAY CALM AND WORK TOGETHER WE CAN--
HE'S LYING!
I CAN SEE IT IN HIS HEAD. FLASH HAS NO IDEA HOW TO STOP THIS, THIS... MONSTER.
AND IT WON'T STOP UNTIL WE'RE ALL DEAD.
AS LONG AS WE DON'T USE OUR POWERS, IT CAN'T FOLLOW US.
I'M NOT GOING TO WAIT FOR THAT THING TO GET ME, STEADFAST!
BUT IF IT TRACKS OUR POWERS...

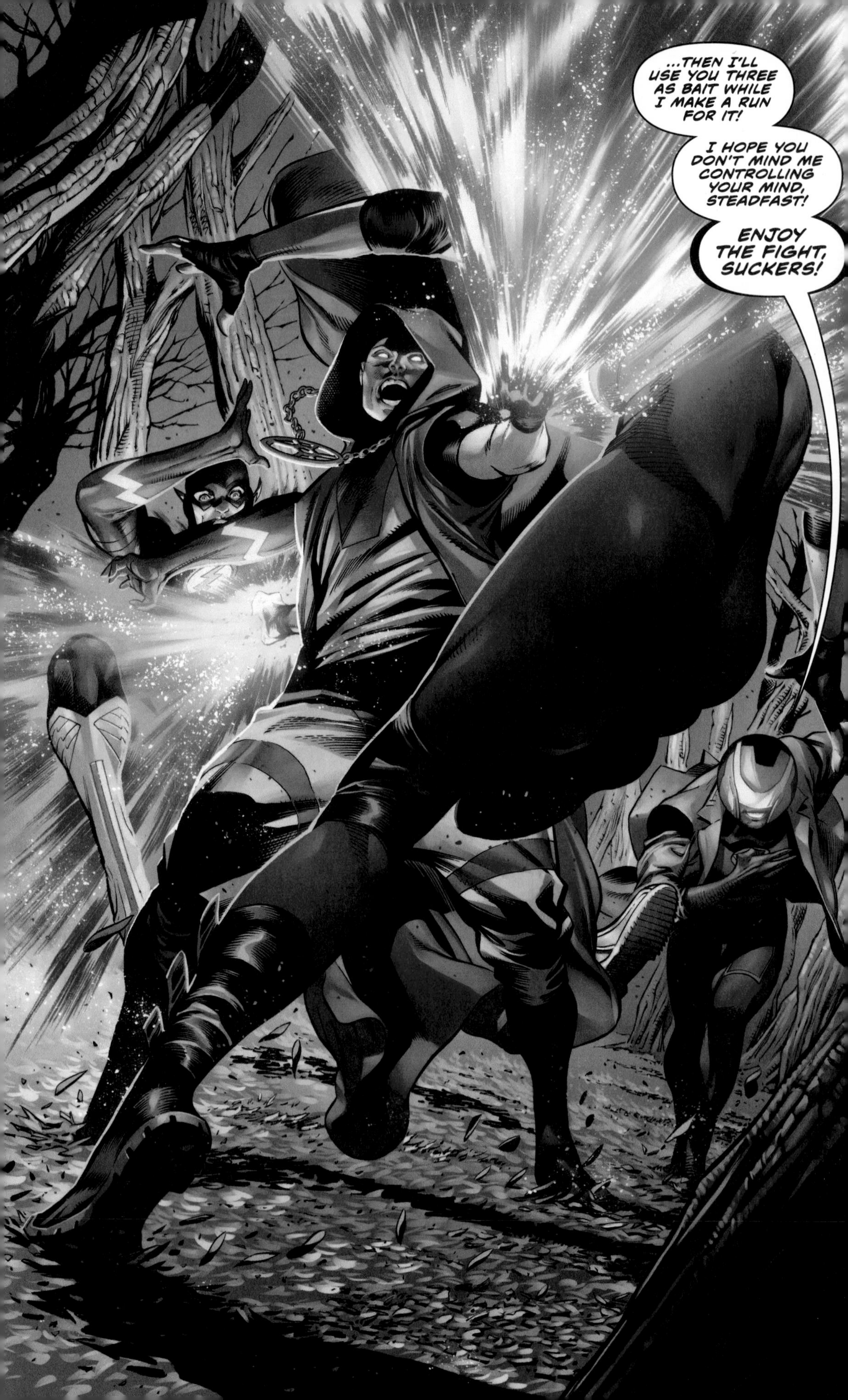
...THEN I'LL USE YOU THREE AS BAIT WHILE I MAKE A RUN FOR IT!
I HOPE YOU DON'T MIND ME CONTROLLING YOUR MIND, STEADFAST!
ENJOY THE FIGHT, SUCKERS!

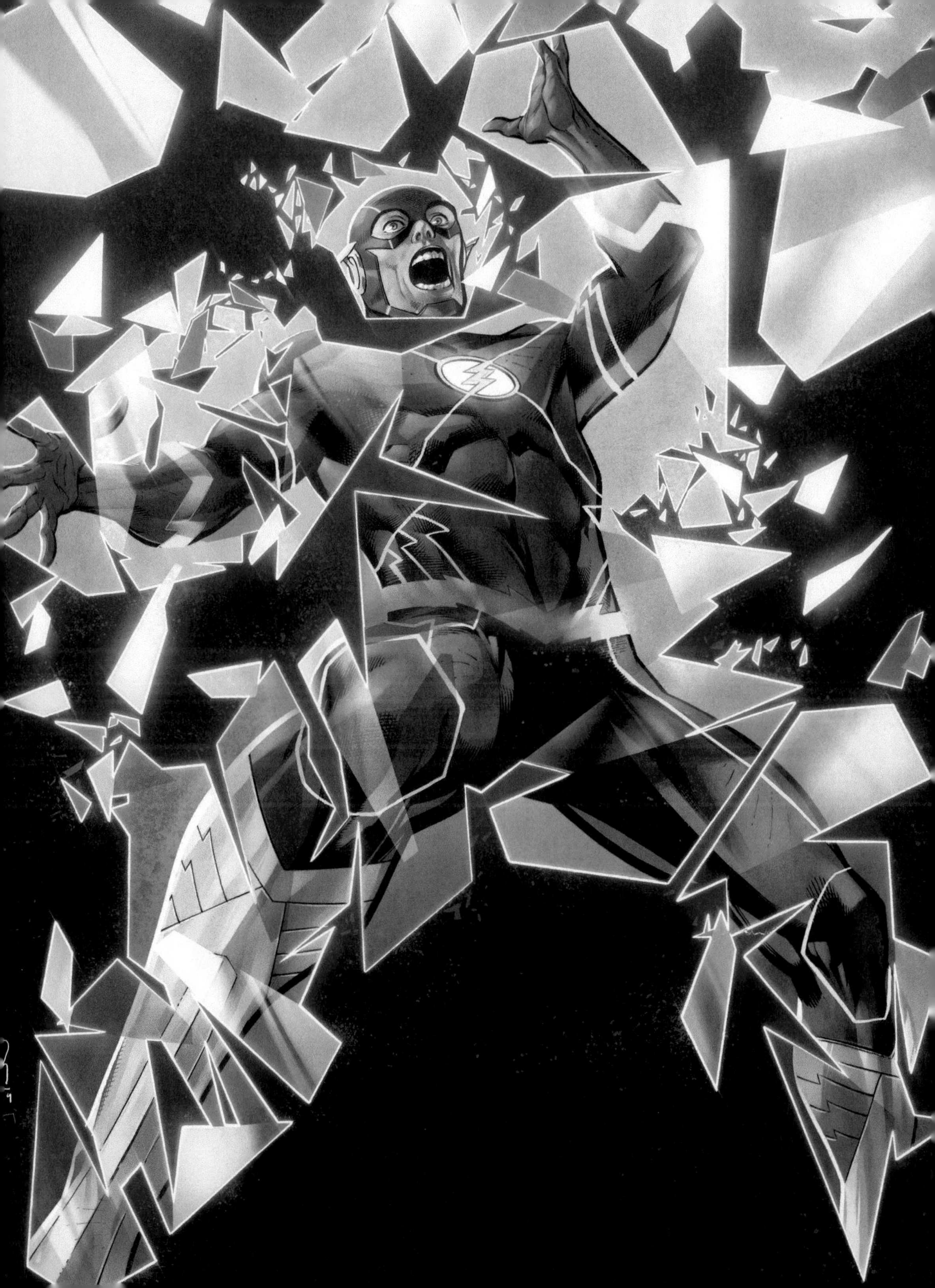

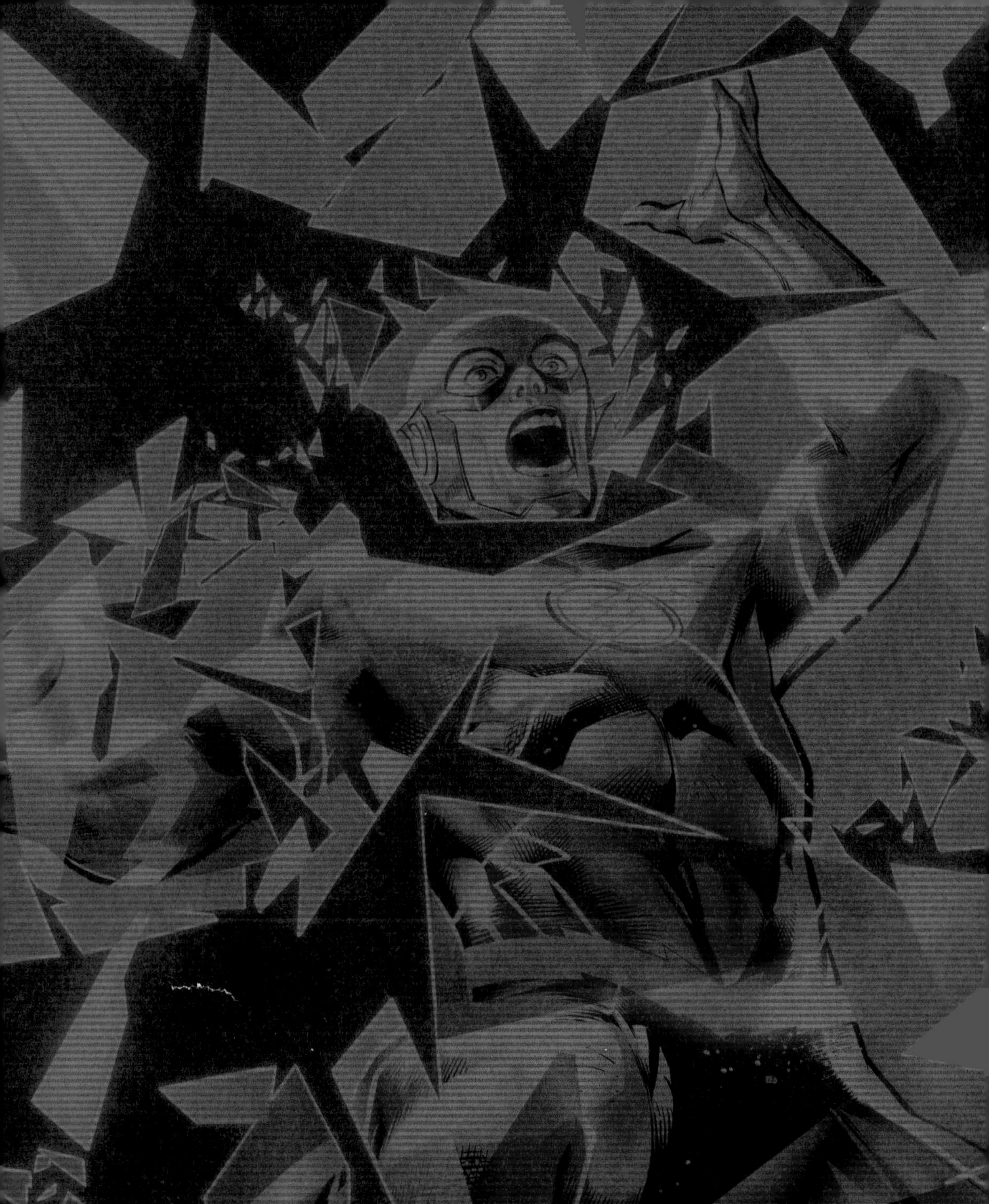

THE FLASH

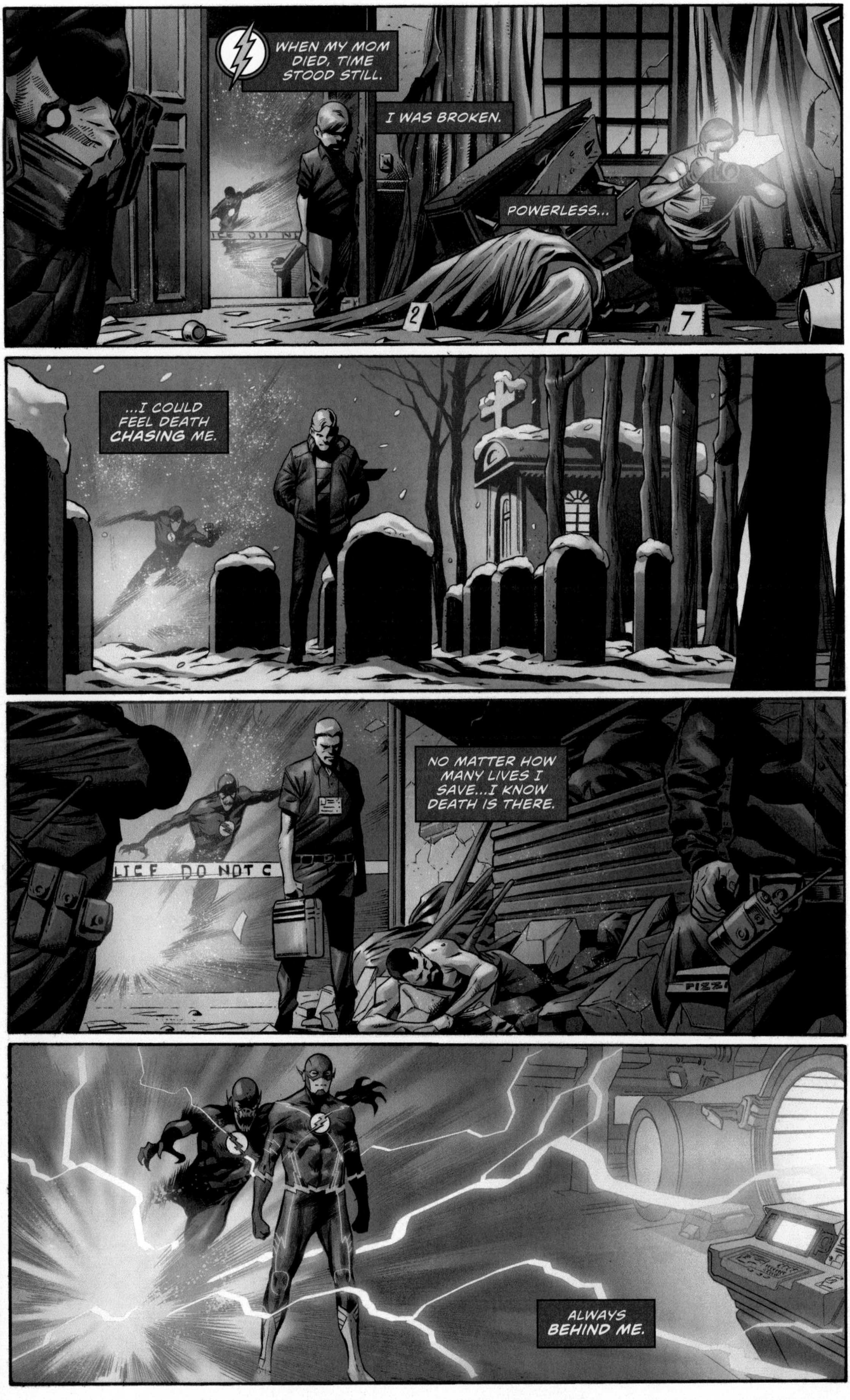
WHEN MY MOM DIED, TIME STOOD STILL.
I WAS BROKEN.
POWERLESS...
...I COULD FEEL DEATH CHASING ME.
NO MATTER HOW MANY LIVES I SAVE...I KNOW DEATH IS THERE.
ALWAYS BEHIND ME.

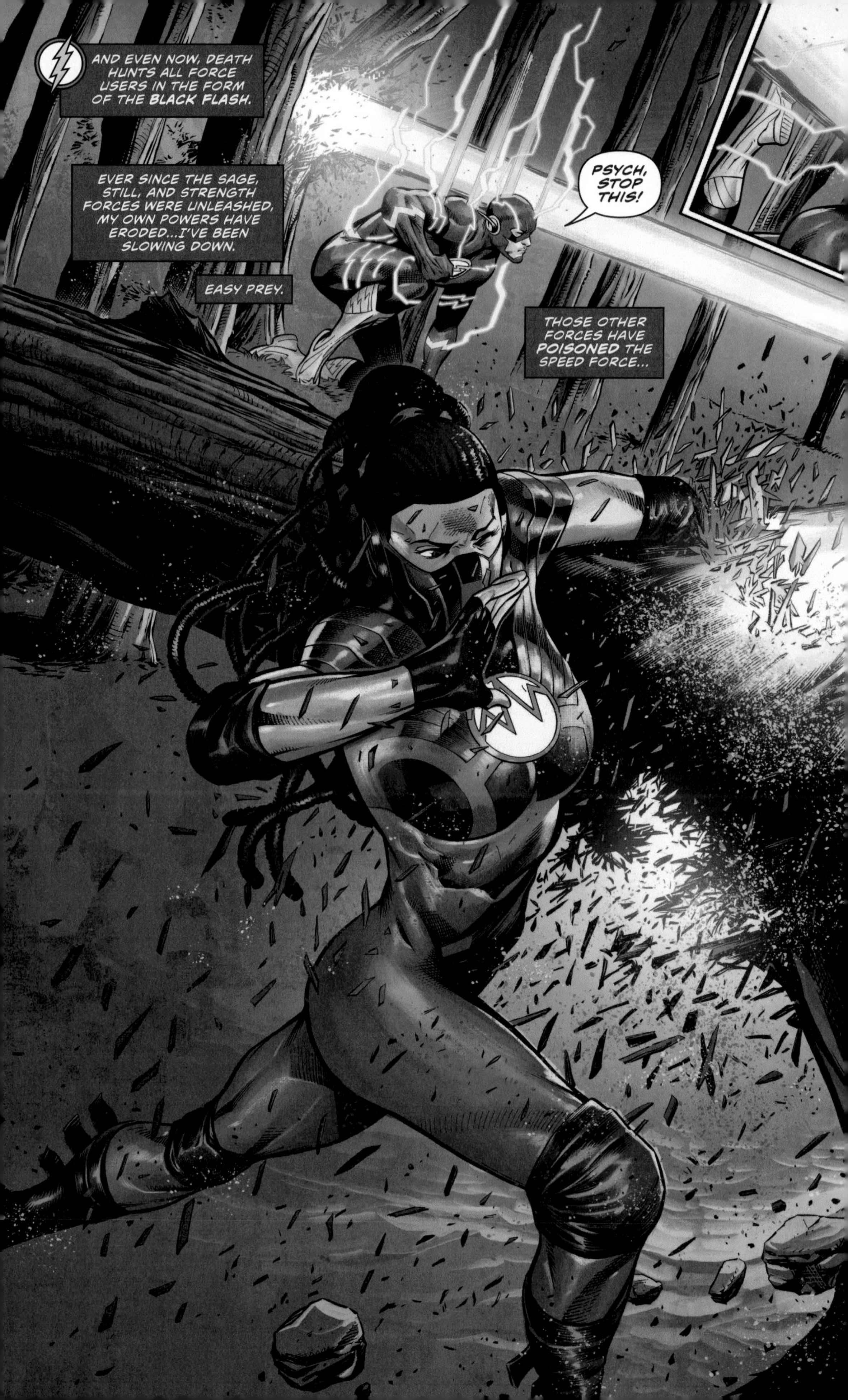
AND EVEN NOW, DEATH HUNTS ALL FORCE USERS IN THE FORM OF THE BLACK FLASH.
EVER SINCE THE SAGE, STILL, AND STRENGTH FORCES WERE UNLEASHED, MY OWN POWERS HAVE ERODED...I'VE BEEN SLOWING DOWN.
EASY PREY.
PSYCH, STOP THIS!
THOSE OTHER FORCES HAVE POISONED THE SPEED FORCE...

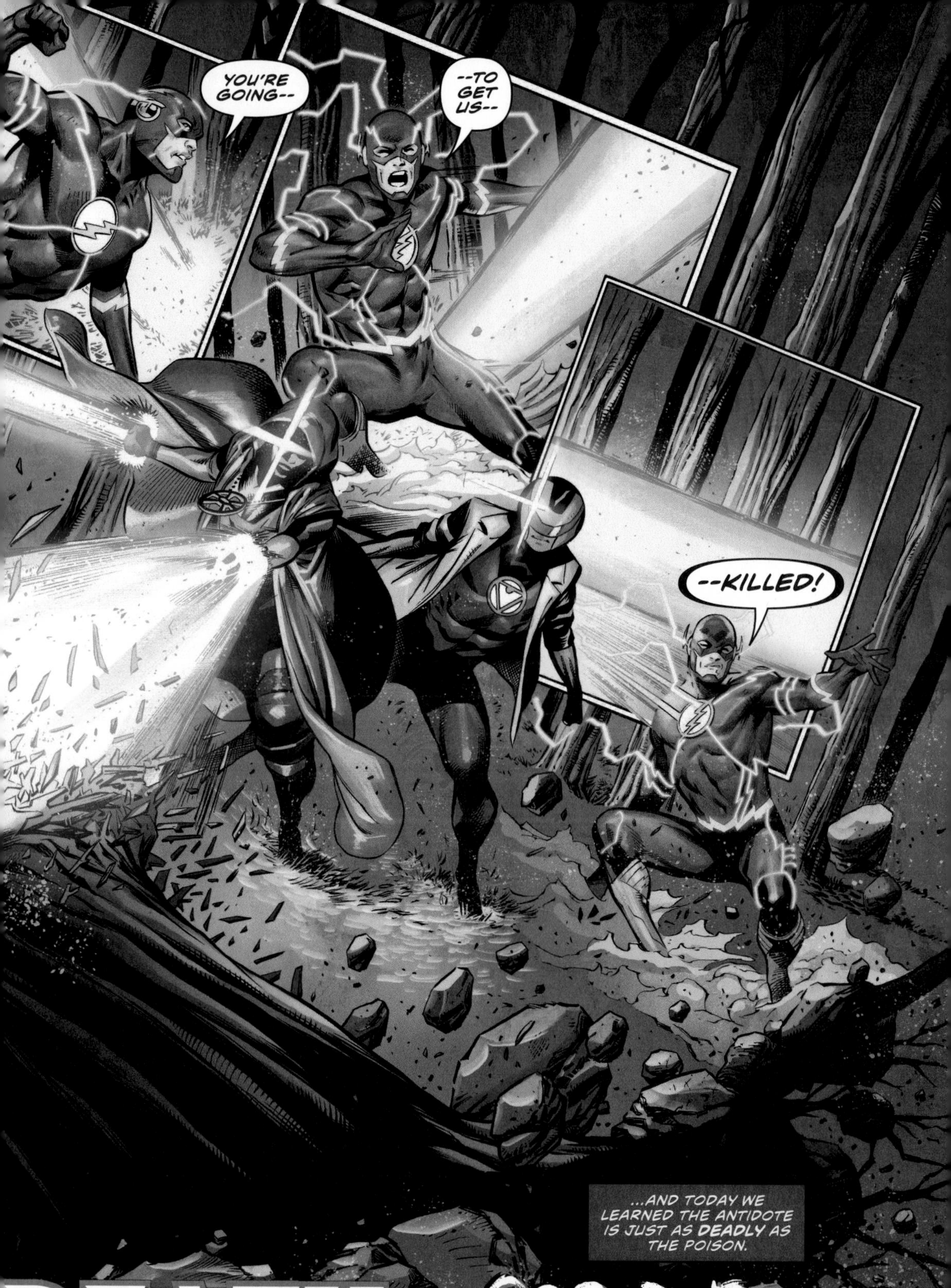
YOU'RE GOING--
--TO GET US--
--KILLED!
...AND TODAY WE LEARNED THE ANTIDOTE IS JUST AS DEADLY AS THE POISON.

DEATH AND THE SPEED FORCE

Part Three

JOSHUA WILLIAMSON WRITER **RAFA SANDOVAL** PENCILS
JORDI TARRAGONA INKS **ARIF PRIANTO** COLORS **STEVE WANDS** LETTERS
SANDOVAL, TARRAGONA & **TOMEU MOREY** COVER
ROB LEVIN ASSOCIATE EDITOR **PAUL KAMINSKI** EDITOR **JAMIE S. RICH** GROUP EDITOR

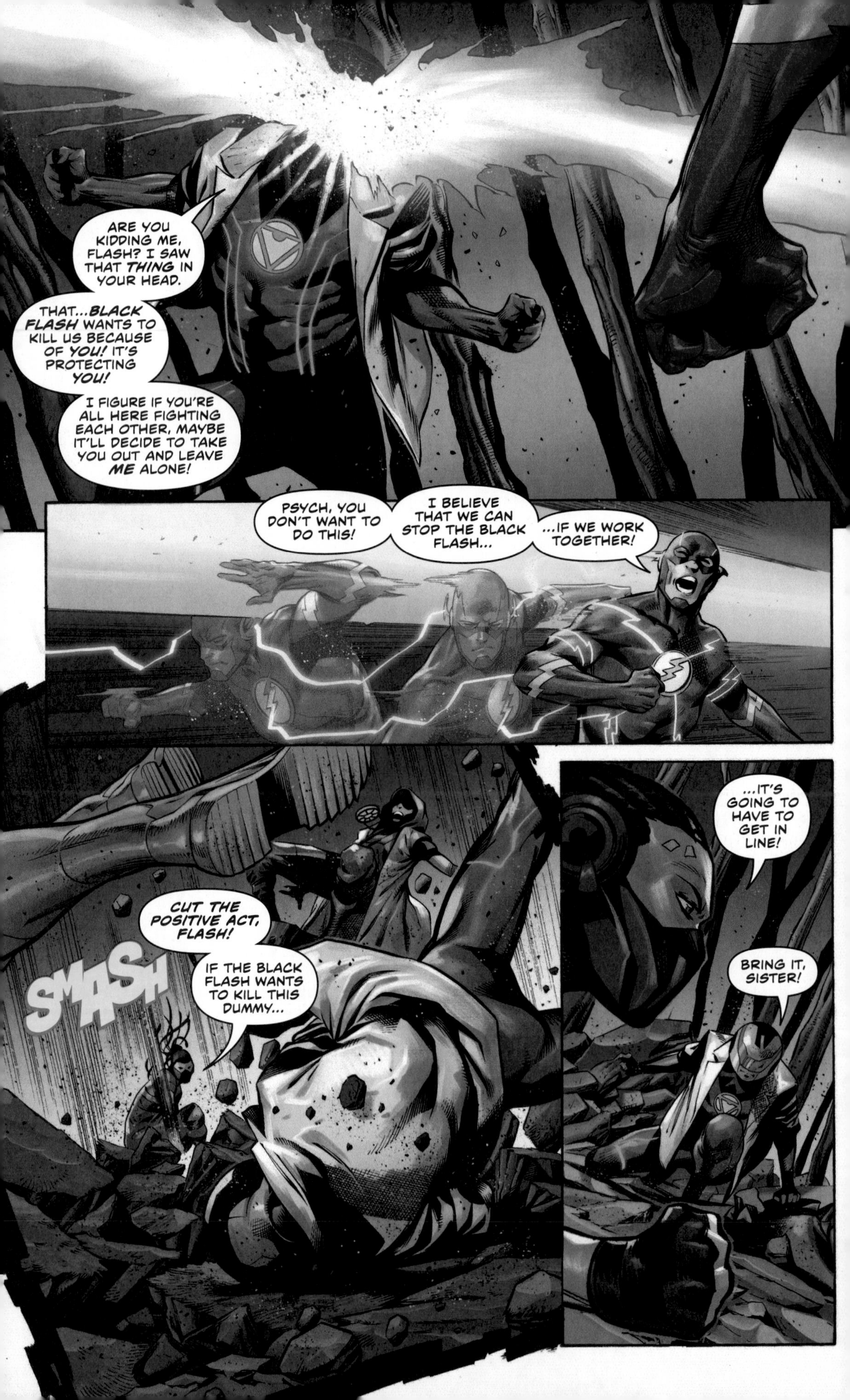
ARE YOU KIDDING ME, FLASH? I SAW THAT THING IN YOUR HEAD.
THAT...BLACK FLASH WANTS TO KILL US BECAUSE OF YOU! IT'S PROTECTING YOU!
I FIGURE IF YOU'RE ALL HERE FIGHTING EACH OTHER, MAYBE IT'LL DECIDE TO TAKE YOU OUT AND LEAVE ME ALONE!
PSYCH, YOU DON'T WANT TO DO THIS!
I BELIEVE THAT WE CAN STOP THE BLACK FLASH...
...IF WE WORK TOGETHER!
CUT THE POSITIVE ACT, FLASH!
IF THE BLACK FLASH WANTS TO KILL THIS DUMMY...
SMASH
...IT'S GOING TO HAVE TO GET IN LINE!
BRING IT, SISTER!

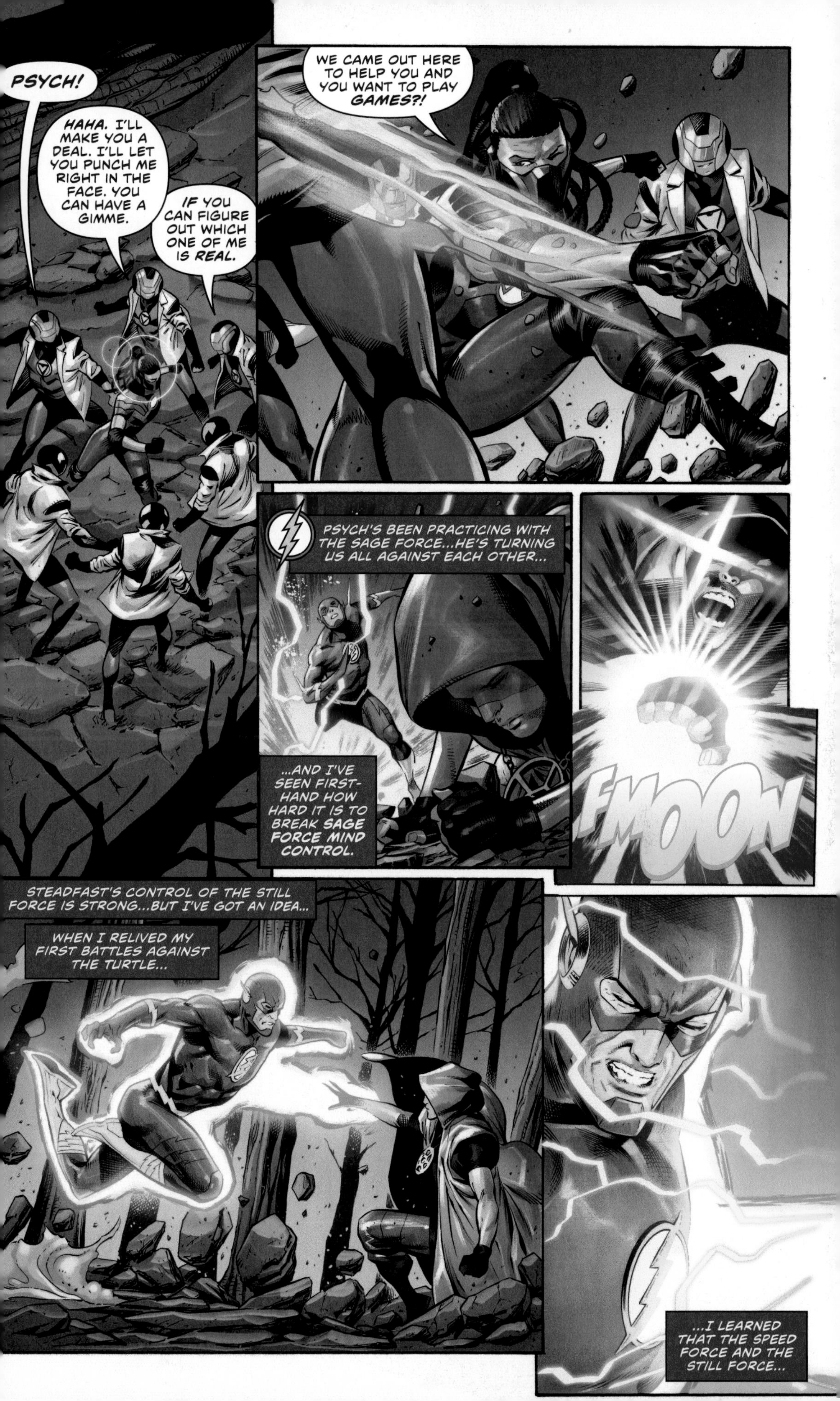
PSYCH!
HAHA. I'LL MAKE YOU A DEAL. I'LL LET YOU PUNCH ME RIGHT IN THE FACE. YOU CAN HAVE A GIMME.
IF YOU CAN FIGURE OUT WHICH ONE OF ME IS REAL.
WE CAME OUT HERE TO HELP YOU AND YOU WANT TO PLAY GAMES?!
PSYCH'S BEEN PRACTICING WITH THE SAGE FORCE...HE'S TURNING US ALL AGAINST EACH OTHER...
...AND I'VE SEEN FIRST-HAND HOW HARD IT IS TO BREAK SAGE FORCE MIND CONTROL.
FMOOON
STEADFAST'S CONTROL OF THE STILL FORCE IS STRONG...BUT I'VE GOT AN IDEA...
WHEN I RELIVED MY FIRST BATTLES AGAINST THE TURTLE...
...I LEARNED THAT THE SPEED FORCE AND THE STILL FORCE...

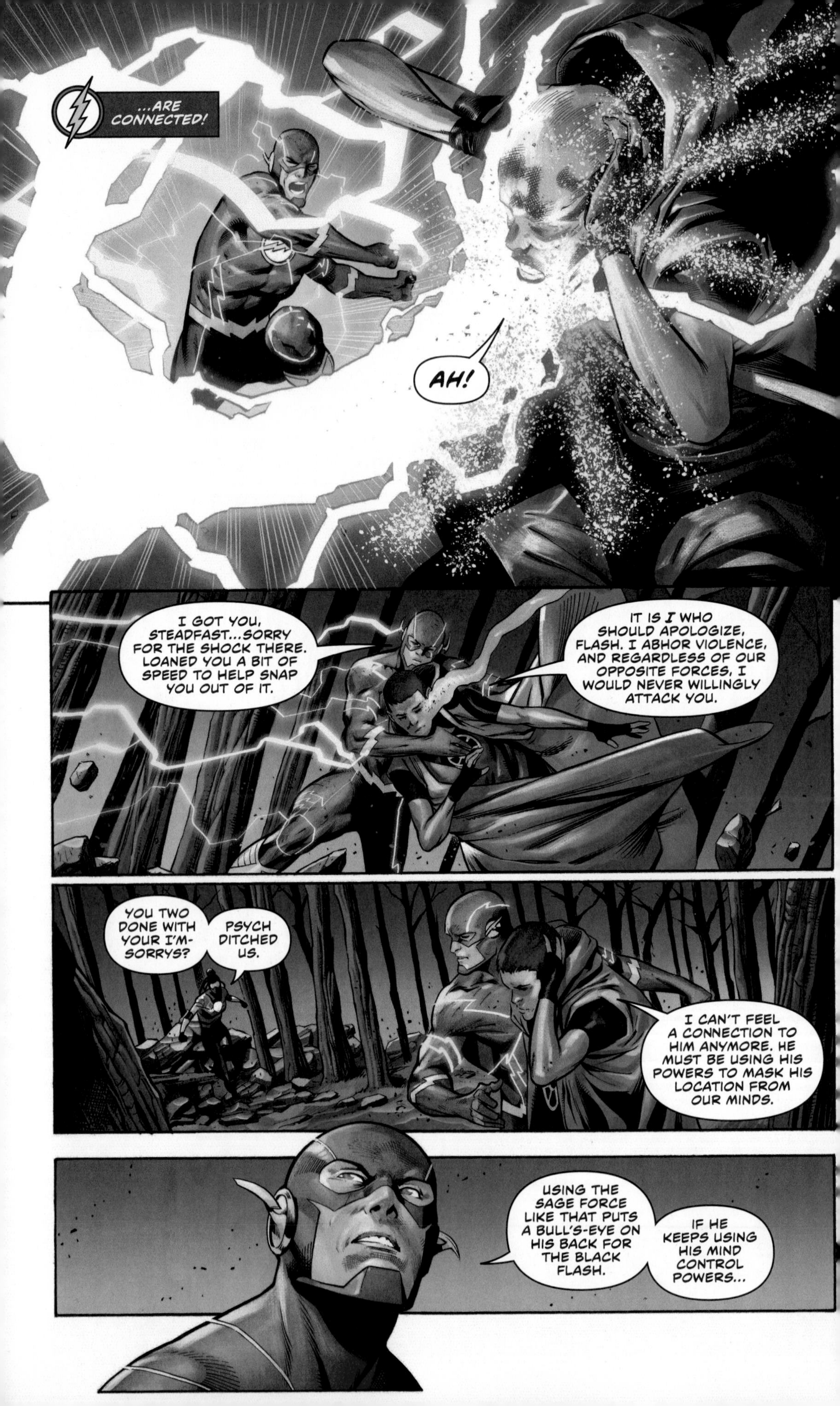

...ARE CONNECTED!
AH!
I GOT YOU, STEADFAST...SORRY FOR THE SHOCK THERE. LOANED YOU A BIT OF SPEED TO HELP SNAP YOU OUT OF IT.
IT IS I WHO SHOULD APOLOGIZE, FLASH. I ABHOR VIOLENCE, AND REGARDLESS OF OUR OPPOSITE FORCES, I WOULD NEVER WILLINGLY ATTACK YOU.
YOU TWO DONE WITH YOUR I'M-SORRYS?
PSYCH DITCHED US.
I CAN'T FEEL A CONNECTION TO HIM ANYMORE. HE MUST BE USING HIS POWERS TO MASK HIS LOCATION FROM OUR MINDS.
USING THE SAGE FORCE LIKE THAT PUTS A BULL'S-EYE ON HIS BACK FOR THE BLACK FLASH.
IF HE KEEPS USING HIS MIND CONTROL POWERS...

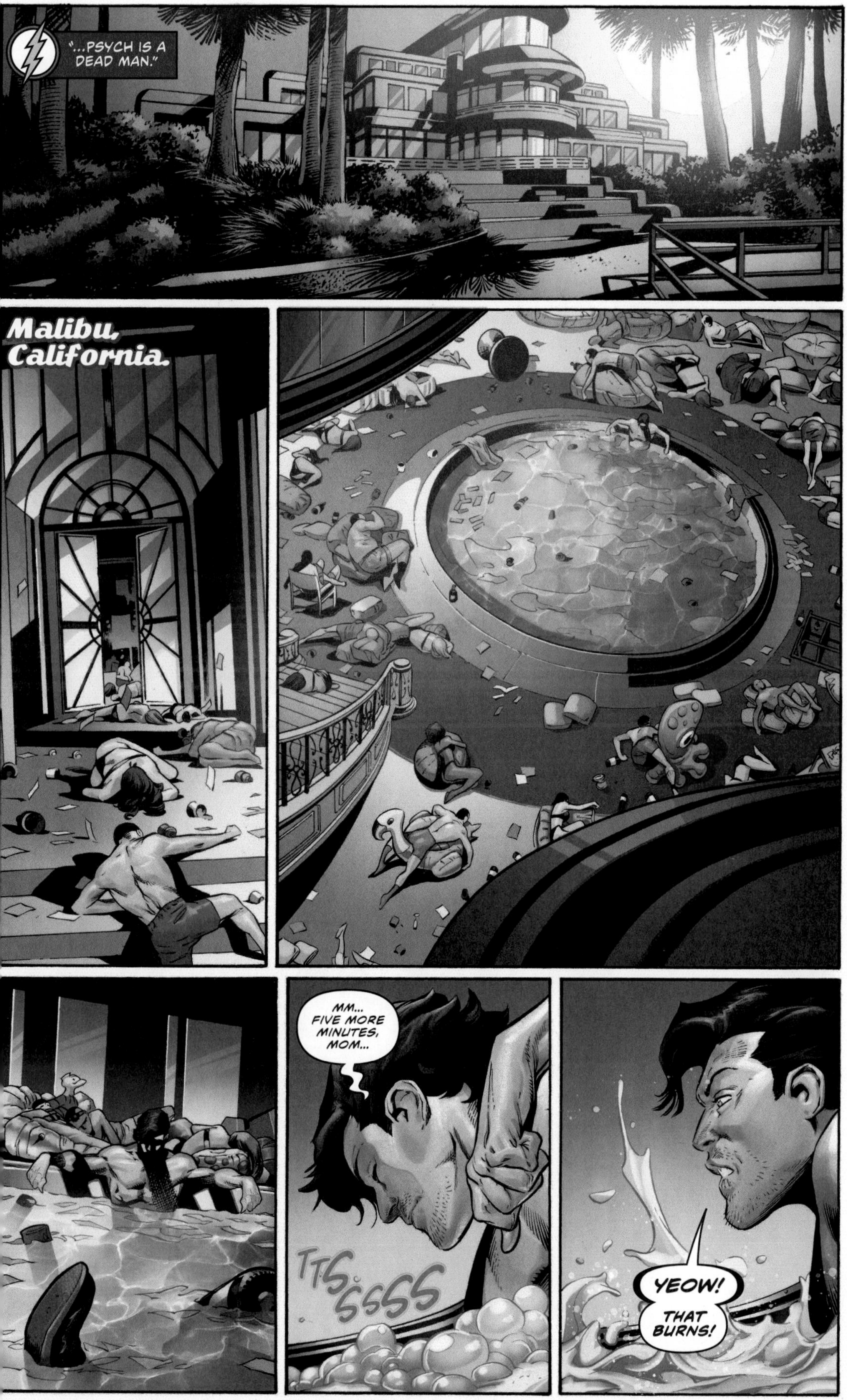
"...PSYCH IS A DEAD MAN."
Malibu, California.
MM... FIVE MORE MINUTES, MOM...
TTSSSSS
YEOW!
THAT BURNS!

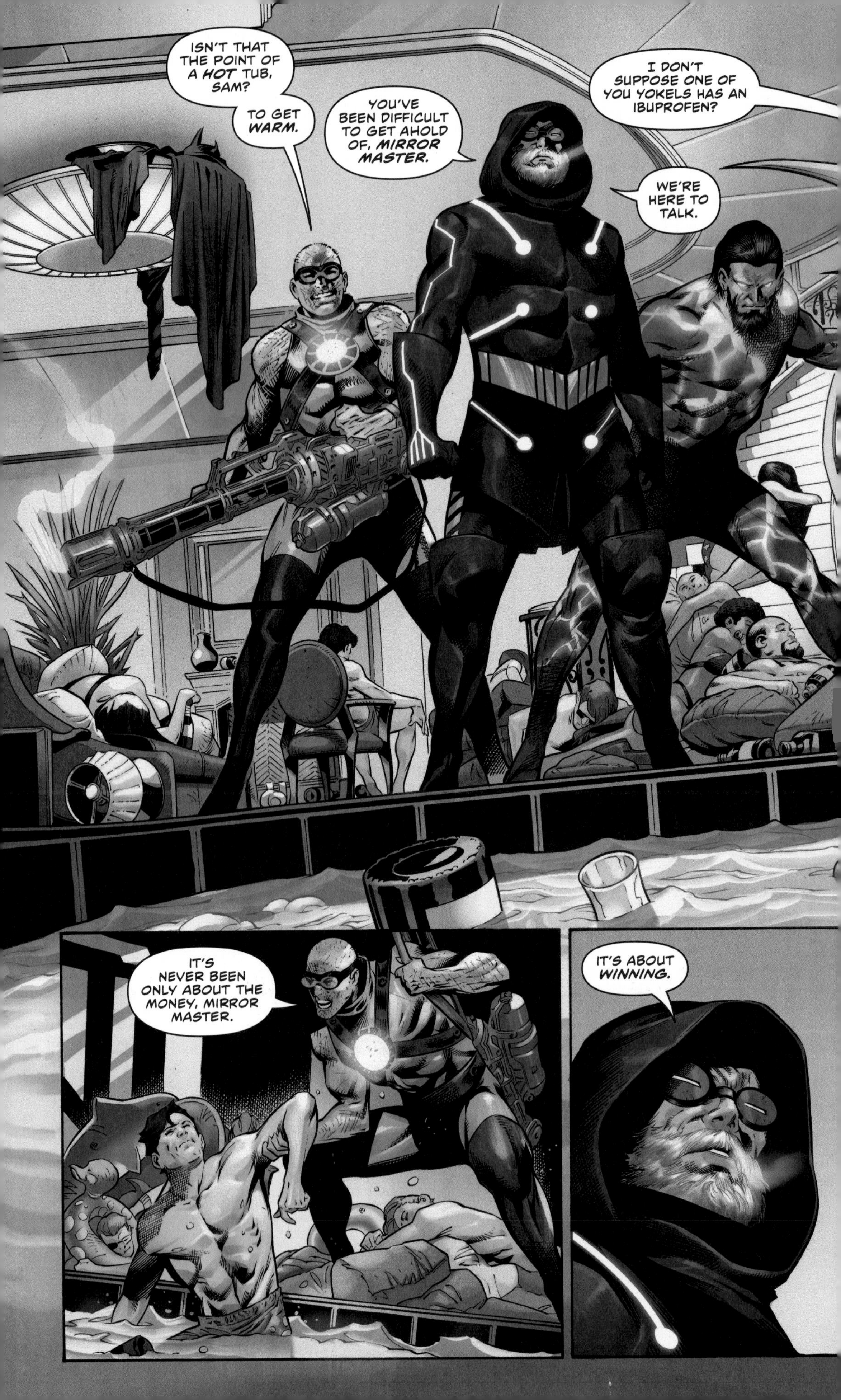

ISN'T THAT THE POINT OF A *HOT* TUB, SAM?
TO GET *WARM.*
YOU'VE BEEN DIFFICULT TO GET AHOLD OF, *MIRROR MASTER.*
I DON'T SUPPOSE ONE OF YOU YOKELS HAS AN IBUPROFEN?
WE'RE HERE TO TALK.
IT'S NEVER BEEN ONLY ABOUT THE MONEY, MIRROR MASTER.
IT'S ABOUT *WINNING.*

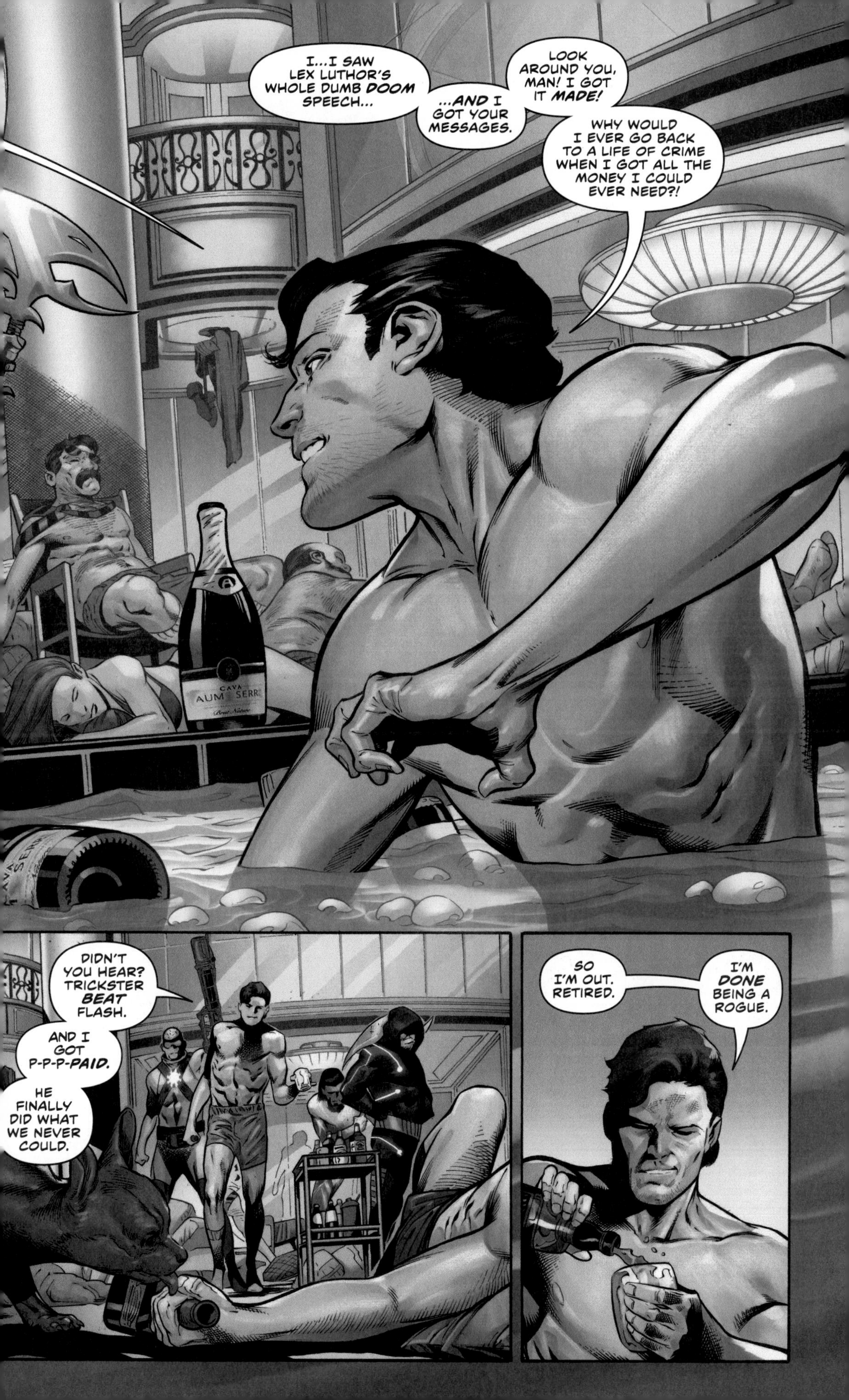
I...I SAW LEX LUTHOR'S WHOLE DUMB *DOOM* SPEECH...
...*AND* I GOT YOUR MESSAGES.
LOOK AROUND YOU, MAN! I GOT IT *MADE!*
WHY WOULD I EVER GO BACK TO A LIFE OF CRIME WHEN I GOT ALL THE MONEY I COULD EVER NEED?!
CAVA
AUM SERR
DIDN'T YOU HEAR? TRICKSTER *BEAT* FLASH.
AND I GOT P-P-P-*PAID.*
HE FINALLY DID WHAT WE NEVER COULD.
SO I'M OUT. RETIRED.
I'M *DONE* BEING A ROGUE.

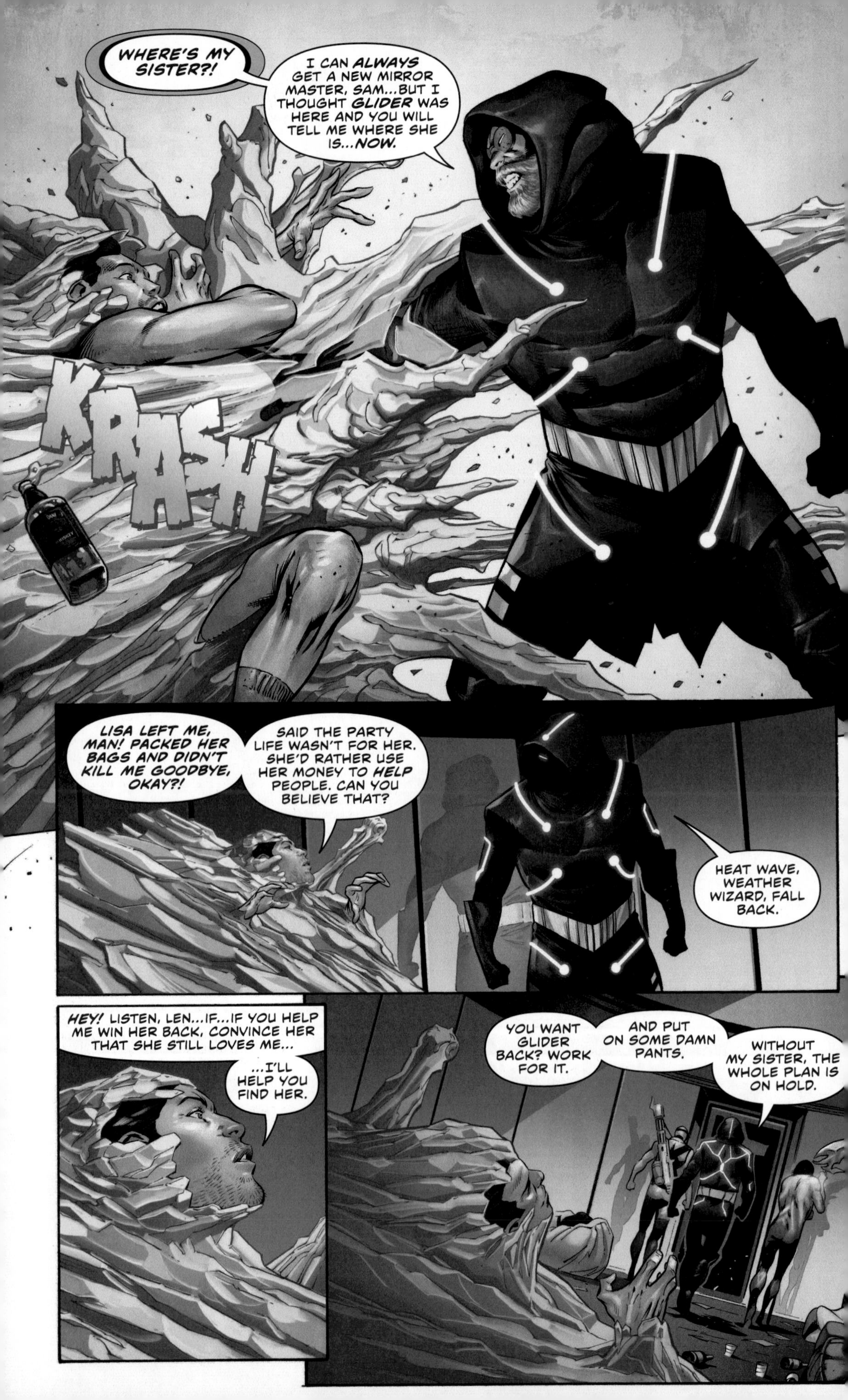
WHERE'S MY SISTER?!
I CAN ALWAYS GET A NEW MIRROR MASTER, SAM...BUT I THOUGHT GLIDER WAS HERE AND YOU WILL TELL ME WHERE SHE IS...NOW.
KRASH
LISA LEFT ME, MAN! PACKED HER BAGS AND DIDN'T KILL ME GOODBYE, OKAY?!
SAID THE PARTY LIFE WASN'T FOR HER. SHE'D RATHER USE HER MONEY TO HELP PEOPLE. CAN YOU BELIEVE THAT?
HEAT WAVE, WEATHER WIZARD, FALL BACK.
HEY! LISTEN, LEN...IF...IF YOU HELP ME WIN HER BACK, CONVINCE HER THAT SHE STILL LOVES ME...
...I'LL HELP YOU FIND HER.
YOU WANT GLIDER BACK? WORK FOR IT.
AND PUT ON SOME DAMN PANTS.
WITHOUT MY SISTER, THE WHOLE PLAN IS ON HOLD.

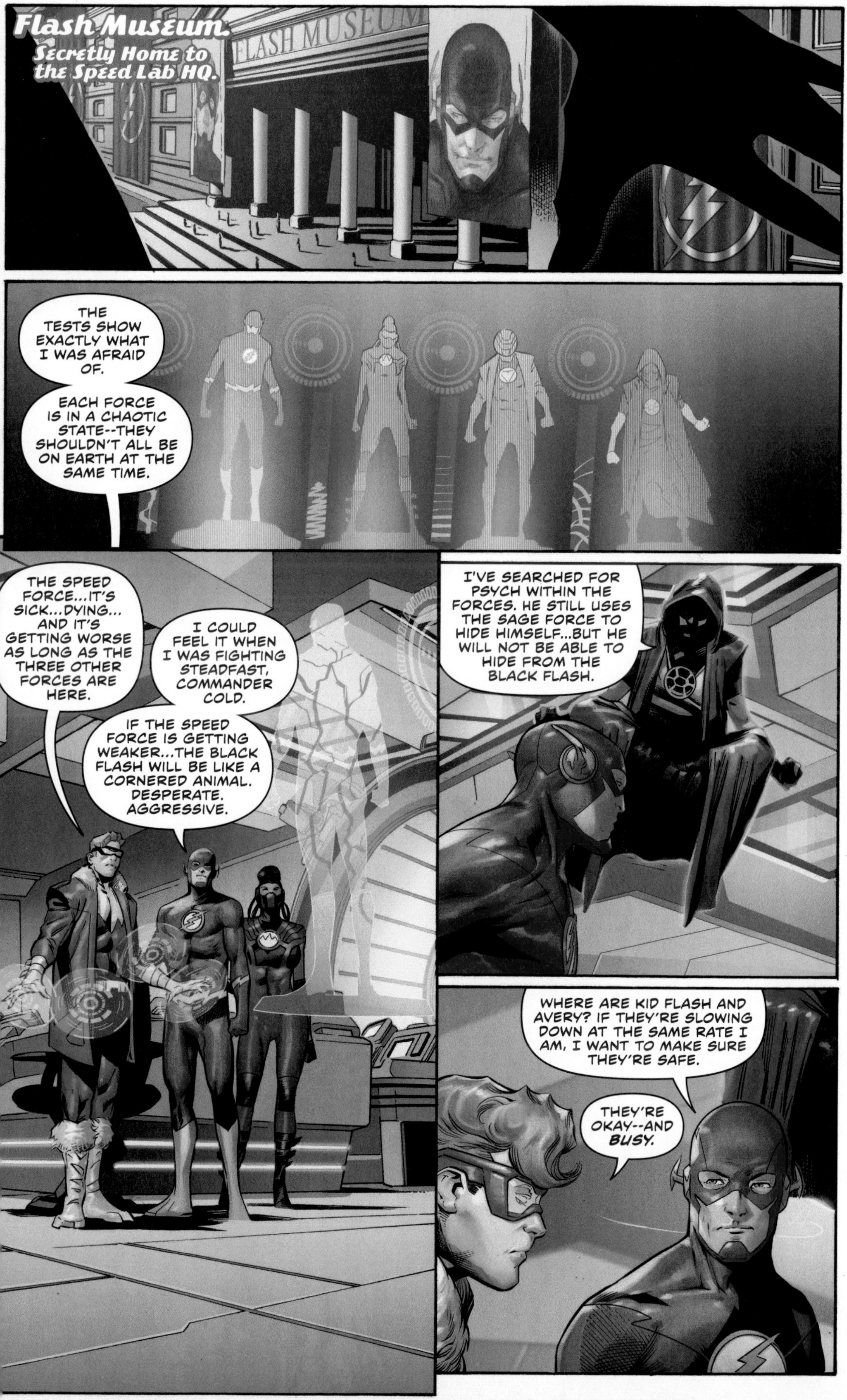

Flash Museum.
Secretly Home to the Speed Lab HQ.
FLASH MUSEUM
THE TESTS SHOW EXACTLY WHAT I WAS AFRAID OF.
EACH FORCE IS IN A CHAOTIC STATE--THEY SHOULDN'T ALL BE ON EARTH AT THE SAME TIME.
THE SPEED FORCE...IT'S SICK...DYING... AND IT'S GETTING WORSE AS LONG AS THE THREE OTHER FORCES ARE HERE.
I COULD FEEL IT WHEN I WAS FIGHTING STEADFAST, COMMANDER COLD.
IF THE SPEED FORCE IS GETTING WEAKER...THE BLACK FLASH WILL BE LIKE A CORNERED ANIMAL. DESPERATE. AGGRESSIVE.
I'VE SEARCHED FOR PSYCH WITHIN THE FORCES. HE STILL USES THE SAGE FORCE TO HIDE HIMSELF...BUT HE WILL NOT BE ABLE TO HIDE FROM THE BLACK FLASH.
WHERE ARE KID FLASH AND AVERY? IF THEY'RE SLOWING DOWN AT THE SAME RATE I AM, I WANT TO MAKE SURE THEY'RE SAFE.
THEY'RE OKAY--AND *BUSY*.

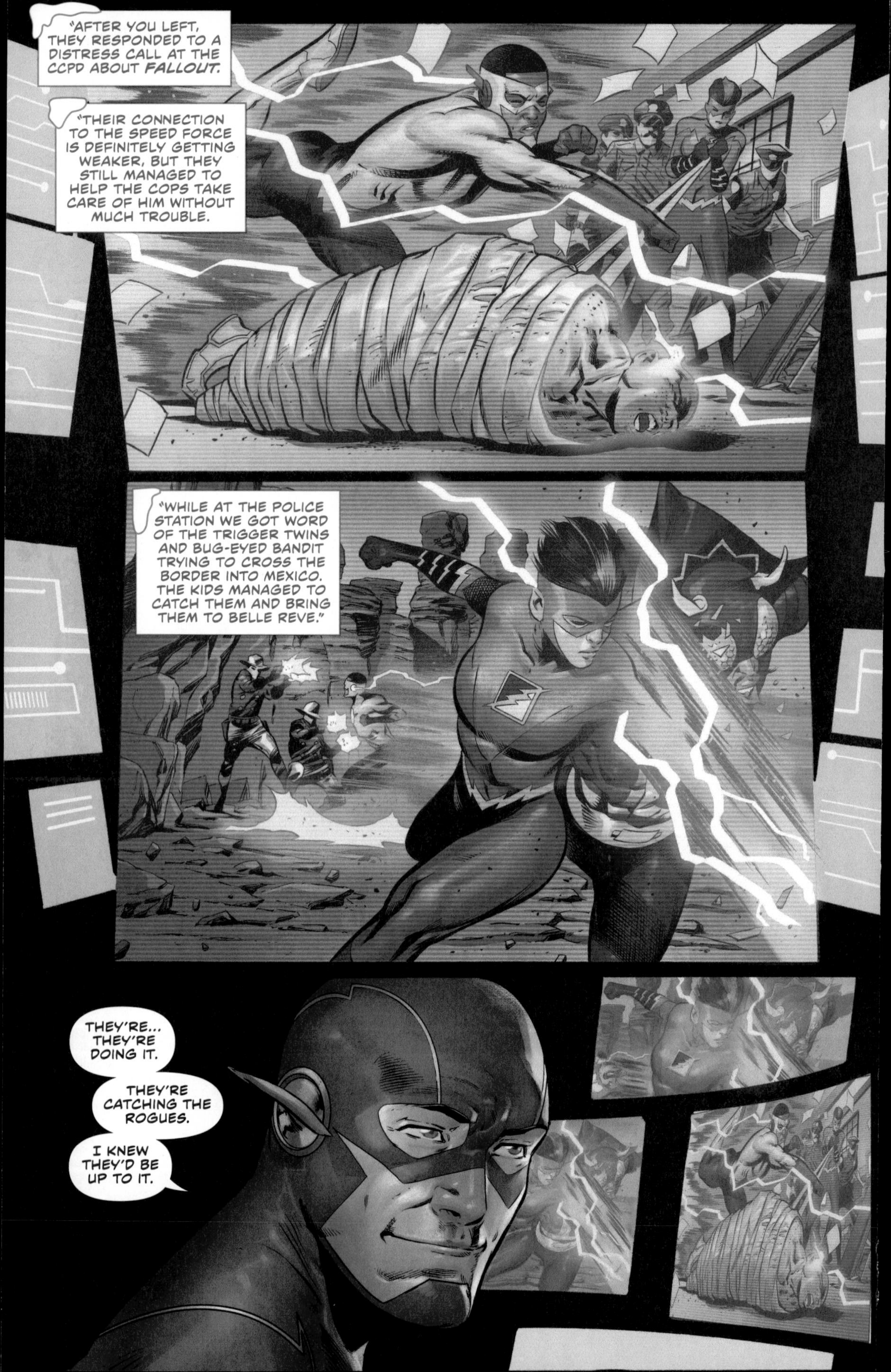
"AFTER YOU LEFT, THEY RESPONDED TO A DISTRESS CALL AT THE CCPD ABOUT *FALLOUT*.
"THEIR CONNECTION TO THE SPEED FORCE IS DEFINITELY GETTING WEAKER, BUT THEY STILL MANAGED TO HELP THE COPS TAKE CARE OF HIM WITHOUT MUCH TROUBLE.
"WHILE AT THE POLICE STATION WE GOT WORD OF THE TRIGGER TWINS AND BUG-EYED BANDIT TRYING TO CROSS THE BORDER INTO MEXICO. THE KIDS MANAGED TO CATCH THEM AND BRING THEM TO BELLE REVE."
THEY'RE... THEY'RE DOING IT.
THEY'RE CATCHING THE ROGUES.
I KNEW THEY'D BE UP TO IT.

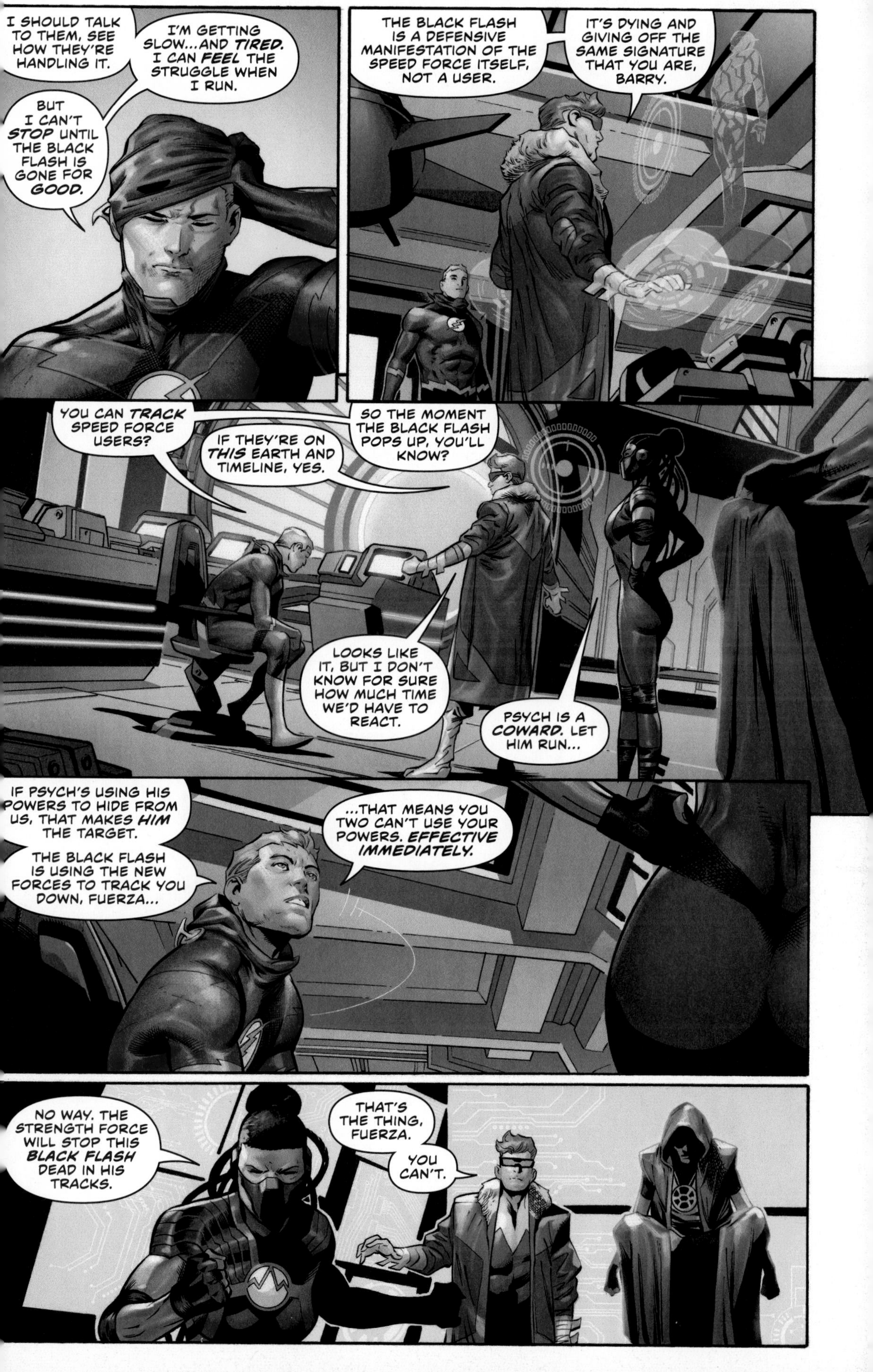
I SHOULD TALK TO THEM, SEE HOW THEY'RE HANDLING IT.
I'M GETTING SLOW...AND TIRED. I CAN FEEL THE STRUGGLE WHEN I RUN.
BUT I CAN'T STOP UNTIL THE BLACK FLASH IS GONE FOR GOOD.
THE BLACK FLASH IS A DEFENSIVE MANIFESTATION OF THE SPEED FORCE ITSELF, NOT A USER.
IT'S DYING AND GIVING OFF THE SAME SIGNATURE THAT YOU ARE, BARRY.
YOU CAN TRACK SPEED FORCE USERS?
IF THEY'RE ON THIS EARTH AND TIMELINE, YES.
SO THE MOMENT THE BLACK FLASH POPS UP, YOU'LL KNOW?
LOOKS LIKE IT, BUT I DON'T KNOW FOR SURE HOW MUCH TIME WE'D HAVE TO REACT.
PSYCH IS A COWARD. LET HIM RUN...
IF PSYCH'S USING HIS POWERS TO HIDE FROM US, THAT MAKES HIM THE TARGET.
THE BLACK FLASH IS USING THE NEW FORCES TO TRACK YOU DOWN, FUERZA...
...THAT MEANS YOU TWO CAN'T USE YOUR POWERS. EFFECTIVE IMMEDIATELY.
NO WAY. THE STRENGTH FORCE WILL STOP THIS BLACK FLASH DEAD IN HIS TRACKS.
THAT'S THE THING, FUERZA.
YOU CAN'T.

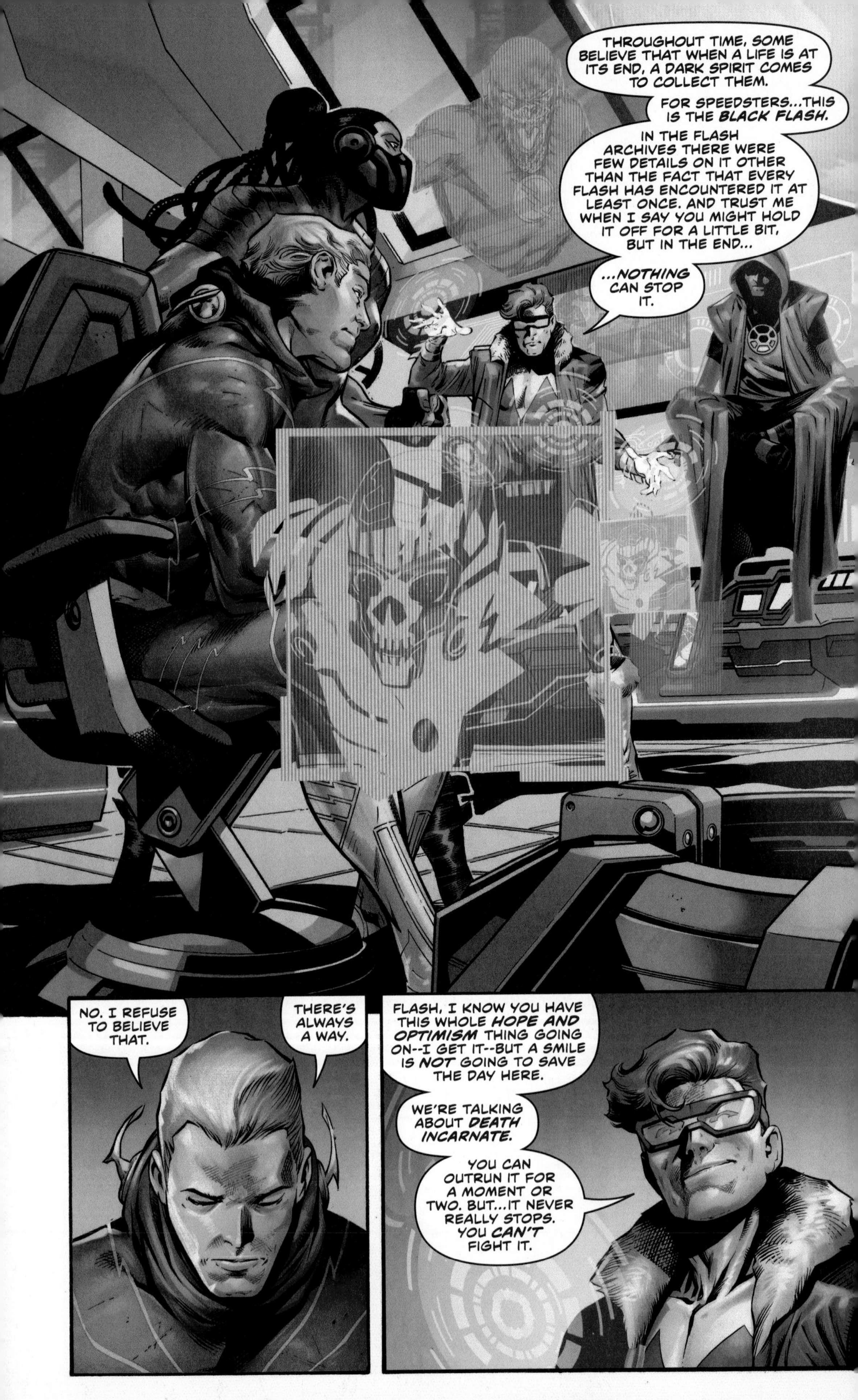
THROUGHOUT TIME, SOME BELIEVE THAT WHEN A LIFE IS AT ITS END, A DARK SPIRIT COMES TO COLLECT THEM.
FOR SPEEDSTERS...THIS IS THE *BLACK FLASH.*
IN THE FLASH ARCHIVES THERE WERE FEW DETAILS ON IT OTHER THAN THE FACT THAT EVERY FLASH HAS ENCOUNTERED IT AT LEAST ONCE. AND TRUST ME WHEN I SAY YOU MIGHT HOLD IT OFF FOR A LITTLE BIT, BUT IN THE END...
...*NOTHING* CAN STOP IT.
NO. I REFUSE TO BELIEVE THAT.
THERE'S ALWAYS A WAY.
FLASH, I KNOW YOU HAVE THIS WHOLE *HOPE AND OPTIMISM* THING GOING ON--I GET IT--BUT A SMILE IS *NOT* GOING TO SAVE THE DAY HERE.
WE'RE TALKING ABOUT *DEATH INCARNATE.*
YOU CAN OUTRUN IT FOR A MOMENT OR TWO. BUT...IT NEVER REALLY STOPS. YOU *CAN'T* FIGHT IT.

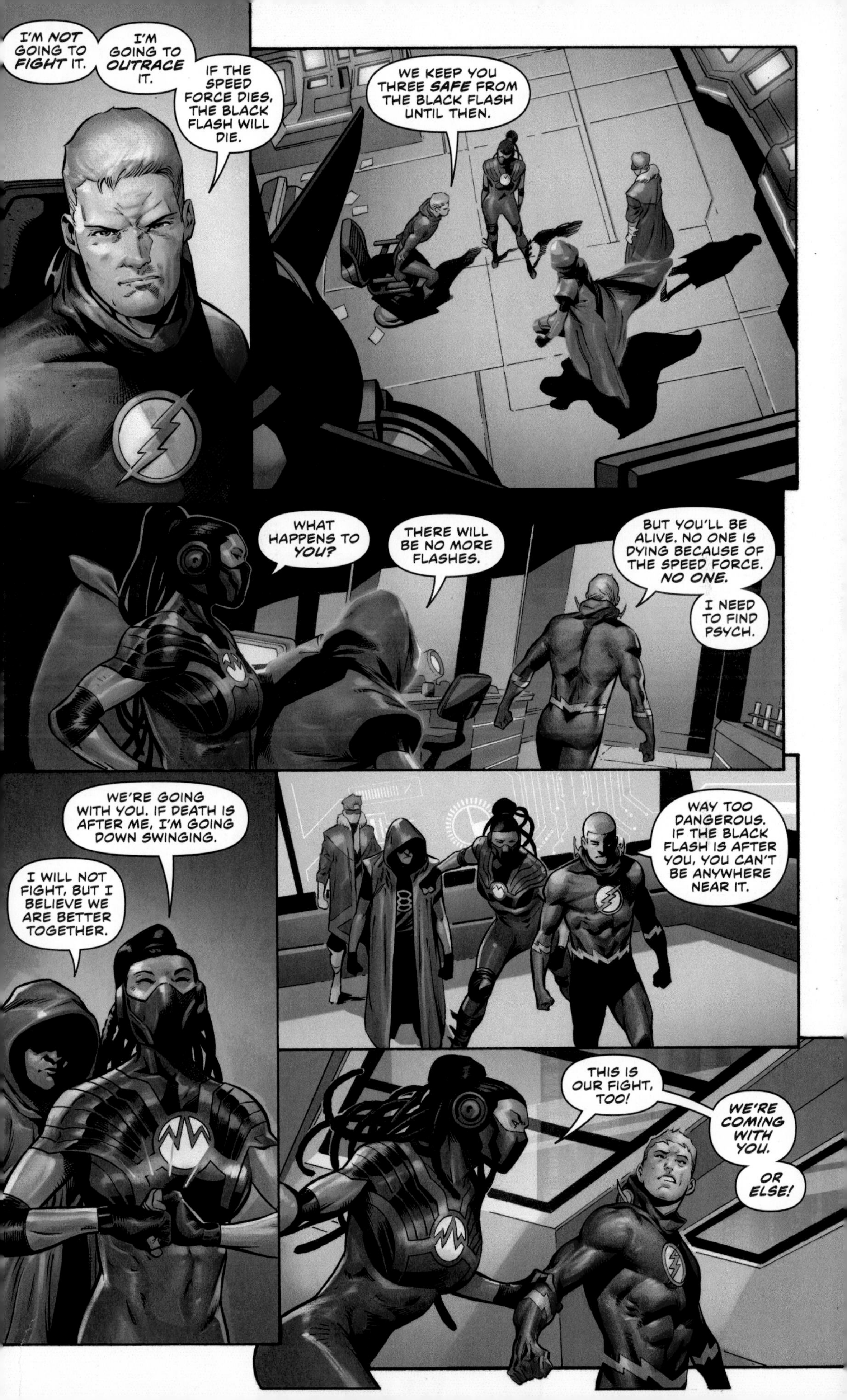

I'M NOT GOING TO FIGHT IT.
I'M GOING TO OUTRACE IT.
IF THE SPEED FORCE DIES, THE BLACK FLASH WILL DIE.
WE KEEP YOU THREE SAFE FROM THE BLACK FLASH UNTIL THEN.
WHAT HAPPENS TO YOU?
THERE WILL BE NO MORE FLASHES.
BUT YOU'LL BE ALIVE. NO ONE IS DYING BECAUSE OF THE SPEED FORCE. NO ONE.
I NEED TO FIND PSYCH.
WE'RE GOING WITH YOU. IF DEATH IS AFTER ME, I'M GOING DOWN SWINGING.
I WILL NOT FIGHT, BUT I BELIEVE WE ARE BETTER TOGETHER.
WAY TOO DANGEROUS. IF THE BLACK FLASH IS AFTER YOU, YOU CAN'T BE ANYWHERE NEAR IT.
THIS IS OUR FIGHT, TOO!
WE'RE COMING WITH YOU.
OR ELSE!

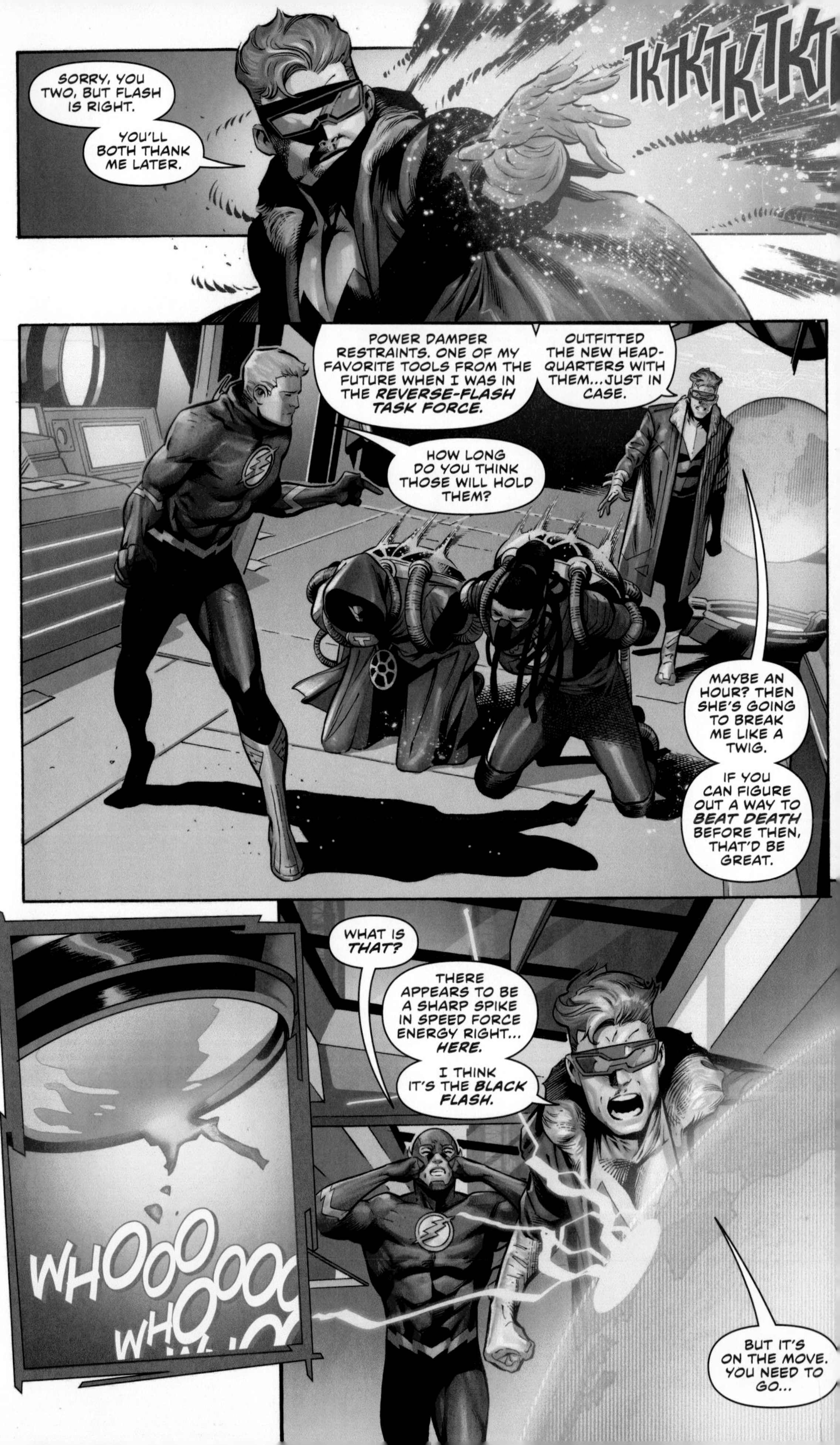
SORRY, YOU TWO, BUT FLASH IS RIGHT.
YOU'LL BOTH THANK ME LATER.
TKTKTKTKTKT
POWER DAMPER RESTRAINTS. ONE OF MY FAVORITE TOOLS FROM THE FUTURE WHEN I WAS IN THE *REVERSE-FLASH TASK FORCE.*
OUTFITTED THE NEW HEAD-QUARTERS WITH THEM...JUST IN CASE.
HOW LONG DO YOU THINK THOSE WILL HOLD THEM?
MAYBE AN HOUR? THEN SHE'S GOING TO BREAK ME LIKE A TWIG.
IF YOU CAN FIGURE OUT A WAY TO *BEAT DEATH* BEFORE THEN, THAT'D BE GREAT.
WHAT IS *THAT?*
THERE APPEARS TO BE A SHARP SPIKE IN SPEED FORCE ENERGY RIGHT... *HERE.*
I THINK IT'S THE *BLACK FLASH.*
WHOOOOO
BUT IT'S ON THE MOVE. YOU NEED TO GO...

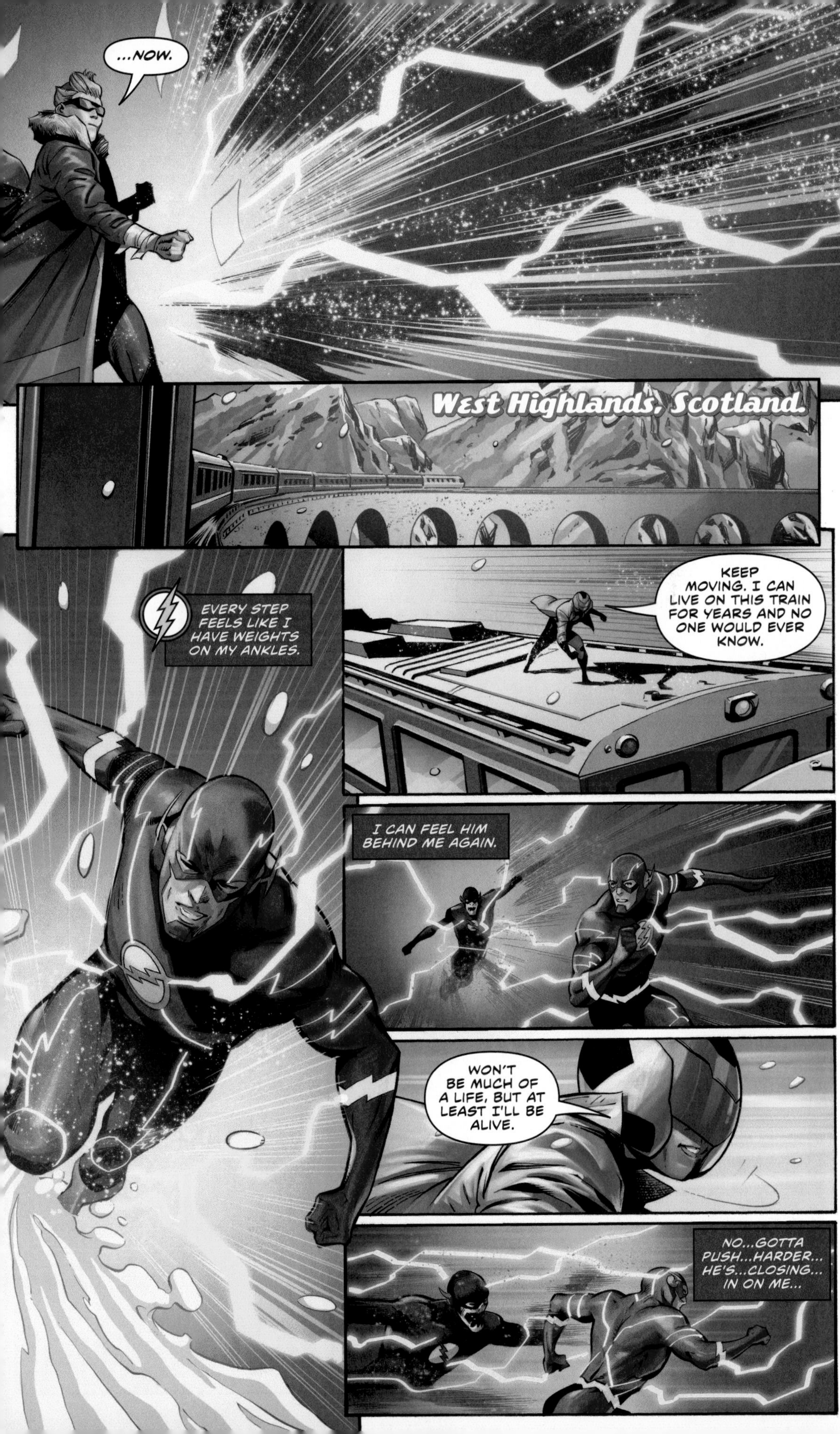
...NOW.
West Highlands, Scotland.
EVERY STEP FEELS LIKE I HAVE WEIGHTS ON MY ANKLES.
KEEP MOVING. I CAN LIVE ON THIS TRAIN FOR YEARS AND NO ONE WOULD EVER KNOW.
I CAN FEEL HIM BEHIND ME AGAIN.
WON'T BE MUCH OF A LIFE, BUT AT LEAST I'LL BE ALIVE.
NO...GOTTA PUSH...HARDER... HE'S...CLOSING... IN ON ME...

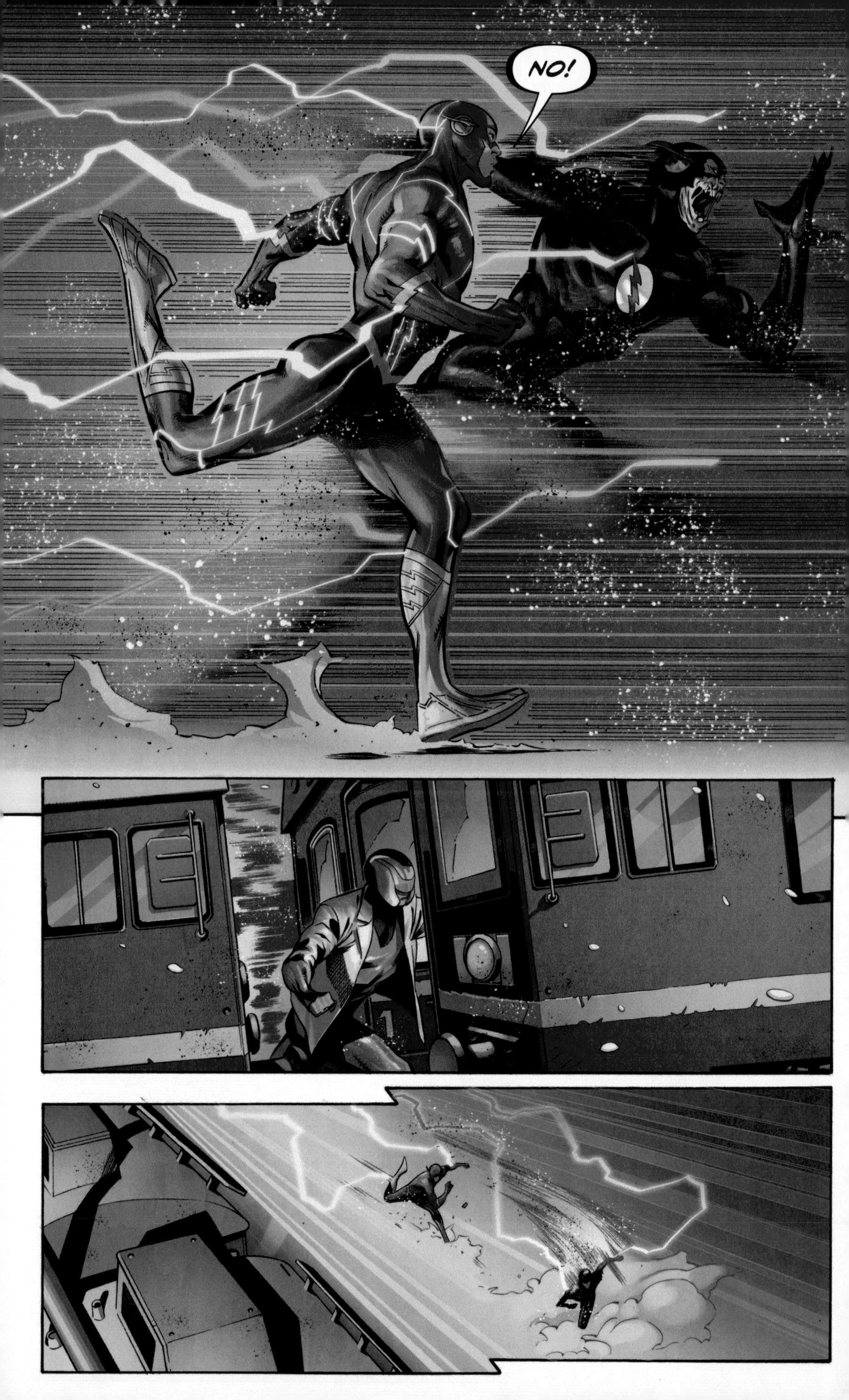
NO!

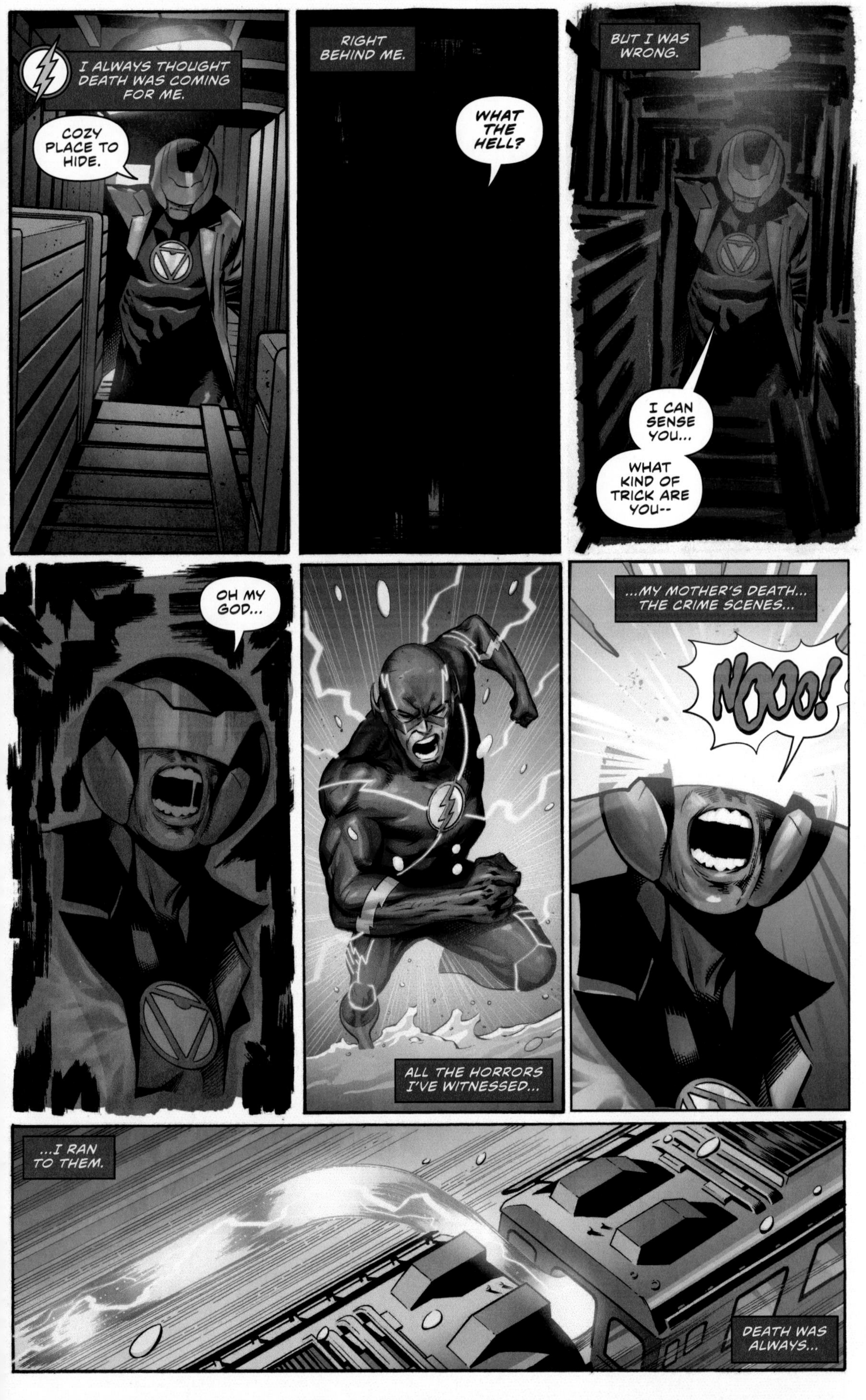
I ALWAYS THOUGHT DEATH WAS COMING FOR ME.
COZY PLACE TO HIDE.
RIGHT BEHIND ME.
WHAT THE HELL?
BUT I WAS WRONG.
I CAN SENSE YOU...
WHAT KIND OF TRICK ARE YOU--
OH MY GOD...
ALL THE HORRORS I'VE WITNESSED...
...MY MOTHER'S DEATH... THE CRIME SCENES...
NOOO!
...I RAN TO THEM.
DEATH WAS ALWAYS...

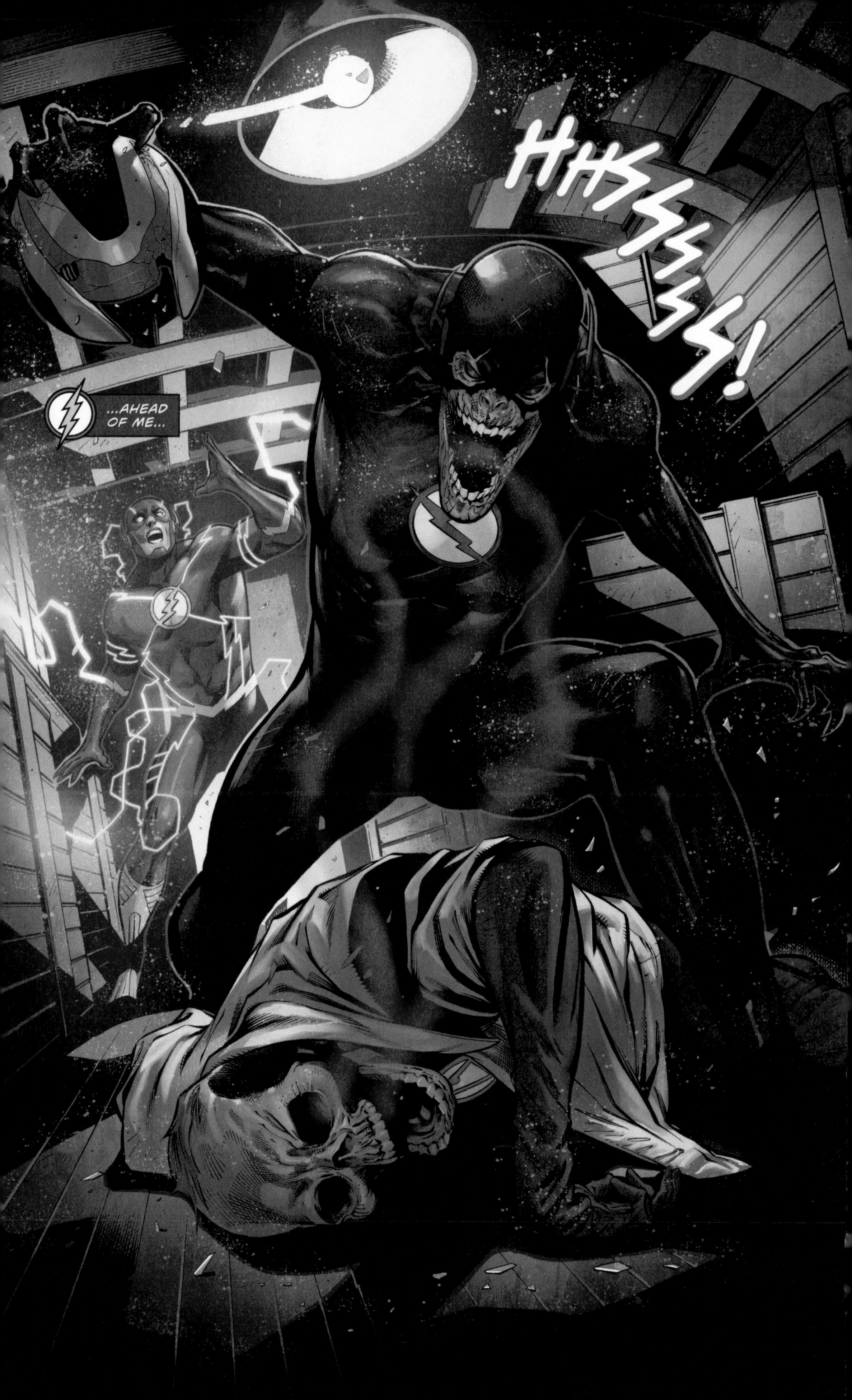
...AHEAD OF ME...
HHSSSSS!

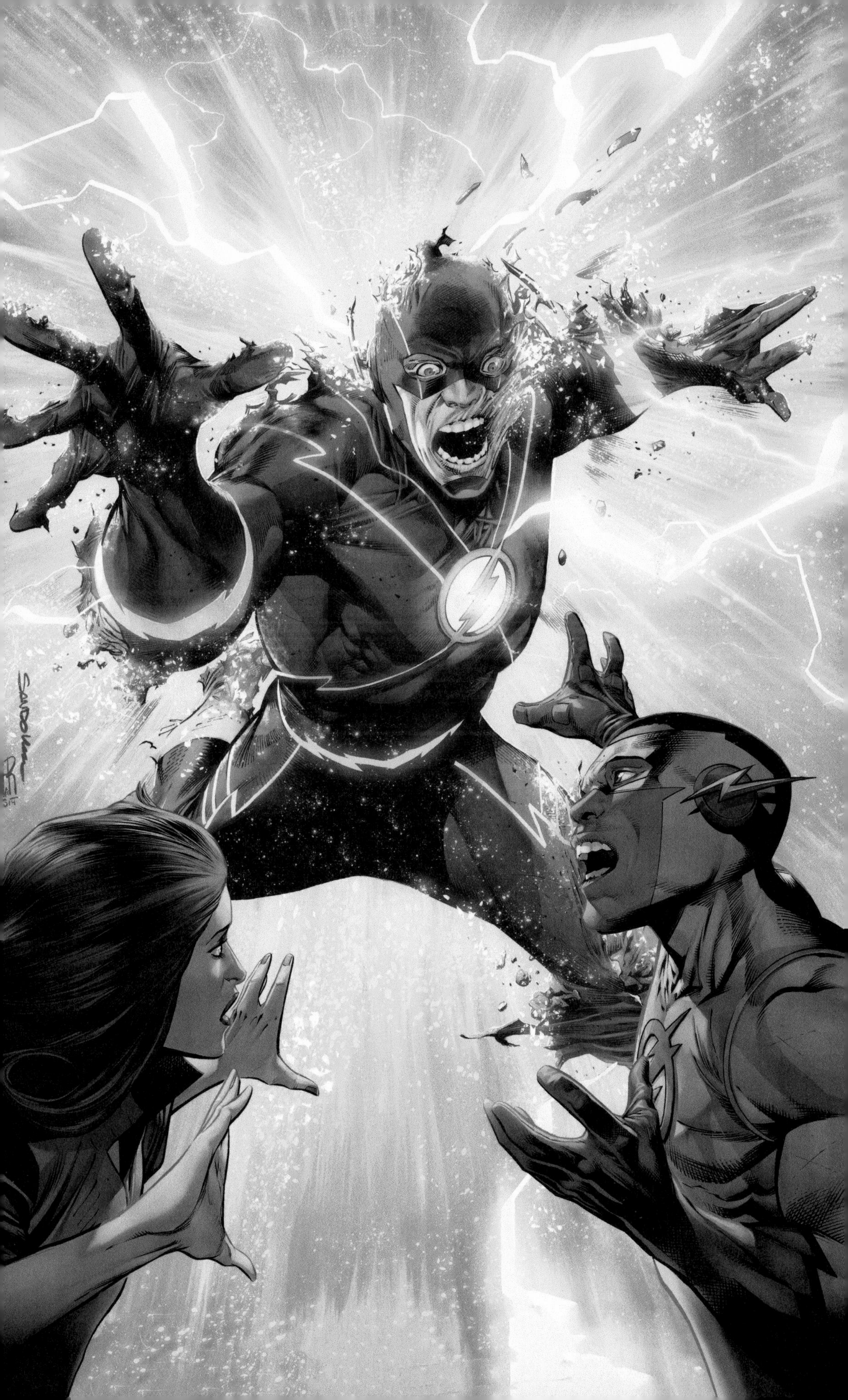

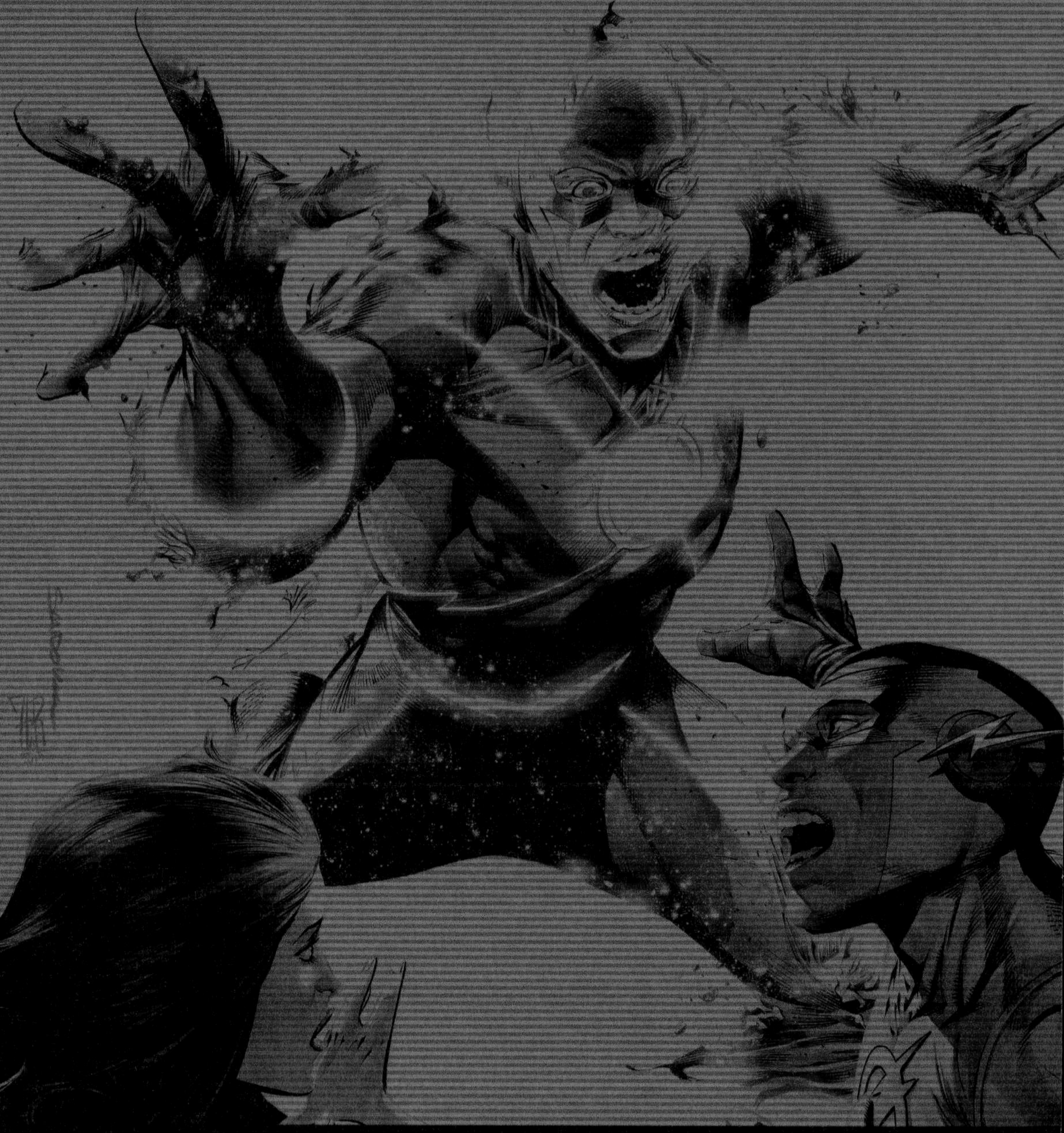

THE FLASH
#79

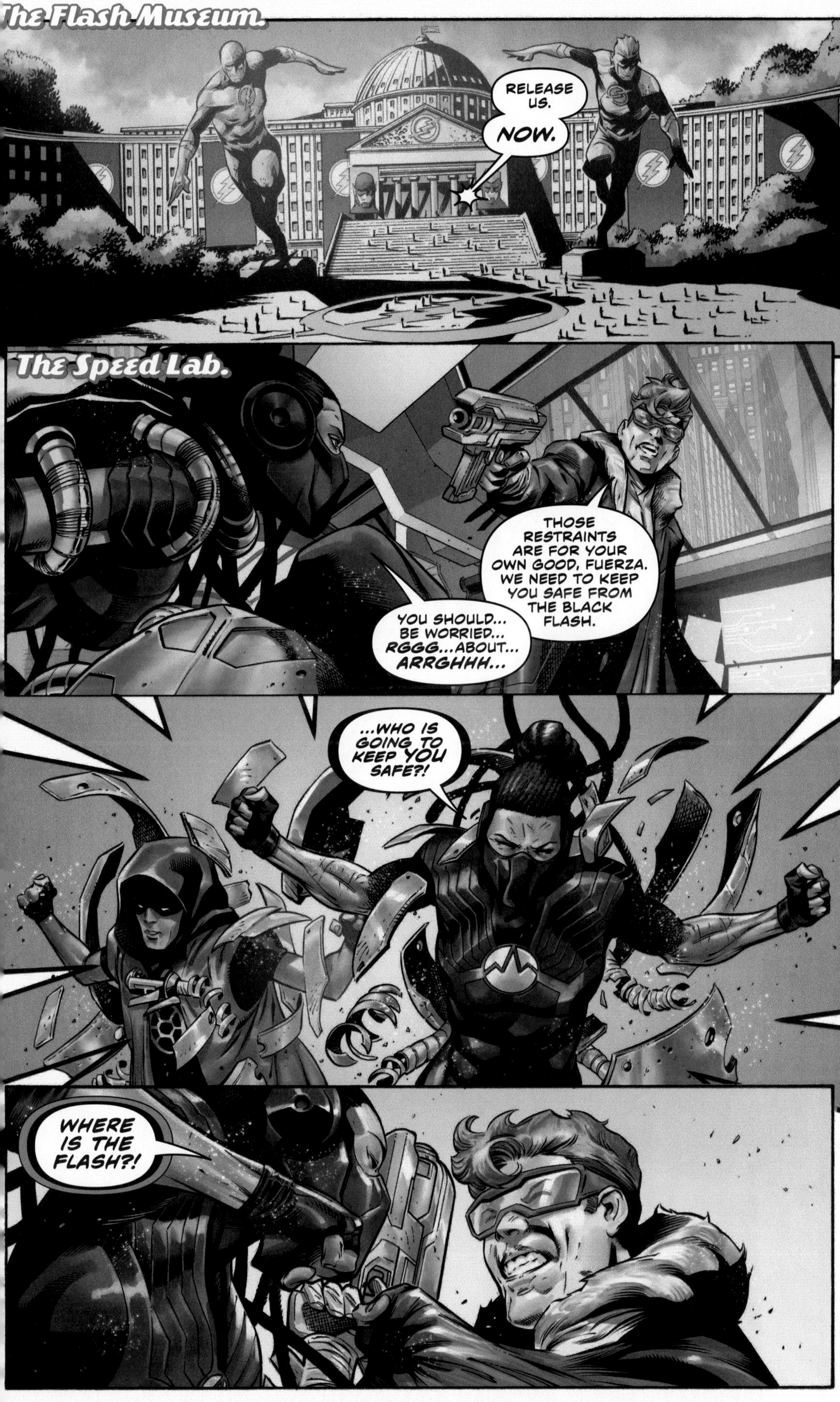
The Flash Museum.
RELEASE US. NOW.
The Speed Lab.
THOSE RESTRAINTS ARE FOR YOUR OWN GOOD, FUERZA. WE NEED TO KEEP YOU SAFE FROM THE BLACK FLASH.
YOU SHOULD... BE WORRIED... RGGG...ABOUT... ARRGHHH...
...WHO IS GOING TO KEEP YOU SAFE?!
WHERE IS THE FLASH?!

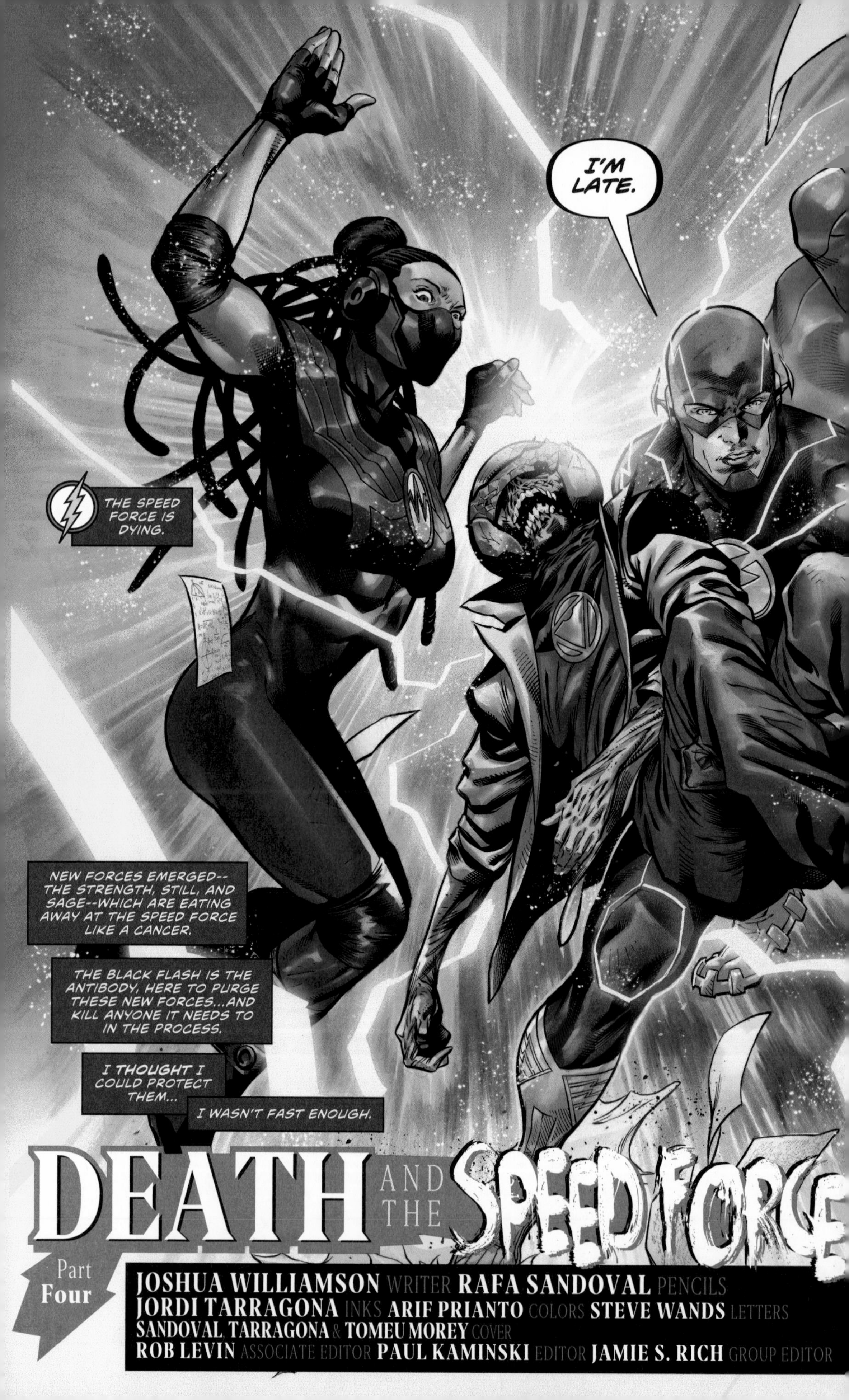
I'M LATE.
THE SPEED FORCE IS DYING.
NEW FORCES EMERGED--THE STRENGTH, STILL, AND SAGE--WHICH ARE EATING AWAY AT THE SPEED FORCE LIKE A CANCER.
THE BLACK FLASH IS THE ANTIBODY, HERE TO PURGE THESE NEW FORCES...AND KILL ANYONE IT NEEDS TO IN THE PROCESS.
I THOUGHT I COULD PROTECT THEM...
I WASN'T FAST ENOUGH.
DEATH AND THE SPEED FORCE
Part Four
JOSHUA WILLIAMSON WRITER RAFA SANDOVAL PENCILS
JORDI TARRAGONA INKS ARIF PRIANTO COLORS STEVE WANDS LETTERS
SANDOVAL, TARRAGONA & TOMEU MOREY COVER
ROB LEVIN ASSOCIATE EDITOR PAUL KAMINSKI EDITOR JAMIE S. RICH GROUP EDITOR

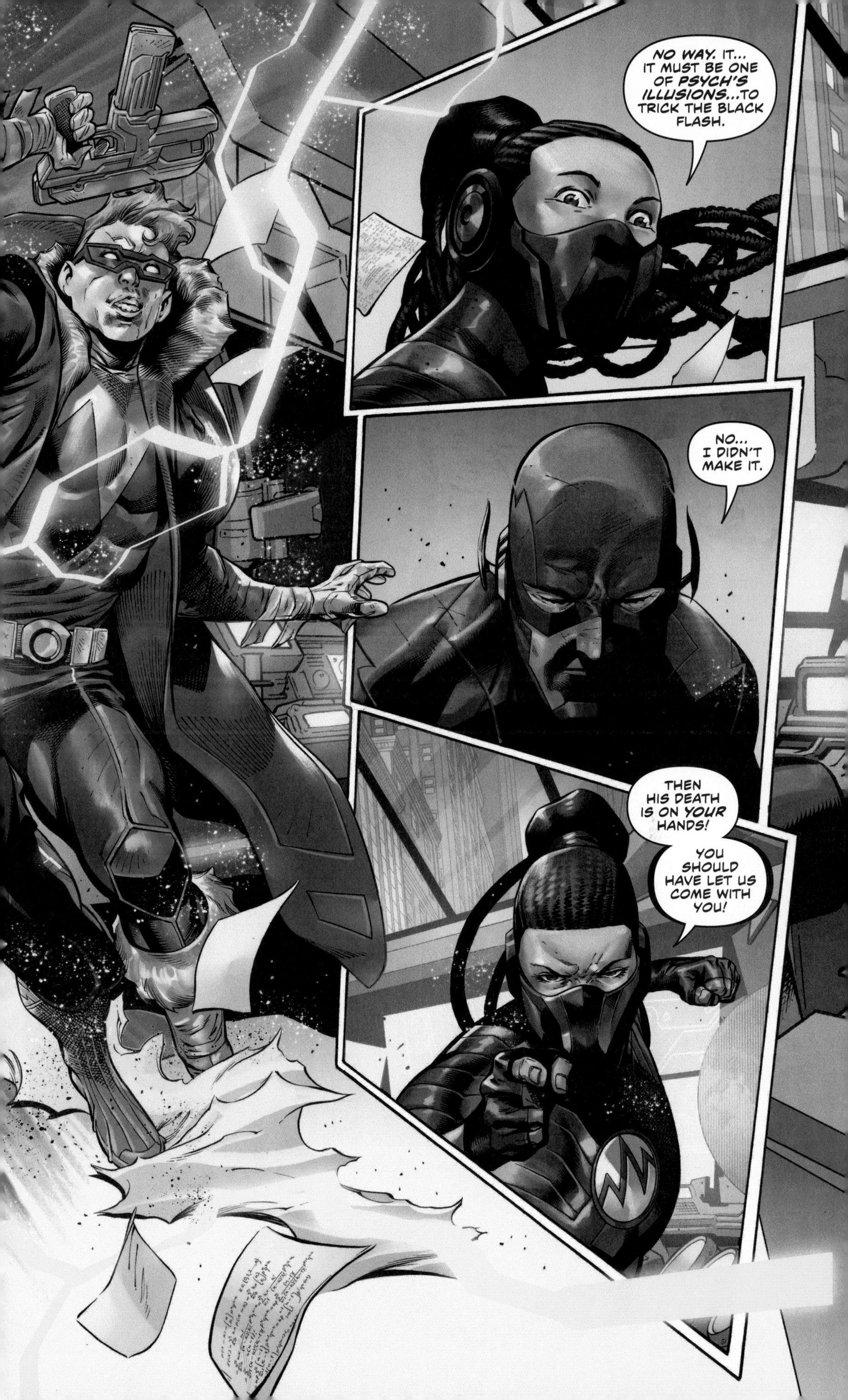

NO WAY. IT... IT MUST BE ONE OF PSYCH'S ILLUSIONS...TO TRICK THE BLACK FLASH.
NO... I DIDN'T MAKE IT.
THEN HIS DEATH IS ON YOUR HANDS!
YOU SHOULD HAVE LET US COME WITH YOU!

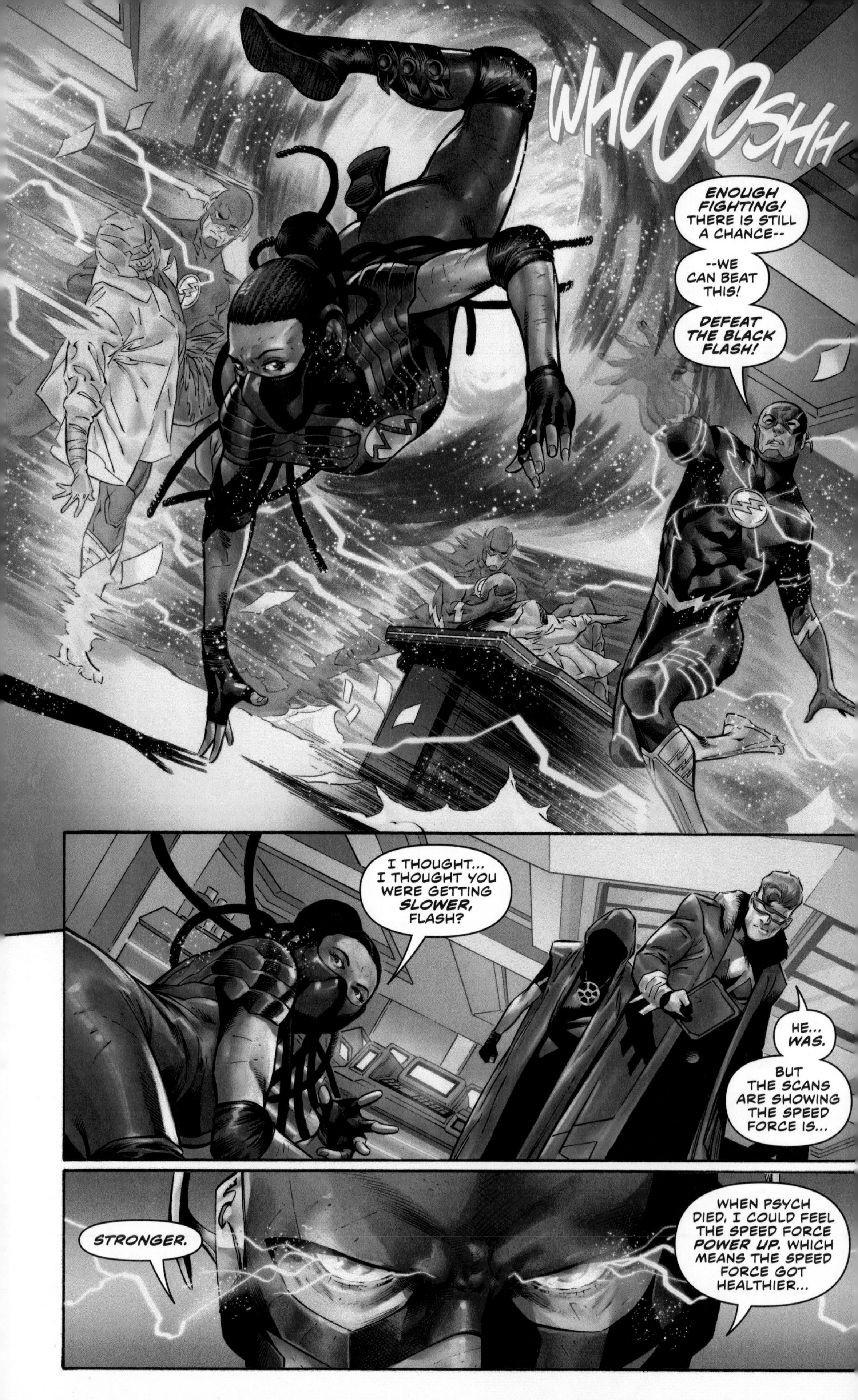
WHOOOOSHH
ENOUGH FIGHTING! THERE IS STILL A CHANCE--
--WE CAN BEAT THIS!
DEFEAT THE BLACK FLASH!
I THOUGHT... I THOUGHT YOU WERE GETTING SLOWER, FLASH?
HE... WAS.
BUT THE SCANS ARE SHOWING THE SPEED FORCE IS...
STRONGER.
WHEN PSYCH DIED, I COULD FEEL THE SPEED FORCE POWER UP. WHICH MEANS THE SPEED FORCE GOT HEALTHIER...

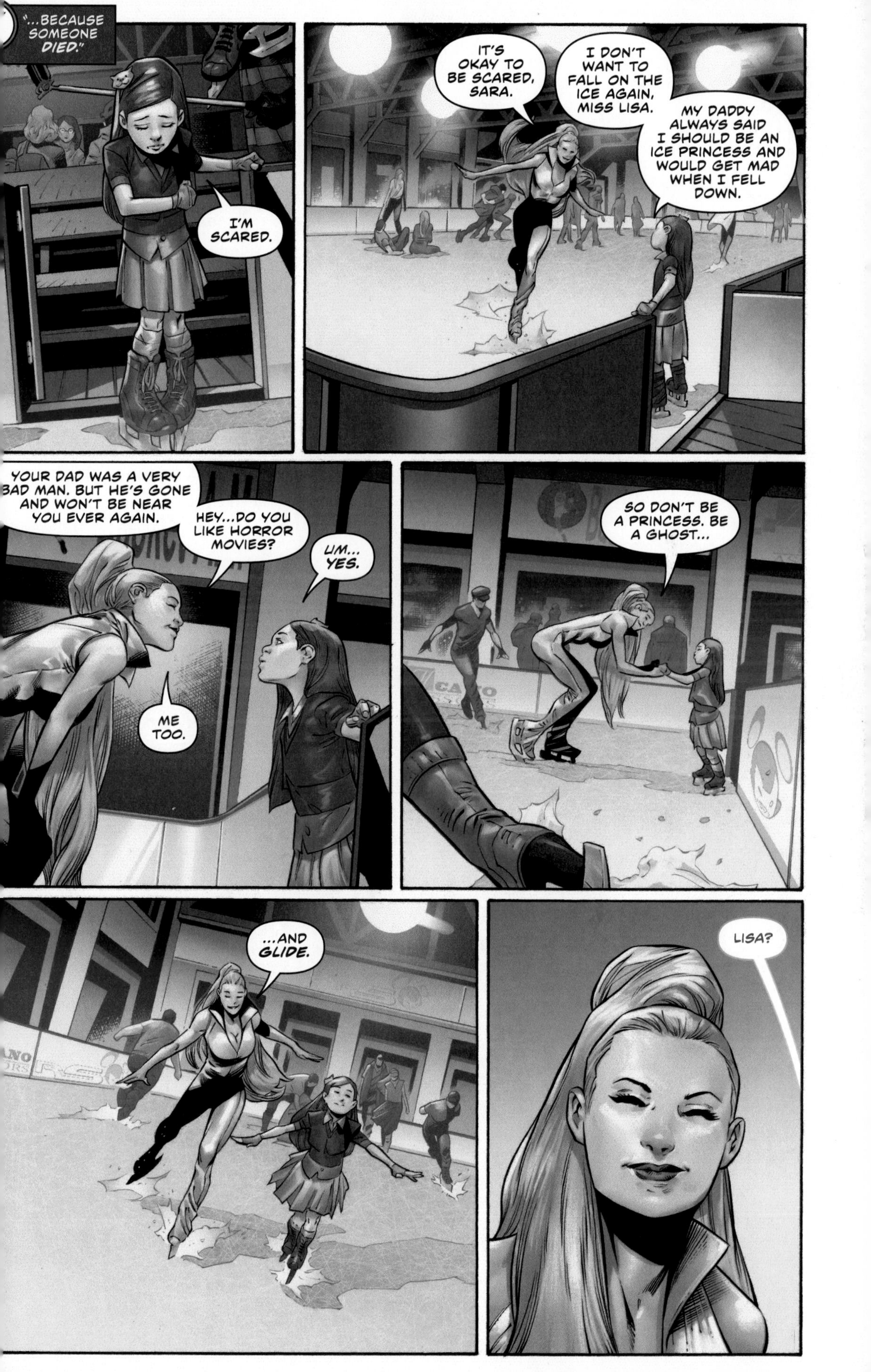
"...BECAUSE SOMEONE DIED."
I'M SCARED.
IT'S OKAY TO BE SCARED, SARA.
I DON'T WANT TO FALL ON THE ICE AGAIN, MISS LISA.
MY DADDY ALWAYS SAID I SHOULD BE AN ICE PRINCESS AND WOULD GET MAD WHEN I FELL DOWN.
YOUR DAD WAS A VERY BAD MAN. BUT HE'S GONE AND WON'T BE NEAR YOU EVER AGAIN.
HEY...DO YOU LIKE HORROR MOVIES?
UM... YES.
ME TOO.
SO DON'T BE A PRINCESS. BE A GHOST...
...AND GLIDE.
LISA?

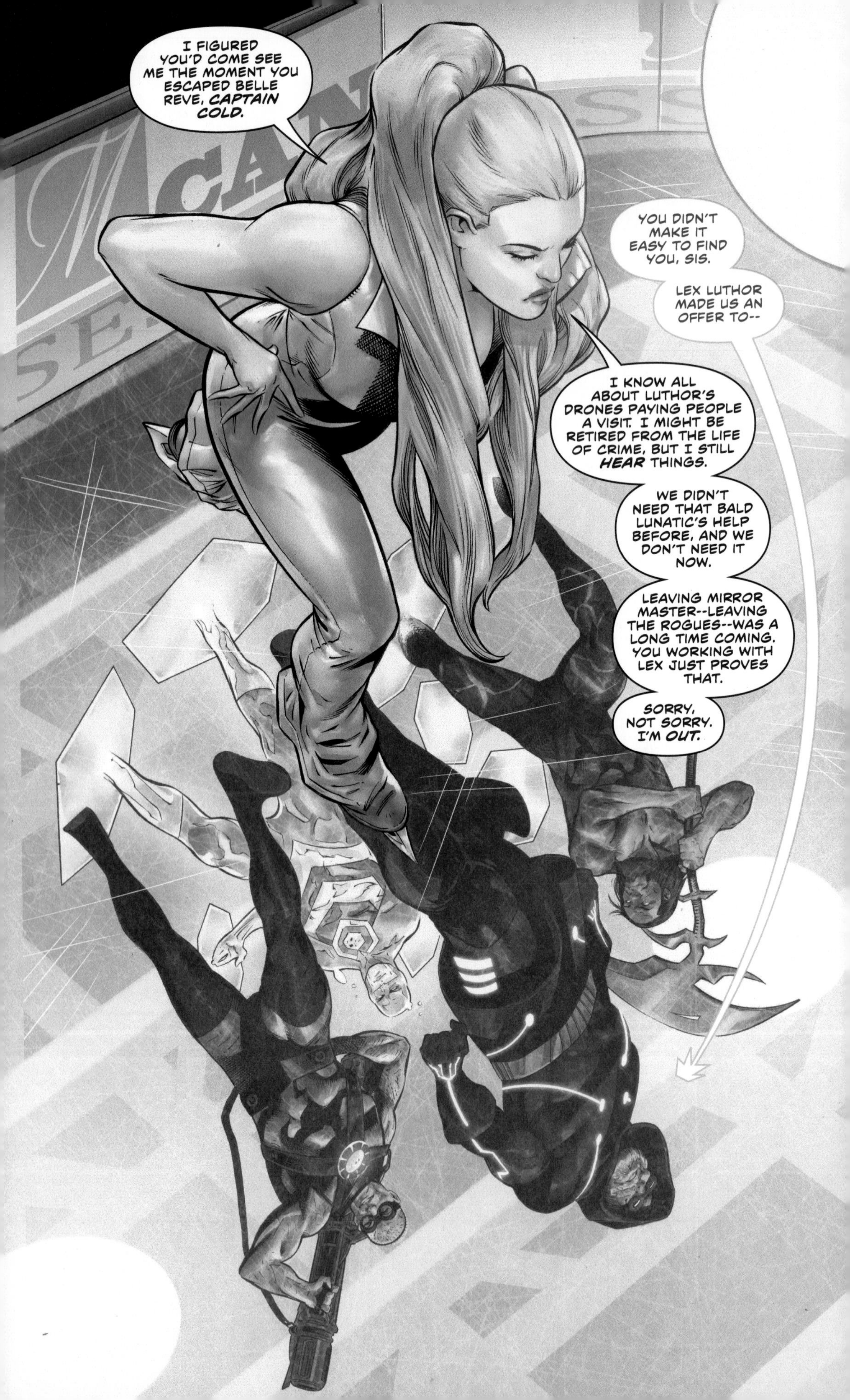

I FIGURED YOU'D COME SEE ME THE MOMENT YOU ESCAPED BELLE REVE, *CAPTAIN COLD.*
YOU DIDN'T MAKE IT EASY TO FIND YOU, SIS.
LEX LUTHOR MADE US AN OFFER TO--
I KNOW ALL ABOUT LUTHOR'S DRONES PAYING PEOPLE A VISIT. I MIGHT BE RETIRED FROM THE LIFE OF CRIME, BUT I STILL ***HEAR*** THINGS.
WE DIDN'T NEED THAT BALD LUNATIC'S HELP BEFORE, AND WE DON'T NEED IT NOW.
LEAVING MIRROR MASTER--LEAVING THE ROGUES--WAS A LONG TIME COMING. YOU WORKING WITH LEX JUST PROVES THAT.
SORRY, NOT SORRY. I'M *OUT.*

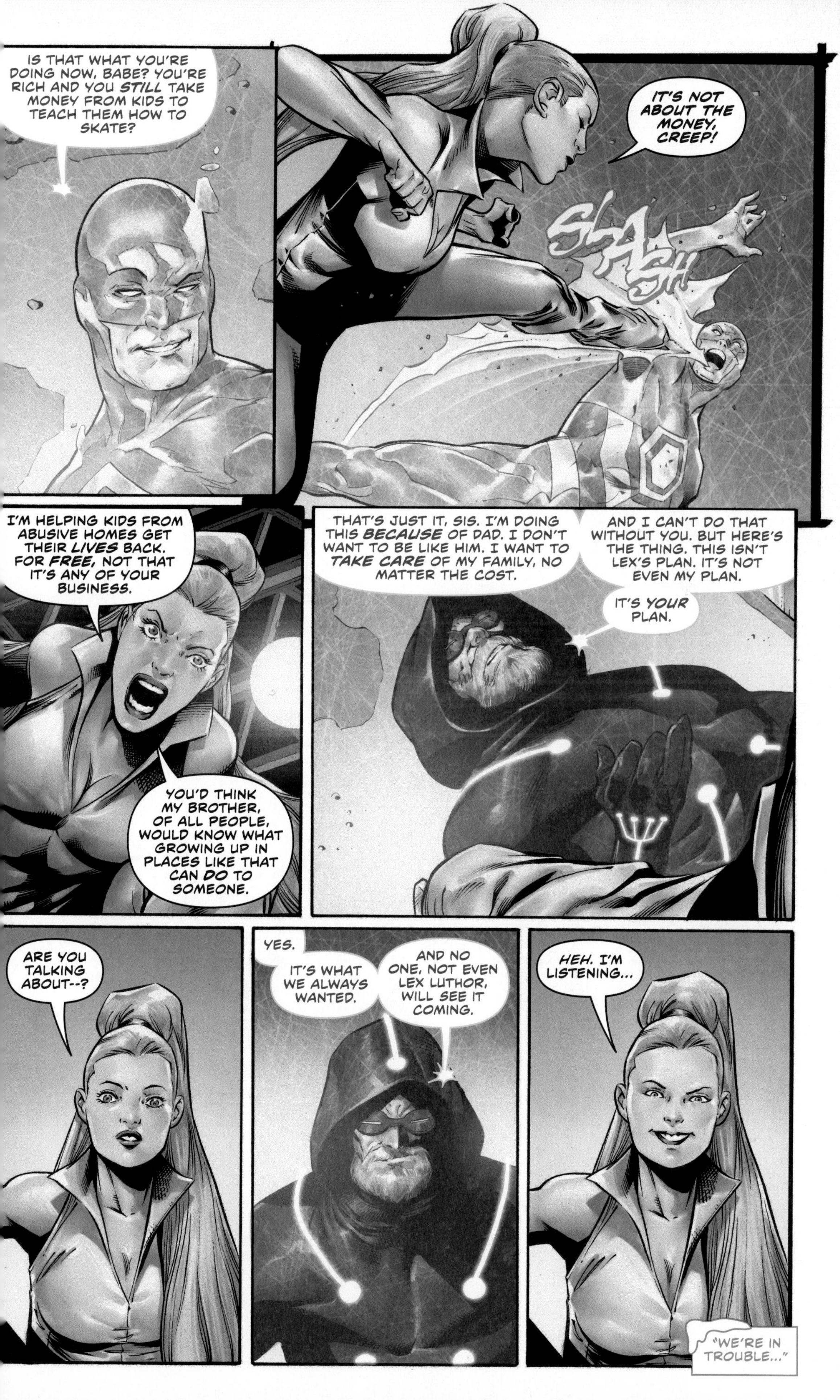
IS THAT WHAT YOU'RE DOING NOW, BABE? YOU'RE RICH AND YOU STILL TAKE MONEY FROM KIDS TO TEACH THEM HOW TO SKATE?
IT'S NOT ABOUT THE MONEY, CREEP!
SLASH
I'M HELPING KIDS FROM ABUSIVE HOMES GET THEIR LIVES BACK. FOR FREE, NOT THAT IT'S ANY OF YOUR BUSINESS.
YOU'D THINK MY BROTHER, OF ALL PEOPLE, WOULD KNOW WHAT GROWING UP IN PLACES LIKE THAT CAN DO TO SOMEONE.
THAT'S JUST IT, SIS. I'M DOING THIS BECAUSE OF DAD. I DON'T WANT TO BE LIKE HIM. I WANT TO TAKE CARE OF MY FAMILY, NO MATTER THE COST.
AND I CAN'T DO THAT WITHOUT YOU. BUT HERE'S THE THING. THIS ISN'T LEX'S PLAN. IT'S NOT EVEN MY PLAN.
IT'S YOUR PLAN.
ARE YOU TALKING ABOUT--?
YES.
IT'S WHAT WE ALWAYS WANTED.
AND NO ONE, NOT EVEN LEX LUTHOR, WILL SEE IT COMING.
HEH. I'M LISTENING...
"WE'RE IN TROUBLE..."

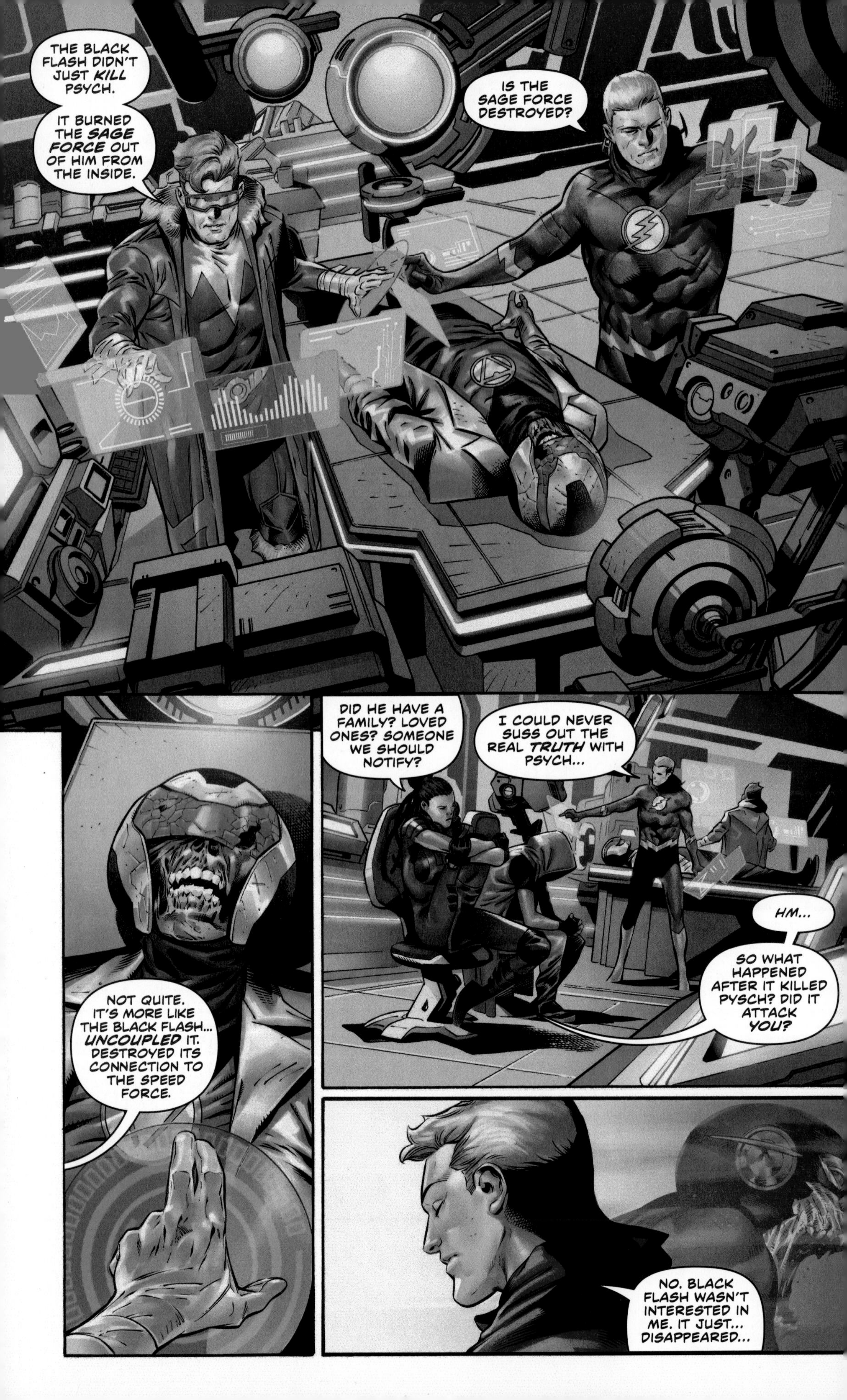
THE BLACK FLASH DIDN'T JUST KILL PSYCH.
IT BURNED THE SAGE FORCE OUT OF HIM FROM THE INSIDE.
IS THE SAGE FORCE DESTROYED?
NOT QUITE. IT'S MORE LIKE THE BLACK FLASH... UNCOUPLED IT. DESTROYED ITS CONNECTION TO THE SPEED FORCE.
DID HE HAVE A FAMILY? LOVED ONES? SOMEONE WE SHOULD NOTIFY?
I COULD NEVER SUSS OUT THE REAL TRUTH WITH PSYCH...
HM...
SO WHAT HAPPENED AFTER IT KILLED PYSCH? DID IT ATTACK YOU?
NO. BLACK FLASH WASN'T INTERESTED IN ME. IT JUST... DISAPPEARED...

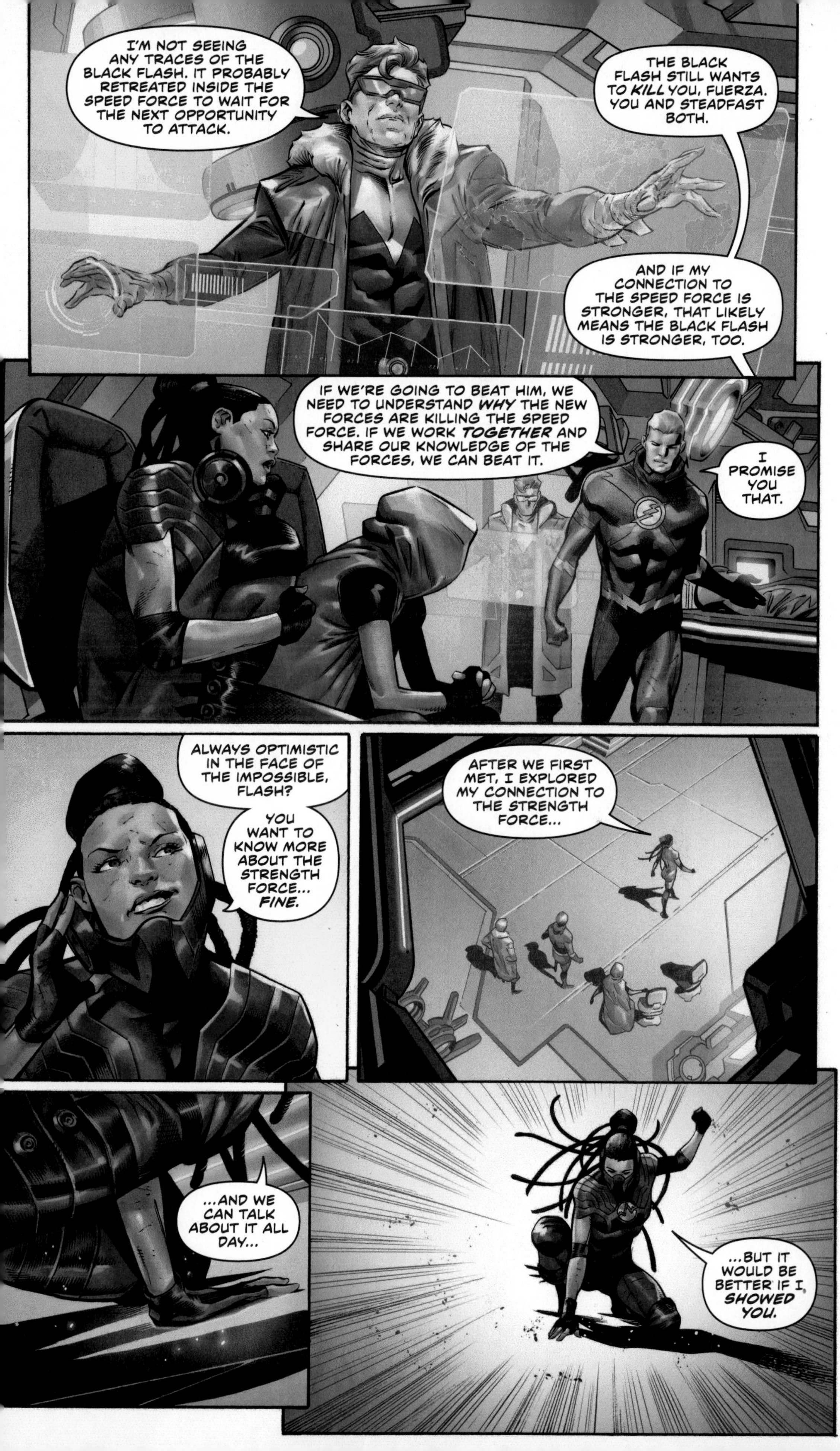
I'M NOT SEEING ANY TRACES OF THE BLACK FLASH. IT PROBABLY RETREATED INSIDE THE SPEED FORCE TO WAIT FOR THE NEXT OPPORTUNITY TO ATTACK.
THE BLACK FLASH STILL WANTS TO *KILL* YOU, FUERZA. YOU AND STEADFAST BOTH.
AND IF MY CONNECTION TO THE SPEED FORCE IS STRONGER, THAT LIKELY MEANS THE BLACK FLASH IS STRONGER, TOO.
IF WE'RE GOING TO BEAT HIM, WE NEED TO UNDERSTAND *WHY* THE NEW FORCES ARE KILLING THE SPEED FORCE. IF WE WORK *TOGETHER* AND SHARE OUR KNOWLEDGE OF THE FORCES, WE CAN BEAT IT.
I PROMISE YOU THAT.
ALWAYS OPTIMISTIC IN THE FACE OF THE IMPOSSIBLE, FLASH?
YOU WANT TO KNOW MORE ABOUT THE STRENGTH FORCE... *FINE.*
AFTER WE FIRST MET, I EXPLORED MY CONNECTION TO THE STRENGTH FORCE...
...AND WE CAN TALK ABOUT IT ALL DAY...
...BUT IT WOULD BE BETTER IF I *SHOWED* YOU.

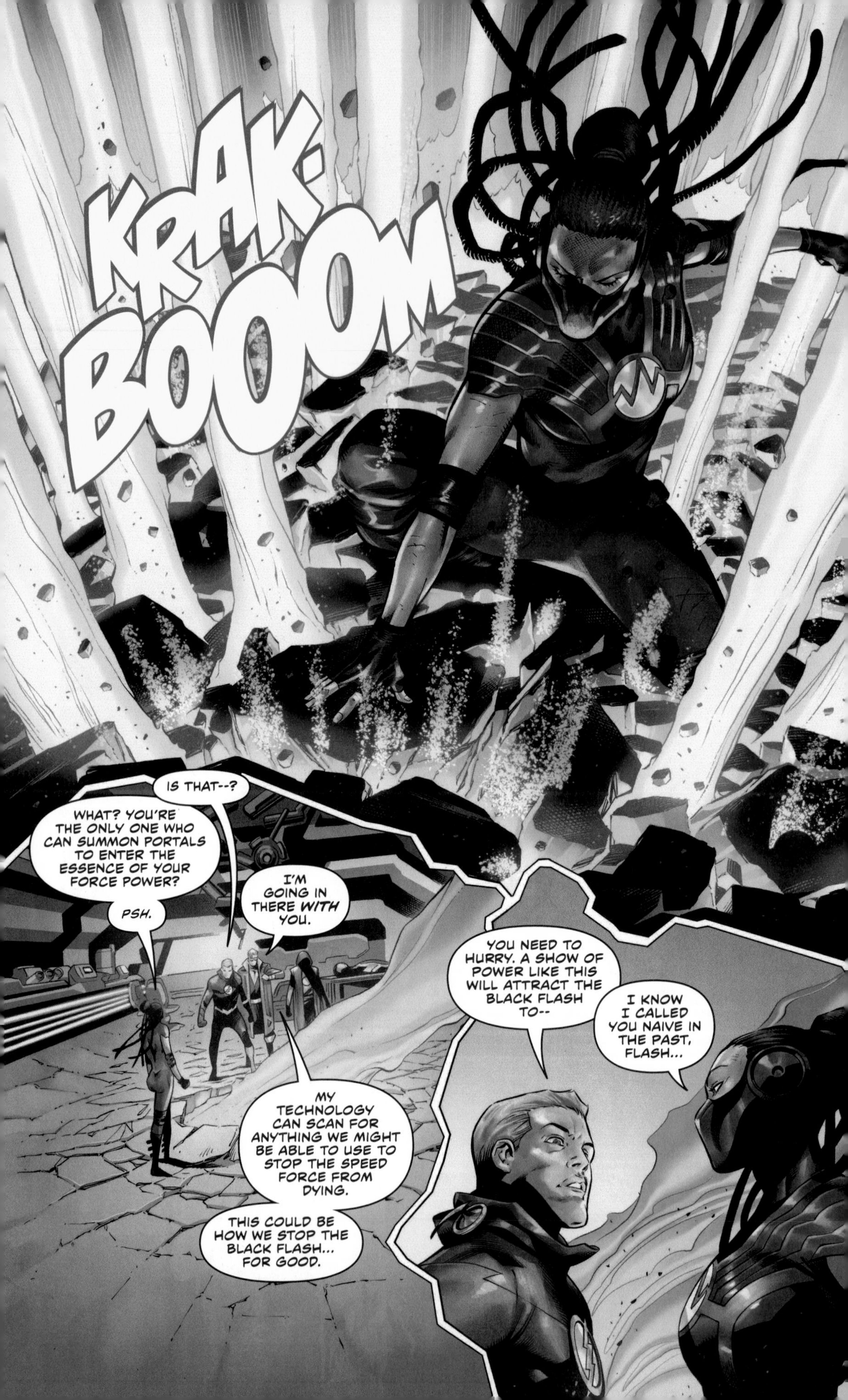
KRAK-BOOOM
IS THAT--?
WHAT? YOU'RE THE ONLY ONE WHO CAN SUMMON PORTALS TO ENTER THE ESSENCE OF YOUR FORCE POWER?
PSH.
I'M GOING IN THERE *WITH* YOU.
MY TECHNOLOGY CAN SCAN FOR ANYTHING WE MIGHT BE ABLE TO USE TO STOP THE SPEED FORCE FROM DYING.
THIS COULD BE HOW WE STOP THE BLACK FLASH... FOR GOOD.
YOU NEED TO HURRY. A SHOW OF POWER LIKE THIS WILL ATTRACT THE BLACK FLASH TO--
I KNOW I CALLED YOU NAIVE IN THE PAST, FLASH...

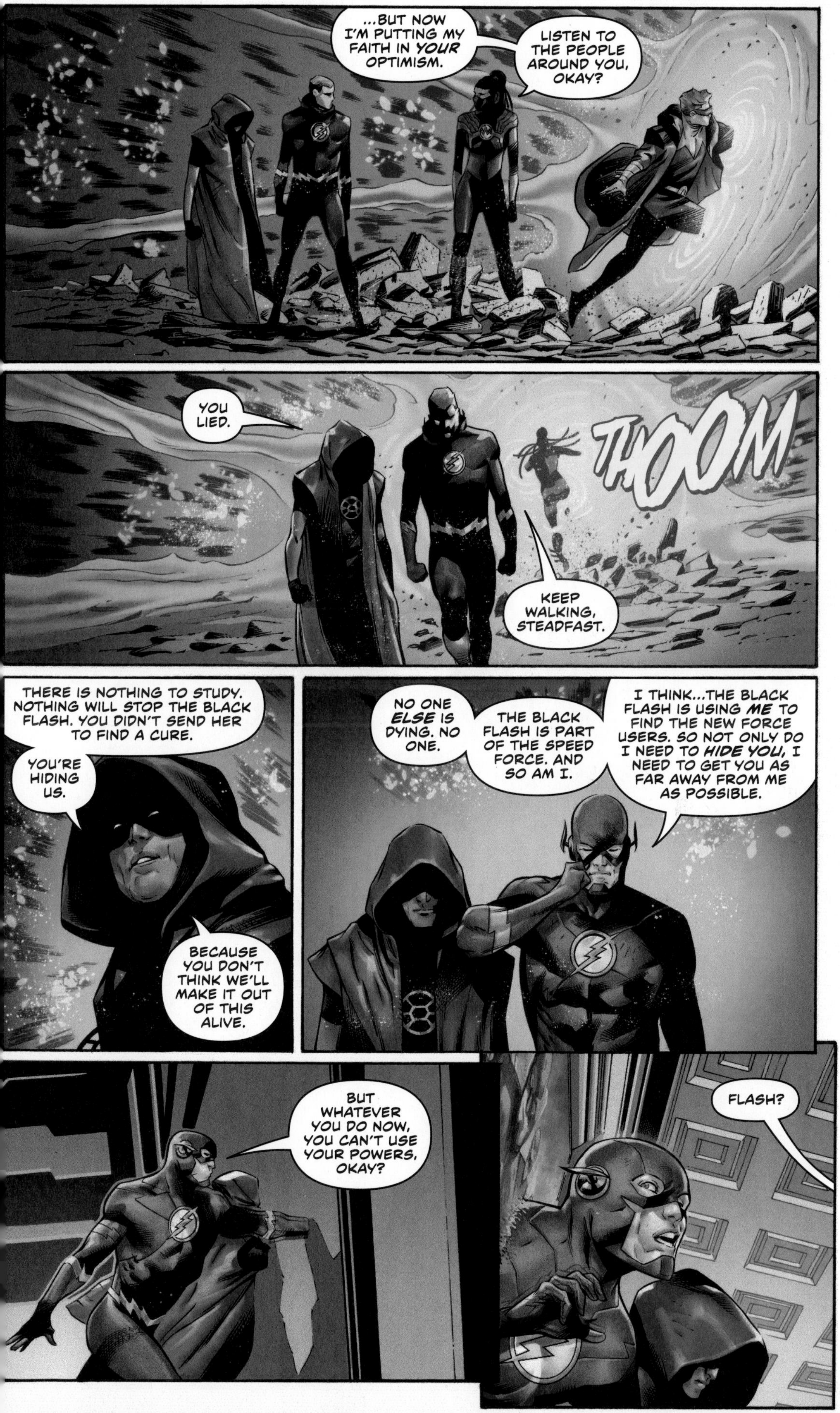

...BUT NOW I'M PUTTING MY FAITH IN YOUR OPTIMISM.
LISTEN TO THE PEOPLE AROUND YOU, OKAY?
YOU LIED.
THOOM
KEEP WALKING, STEADFAST.
THERE IS NOTHING TO STUDY. NOTHING WILL STOP THE BLACK FLASH. YOU DIDN'T SEND HER TO FIND A CURE.
YOU'RE HIDING US.
BECAUSE YOU DON'T THINK WE'LL MAKE IT OUT OF THIS ALIVE.
NO ONE ELSE IS DYING. NO ONE.
THE BLACK FLASH IS PART OF THE SPEED FORCE. AND SO AM I.
I THINK...THE BLACK FLASH IS USING ME TO FIND THE NEW FORCE USERS. SO NOT ONLY DO I NEED TO HIDE YOU, I NEED TO GET YOU AS FAR AWAY FROM ME AS POSSIBLE.
BUT WHATEVER YOU DO NOW, YOU CAN'T USE YOUR POWERS, OKAY?
FLASH?

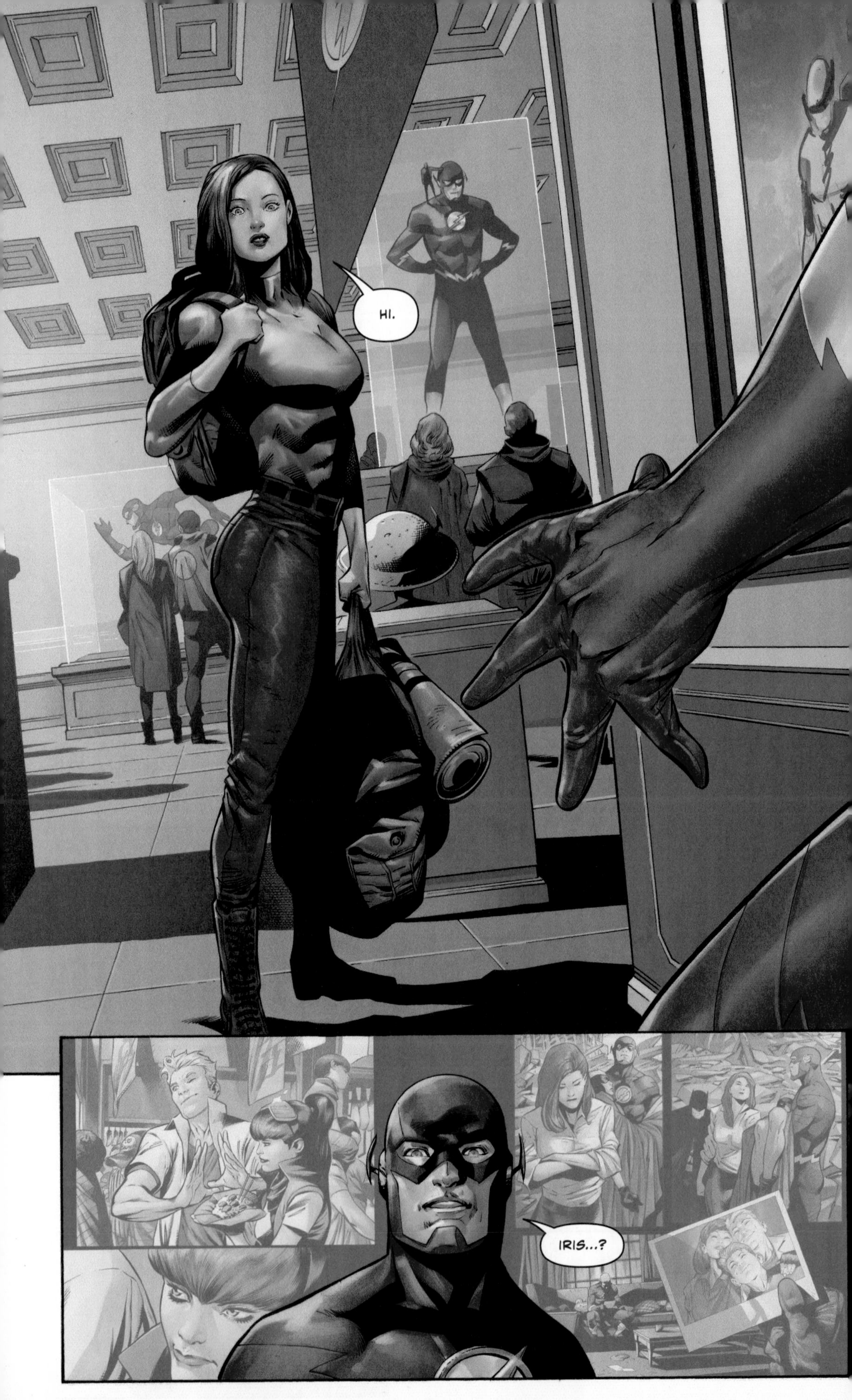
HI.
IRIS...?

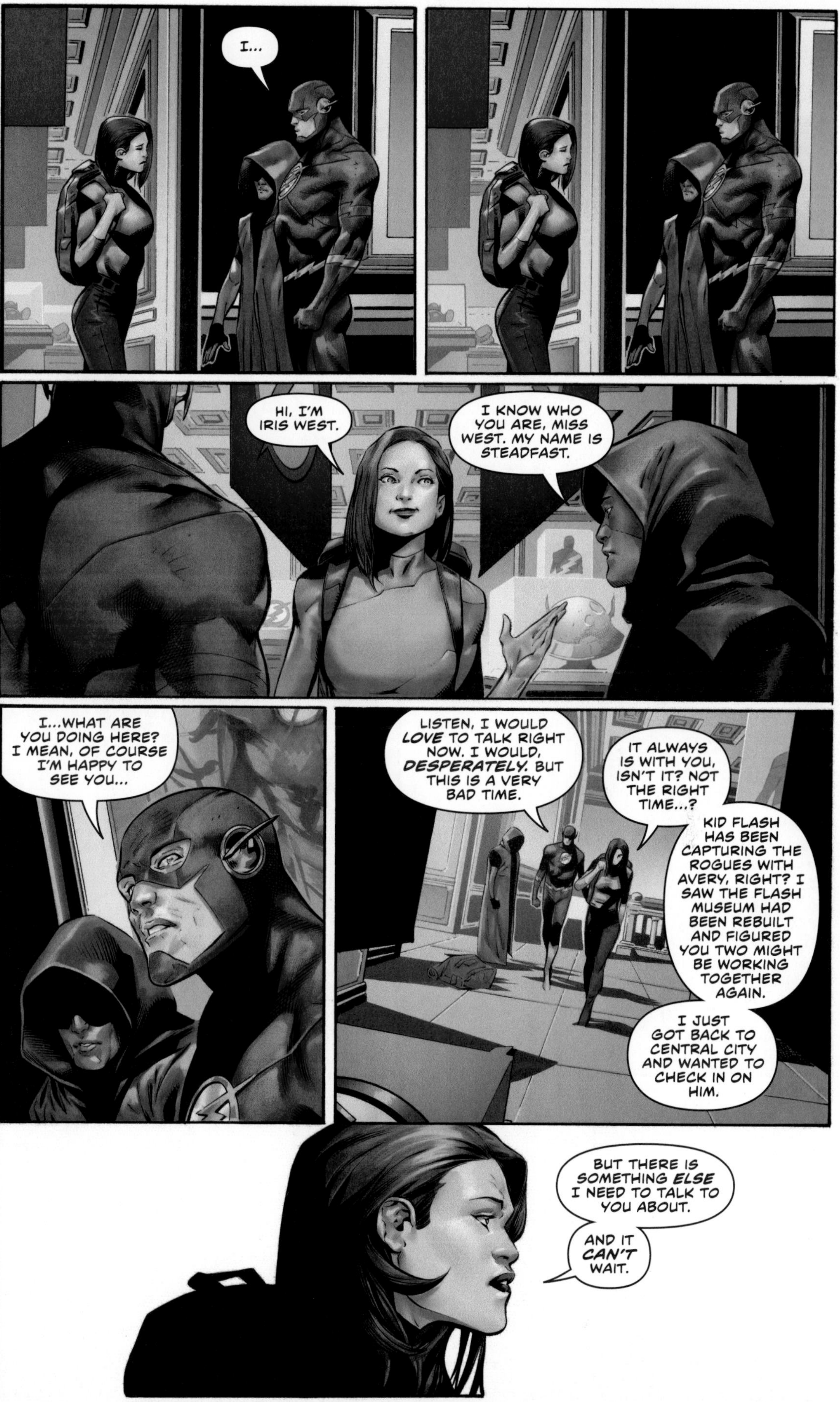
I...
HI, I'M IRIS WEST.
I KNOW WHO YOU ARE, MISS WEST. MY NAME IS STEADFAST.
I...WHAT ARE YOU DOING HERE? I MEAN, OF COURSE I'M HAPPY TO SEE YOU...
LISTEN, I WOULD LOVE TO TALK RIGHT NOW. I WOULD, DESPERATELY. BUT THIS IS A VERY BAD TIME.
IT ALWAYS IS WITH YOU, ISN'T IT? NOT THE RIGHT TIME...?
KID FLASH HAS BEEN CAPTURING THE ROGUES WITH AVERY, RIGHT? I SAW THE FLASH MUSEUM HAD BEEN REBUILT AND FIGURED YOU TWO MIGHT BE WORKING TOGETHER AGAIN.
I JUST GOT BACK TO CENTRAL CITY AND WANTED TO CHECK IN ON HIM.
BUT THERE IS SOMETHING ELSE I NEED TO TALK TO YOU ABOUT.
AND IT CAN'T WAIT.

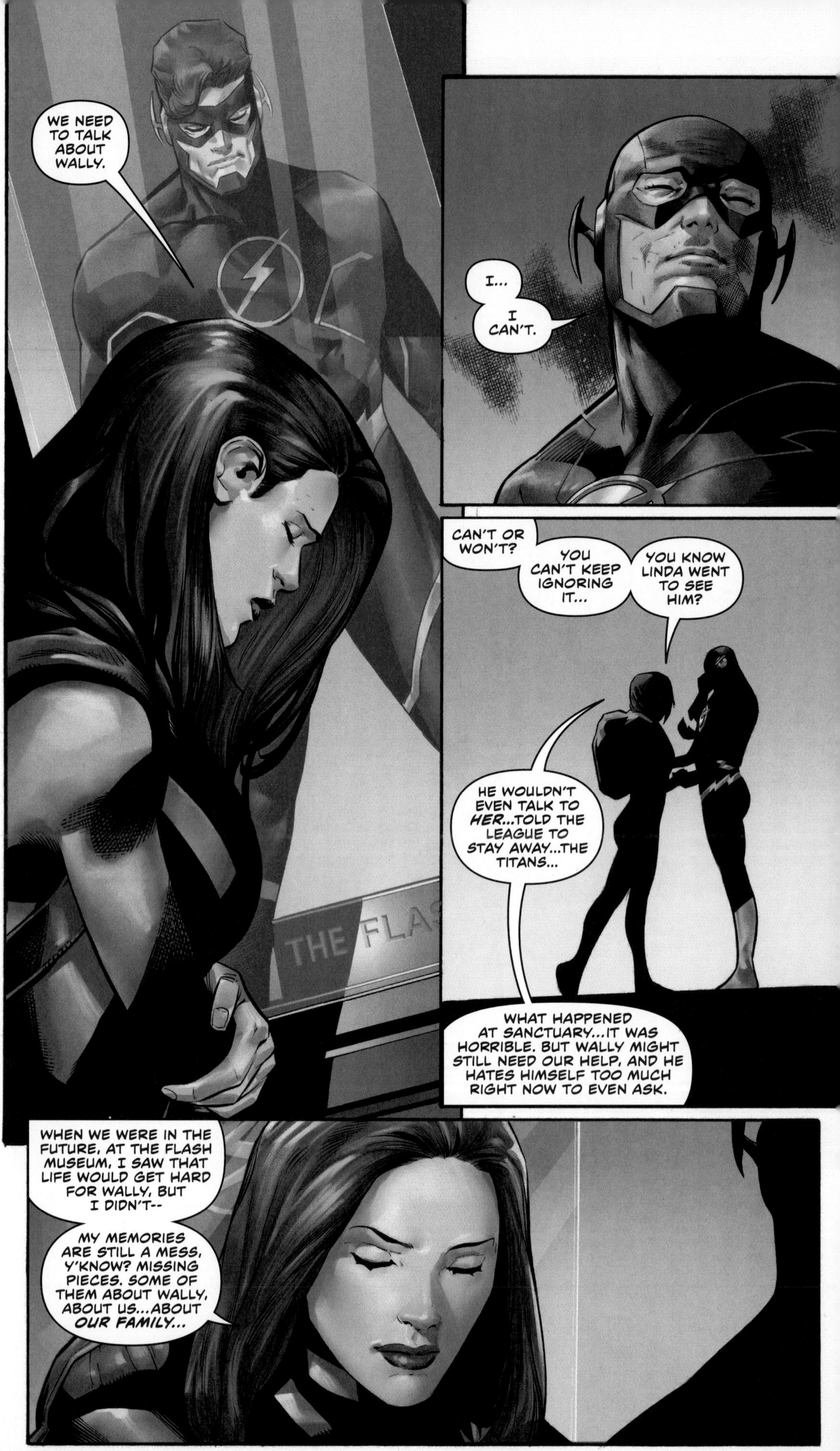
WE NEED TO TALK ABOUT WALLY.
I...
I CAN'T.
CAN'T OR WON'T?
YOU CAN'T KEEP IGNORING IT...
YOU KNOW LINDA WENT TO SEE HIM?
HE WOULDN'T EVEN TALK TO *HER*...TOLD THE LEAGUE TO STAY AWAY...THE TITANS...
WHAT HAPPENED AT SANCTUARY...IT WAS HORRIBLE. BUT WALLY MIGHT STILL NEED OUR HELP, AND HE HATES HIMSELF TOO MUCH RIGHT NOW TO EVEN ASK.
THE FLAS
WHEN WE WERE IN THE FUTURE, AT THE FLASH MUSEUM, I SAW THAT LIFE WOULD GET HARD FOR WALLY, BUT I DIDN'T--
MY MEMORIES ARE STILL A MESS, Y'KNOW? MISSING PIECES. SOME OF THEM ABOUT WALLY, ABOUT US...ABOUT *OUR FAMILY*...

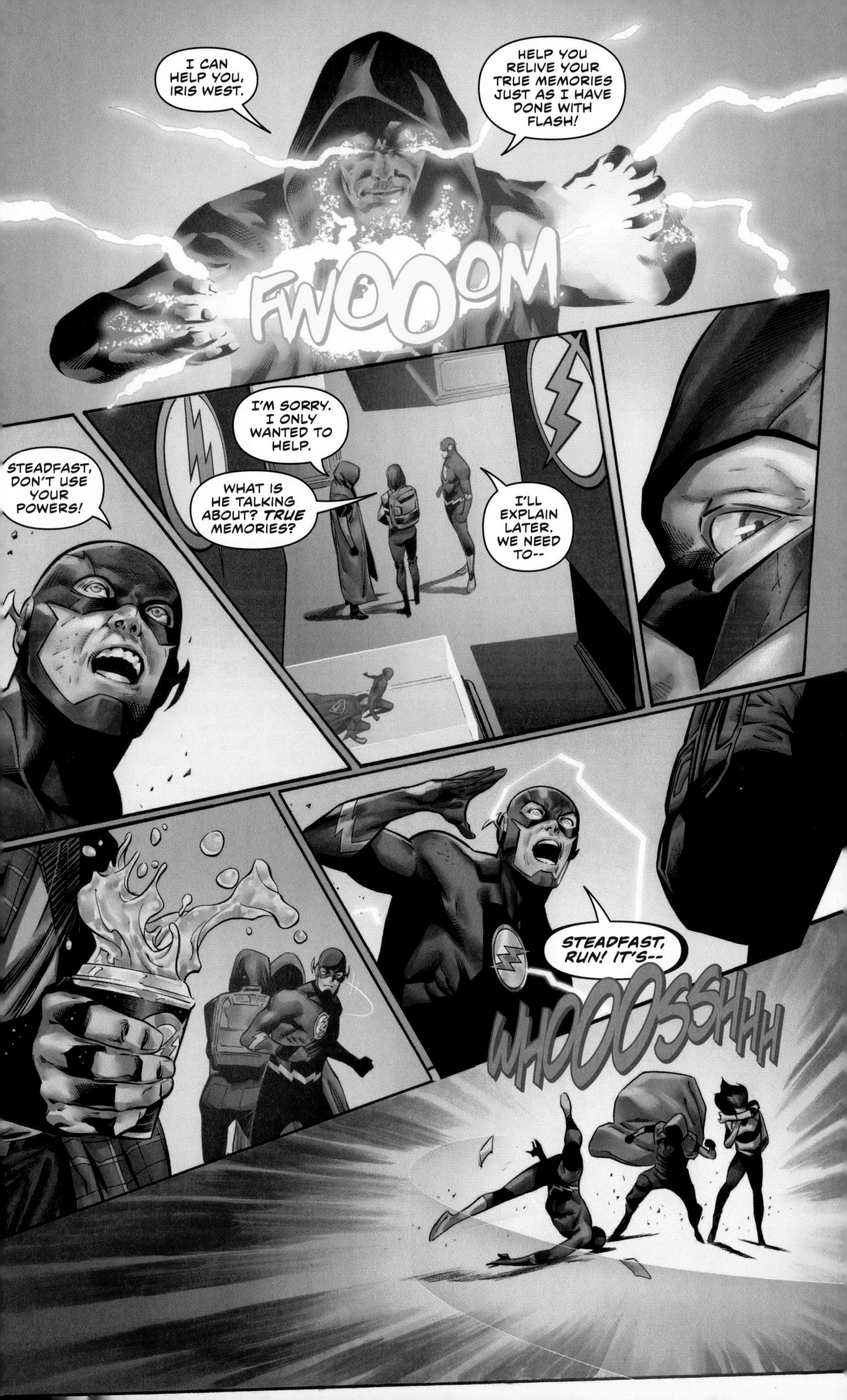
I CAN HELP YOU, IRIS WEST.
HELP YOU RELIVE YOUR TRUE MEMORIES JUST AS I HAVE DONE WITH FLASH!
FWOOOM
STEADFAST, DON'T USE YOUR POWERS!
I'M SORRY. I ONLY WANTED TO HELP.
WHAT IS HE TALKING ABOUT? *TRUE* MEMORIES?
I'LL EXPLAIN LATER. WE NEED TO--
STEADFAST, RUN! IT'S--
WHOOOSSHHH

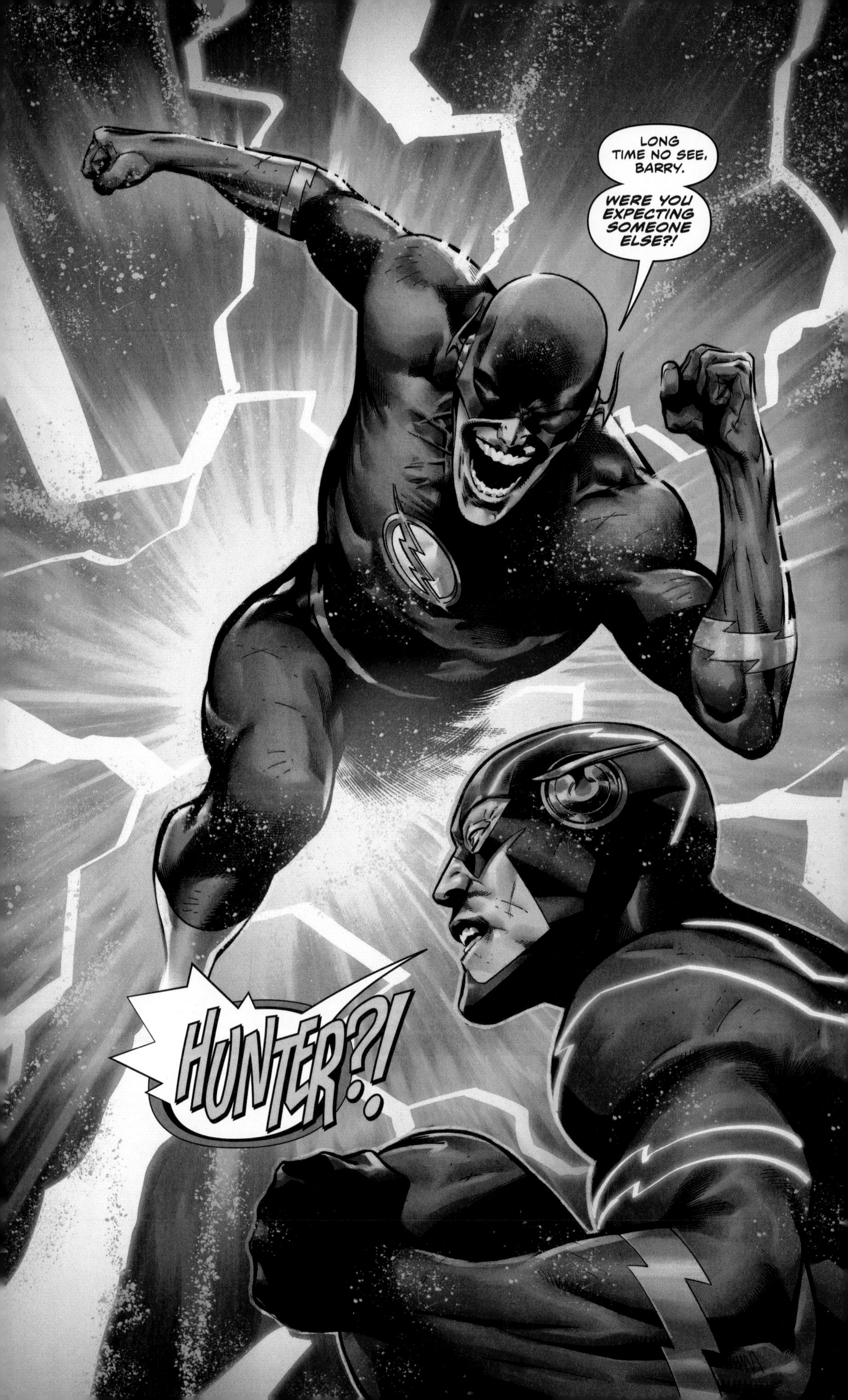

LONG TIME NO SEE, BARRY.
WERE YOU EXPECTING SOMEONE ELSE?!
HUNTER?!

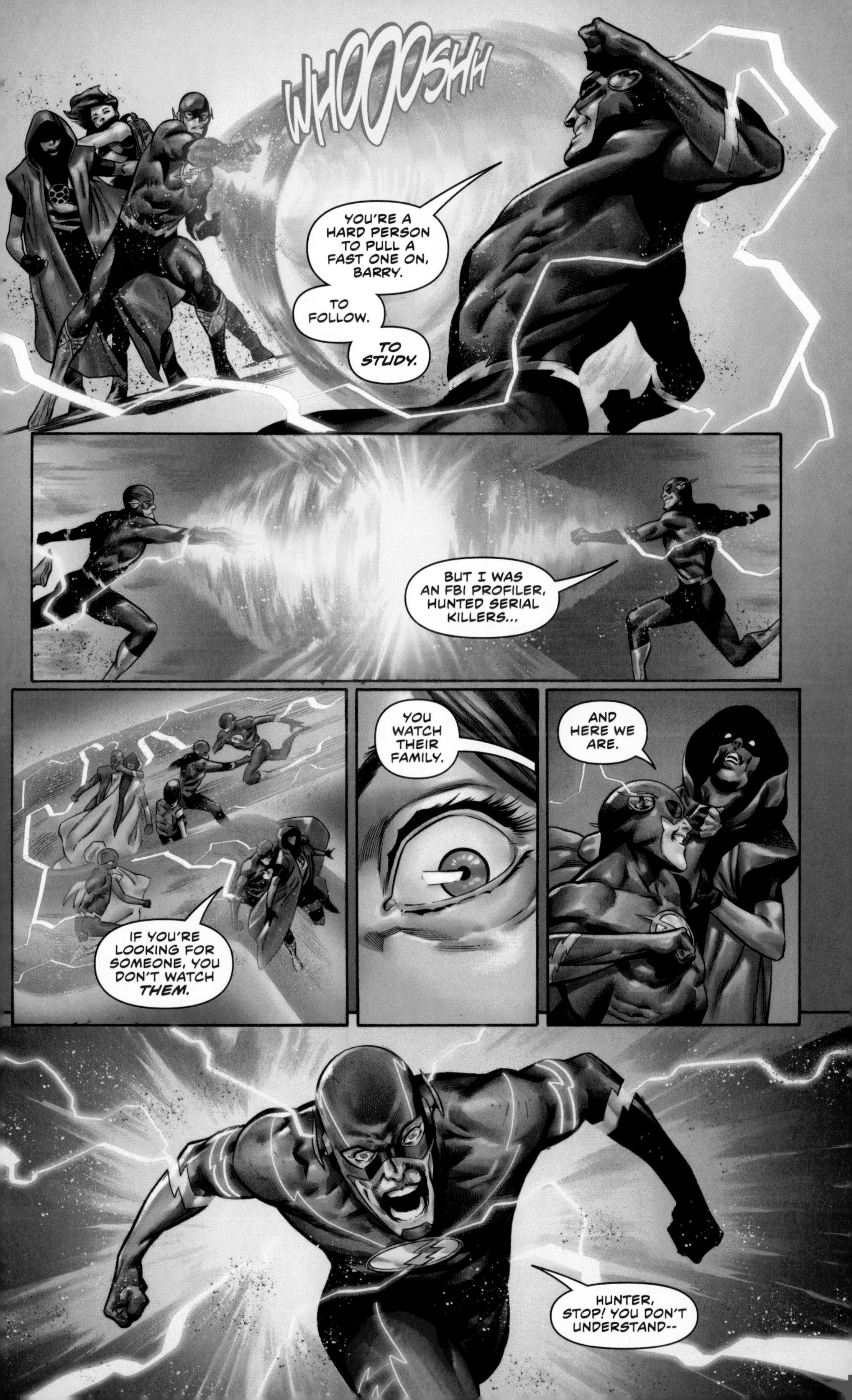
WHOOOOSHH
YOU'RE A HARD PERSON TO PULL A FAST ONE ON, BARRY.
TO FOLLOW.
TO STUDY.
BUT I WAS AN FBI PROFILER, HUNTED SERIAL KILLERS...
IF YOU'RE LOOKING FOR SOMEONE, YOU DON'T WATCH THEM.
YOU WATCH THEIR FAMILY.
AND HERE WE ARE.
HUNTER, STOP! YOU DON'T UNDERSTAND--

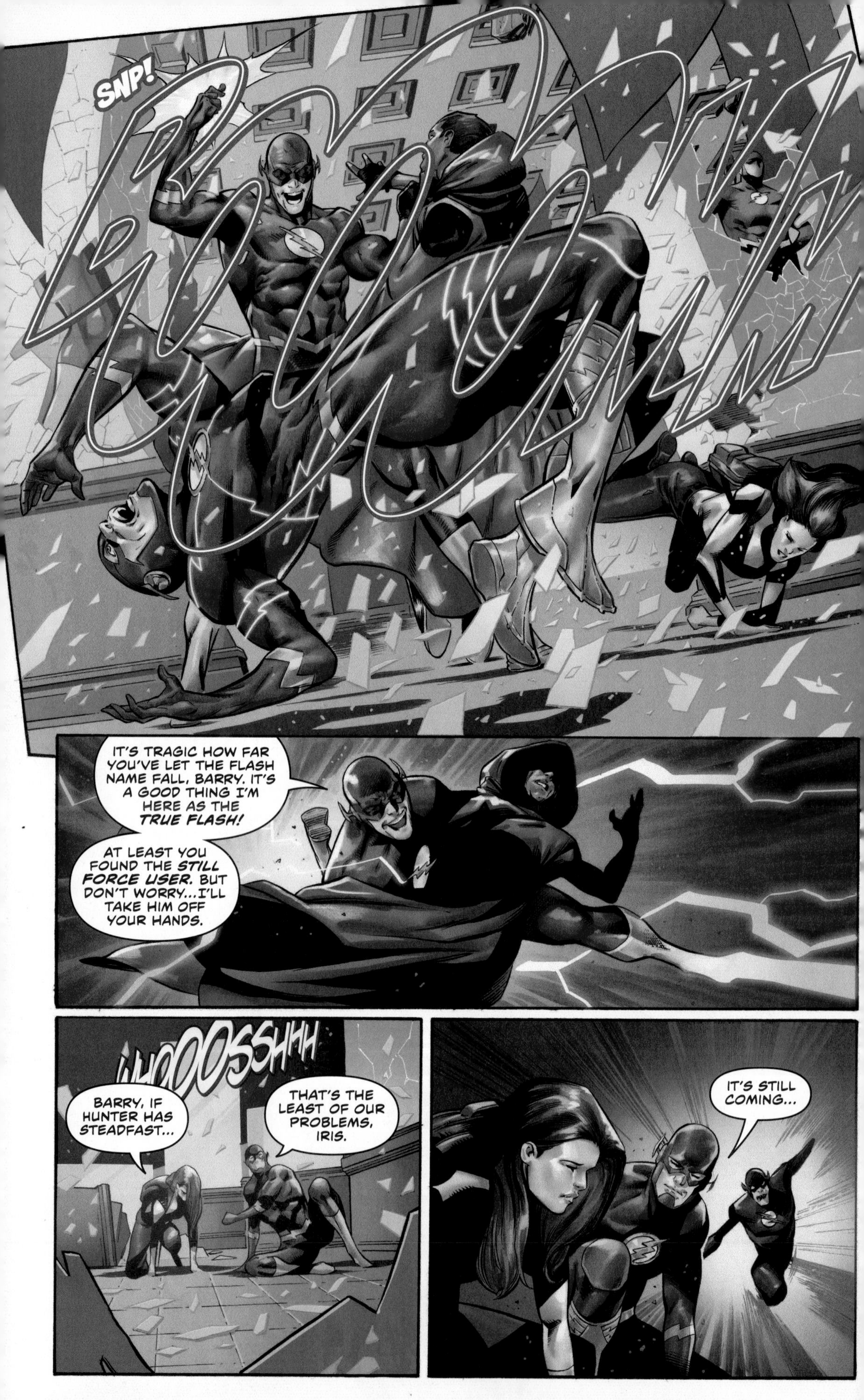
SNP!
IT'S TRAGIC HOW FAR YOU'VE LET THE FLASH NAME FALL, BARRY. IT'S A GOOD THING I'M HERE AS THE TRUE FLASH!
AT LEAST YOU FOUND THE STILL FORCE USER. BUT DON'T WORRY...I'LL TAKE HIM OFF YOUR HANDS.
WHOOOSSHHH
BARRY, IF HUNTER HAS STEADFAST...
THAT'S THE LEAST OF OUR PROBLEMS, IRIS.
IT'S STILL COMING...

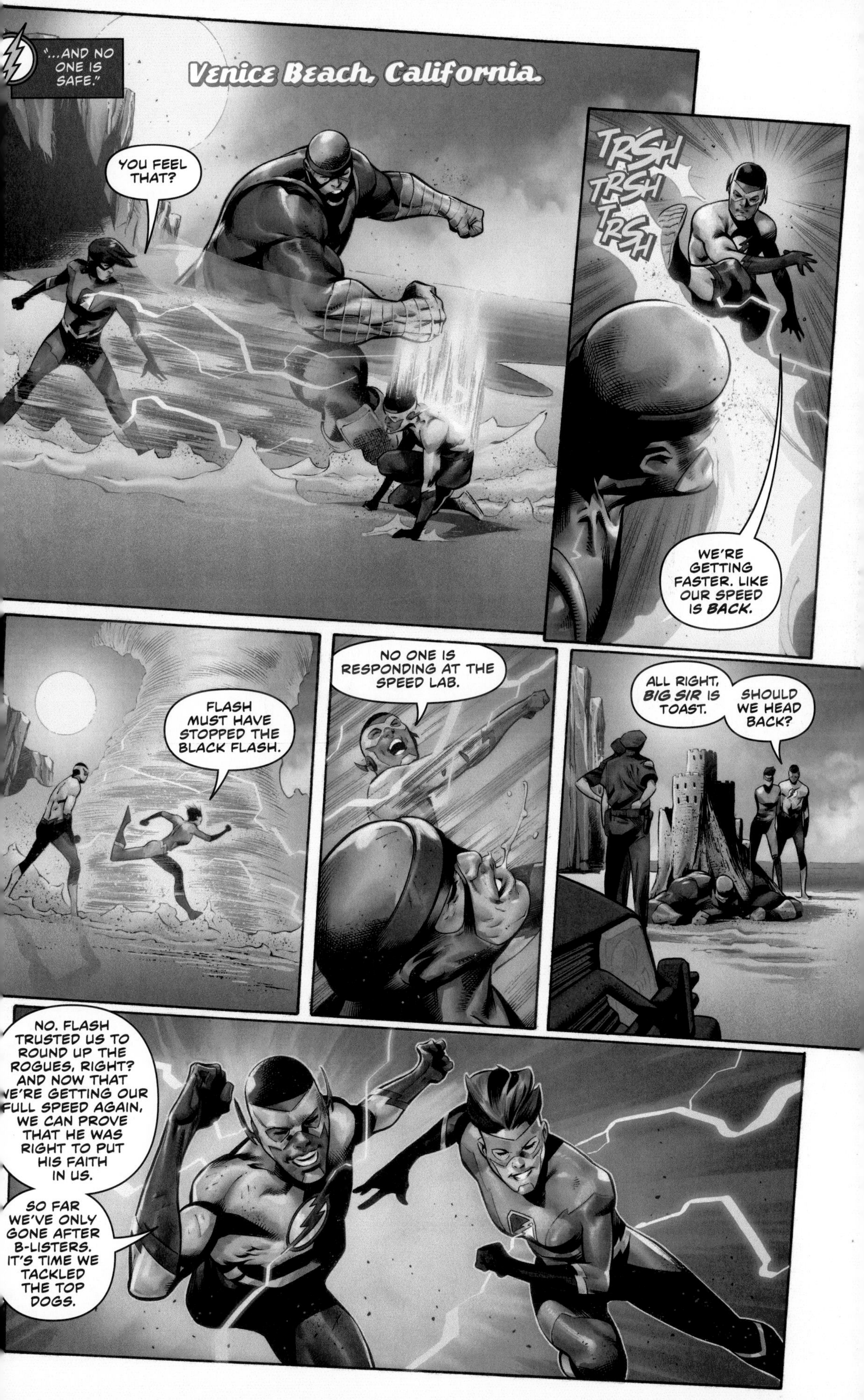
"...AND NO ONE IS SAFE."
Venice Beach, California.
YOU FEEL THAT?
TRSH TRSH TRSH
WE'RE GETTING FASTER. LIKE OUR SPEED IS BACK.
FLASH MUST HAVE STOPPED THE BLACK FLASH.
NO ONE IS RESPONDING AT THE SPEED LAB.
ALL RIGHT, BIG SIR IS TOAST.
SHOULD WE HEAD BACK?
NO. FLASH TRUSTED US TO ROUND UP THE ROGUES, RIGHT? AND NOW THAT WE'RE GETTING OUR FULL SPEED AGAIN, WE CAN PROVE THAT HE WAS RIGHT TO PUT HIS FAITH IN US.
SO FAR WE'VE ONLY GONE AFTER B-LISTERS. IT'S TIME WE TACKLED THE TOP DOGS.

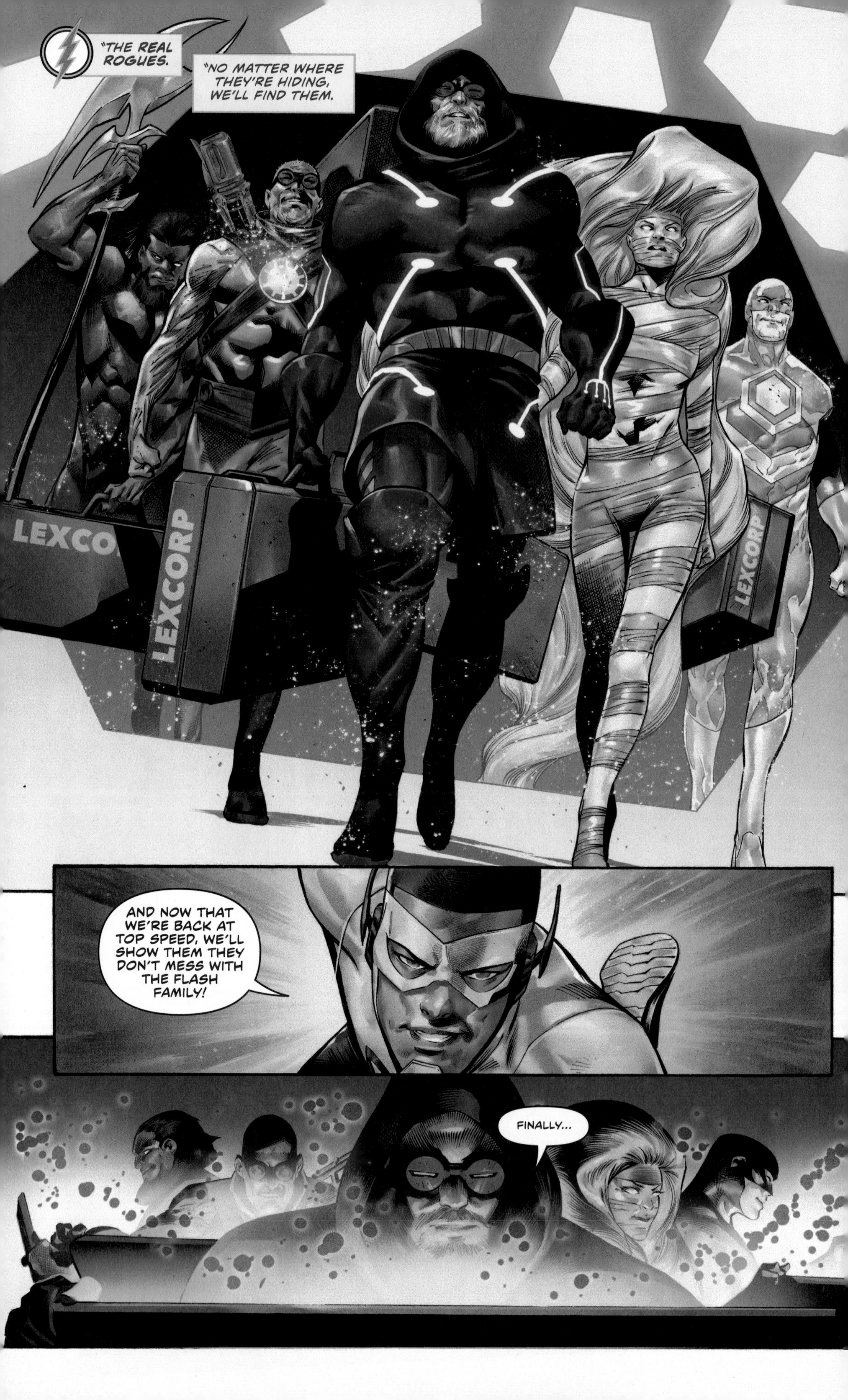
"THE REAL ROGUES.
"NO MATTER WHERE THEY'RE HIDING, WE'LL FIND THEM.
LEXCORP
LEXCORP
LEXCORP
AND NOW THAT WE'RE BACK AT TOP SPEED, WE'LL SHOW THEM THEY DON'T MESS WITH THE FLASH FAMILY!
FINALLY...

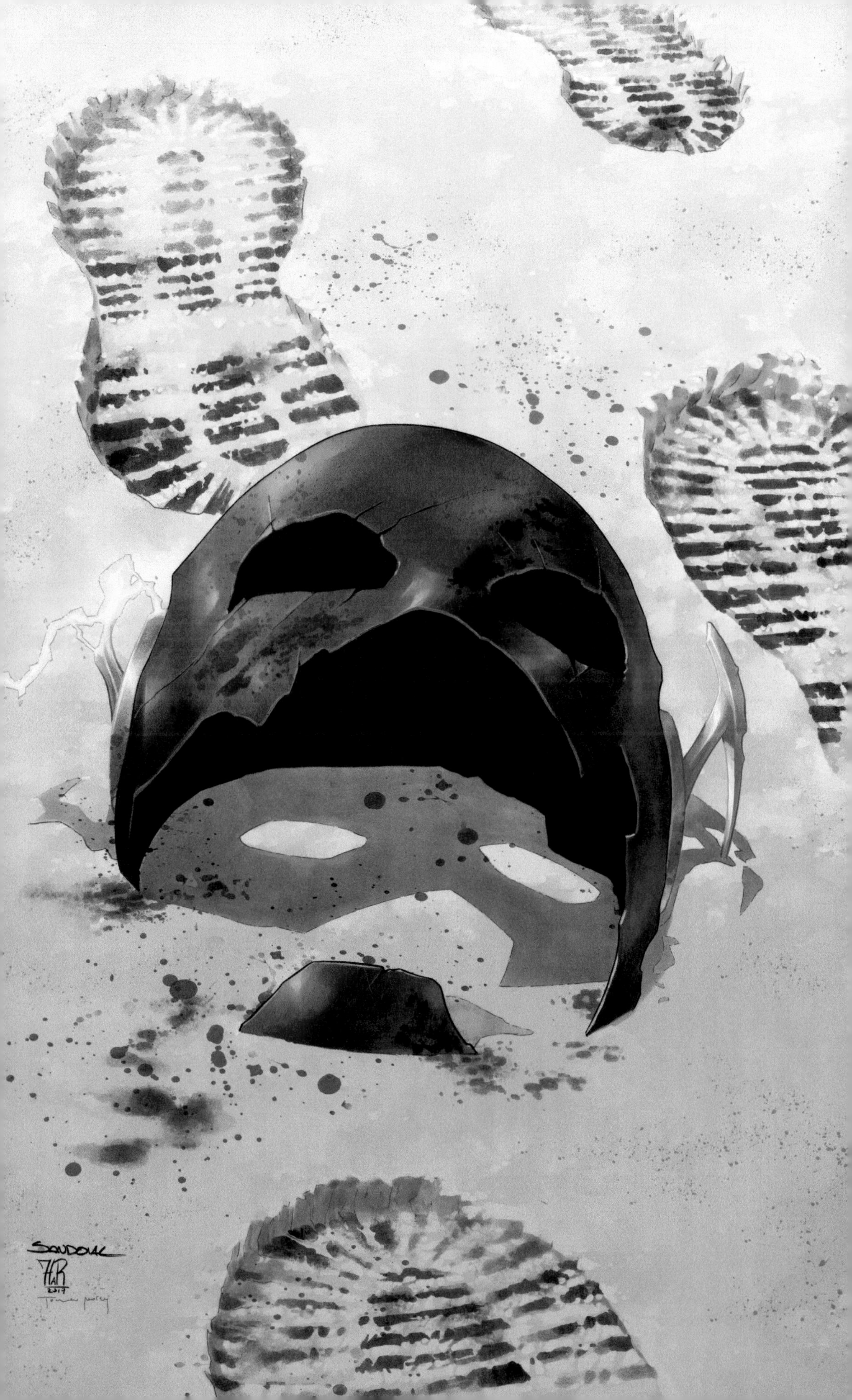

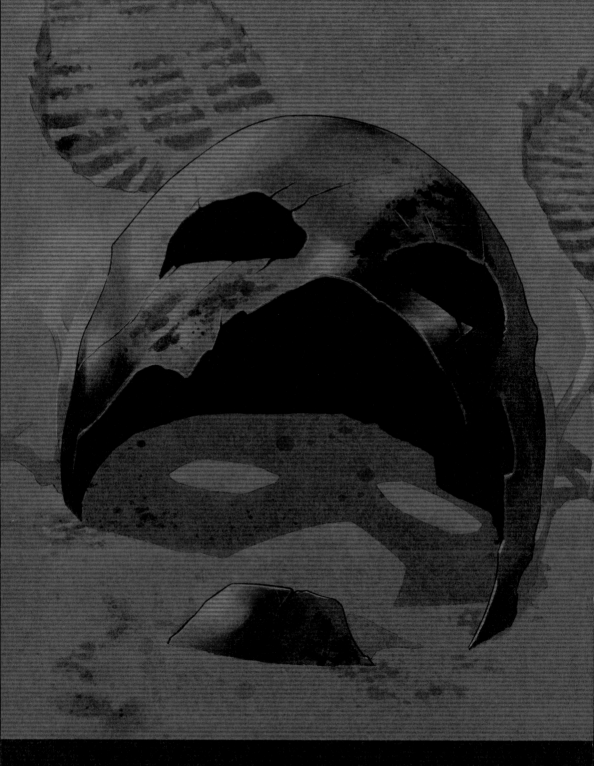

THE FLASH

#80

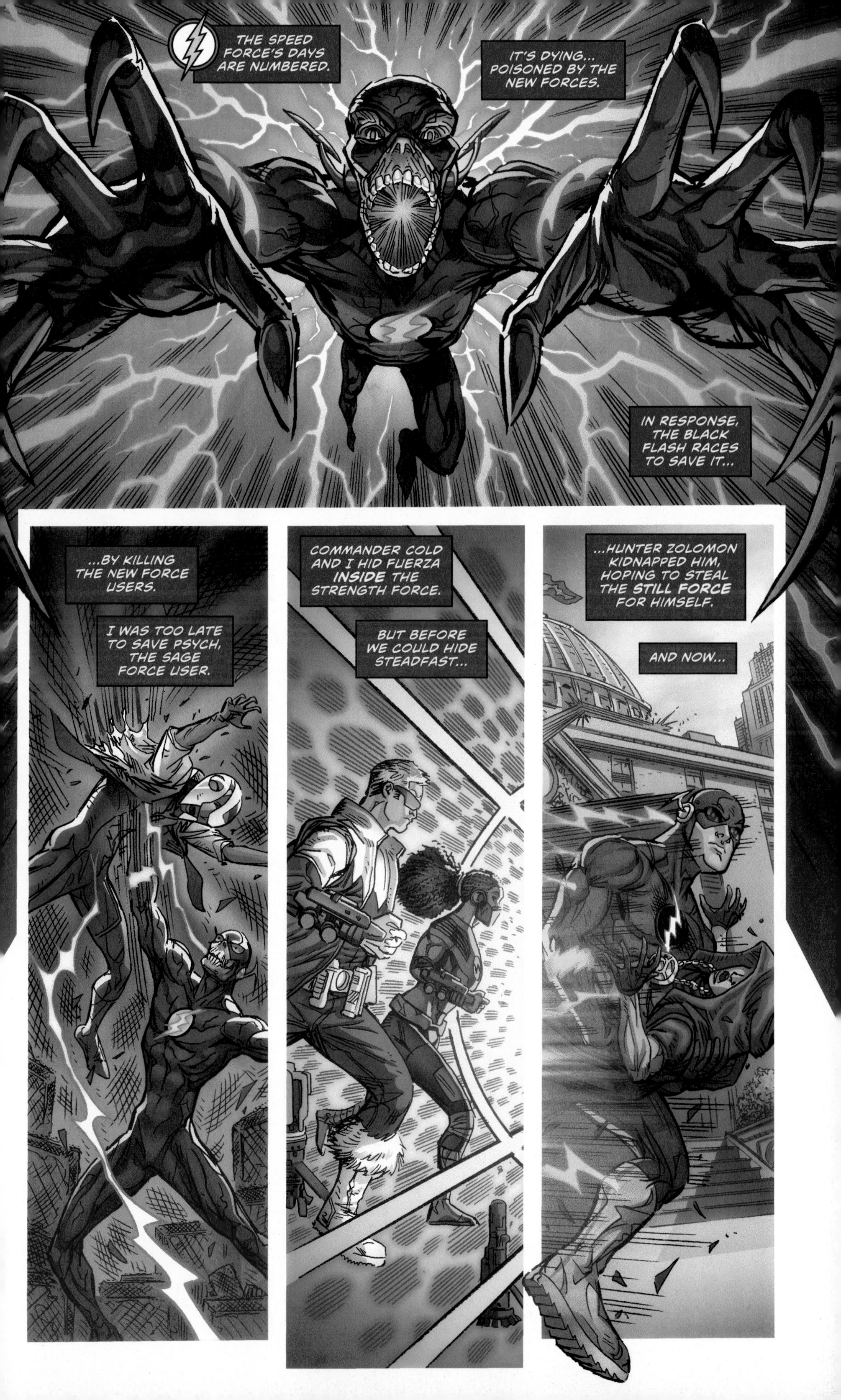
THE SPEED FORCE'S DAYS ARE NUMBERED.
IT'S DYING... POISONED BY THE NEW FORCES.
IN RESPONSE, THE BLACK FLASH RACES TO SAVE IT...
...BY KILLING THE NEW FORCE USERS.
I WAS TOO LATE TO SAVE PSYCH, THE SAGE FORCE USER.
COMMANDER COLD AND I HID FUERZA INSIDE THE STRENGTH FORCE.
BUT BEFORE WE COULD HIDE STEADFAST...
...HUNTER ZOLOMON KIDNAPPED HIM, HOPING TO STEAL THE STILL FORCE FOR HIMSELF.
AND NOW...

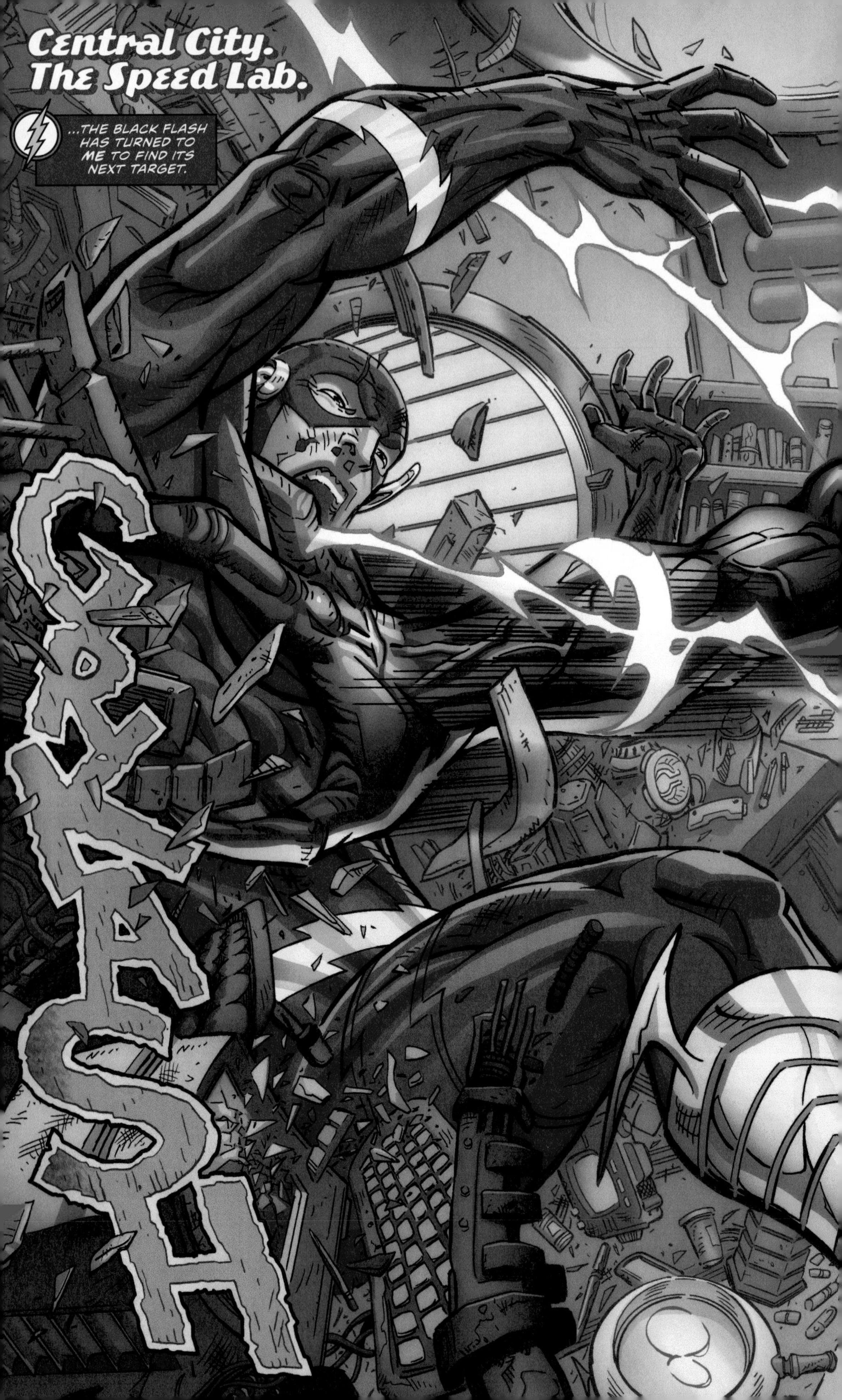
Central City.
The Speed Lab.
...THE BLACK FLASH HAS TURNED TO ME TO FIND ITS NEXT TARGET.
CRASH

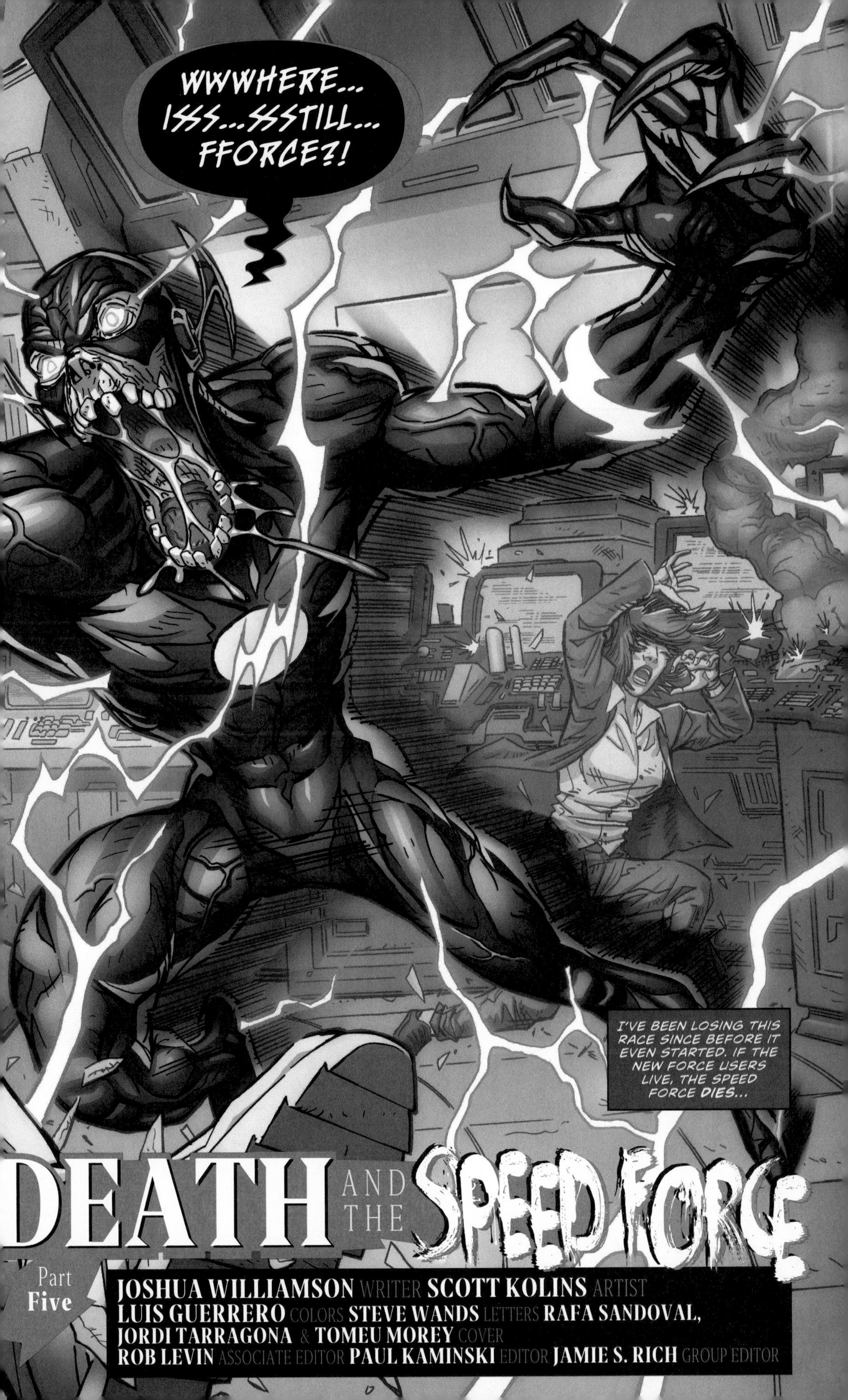
WWWHERE... ISSS...SSSTILL... FFORCE?!
I'VE BEEN LOSING THIS RACE SINCE BEFORE IT EVEN STARTED. IF THE NEW FORCE USERS LIVE, THE SPEED FORCE DIES...
DEATH AND THE SPEED FORCE
Part Five
JOSHUA WILLIAMSON WRITER SCOTT KOLINS ARTIST
LUIS GUERRERO COLORS STEVE WANDS LETTERS RAFA SANDOVAL,
JORDI TARRAGONA & TOMEU MOREY COVER
ROB LEVIN ASSOCIATE EDITOR PAUL KAMINSKI EDITOR JAMIE S. RICH GROUP EDITOR

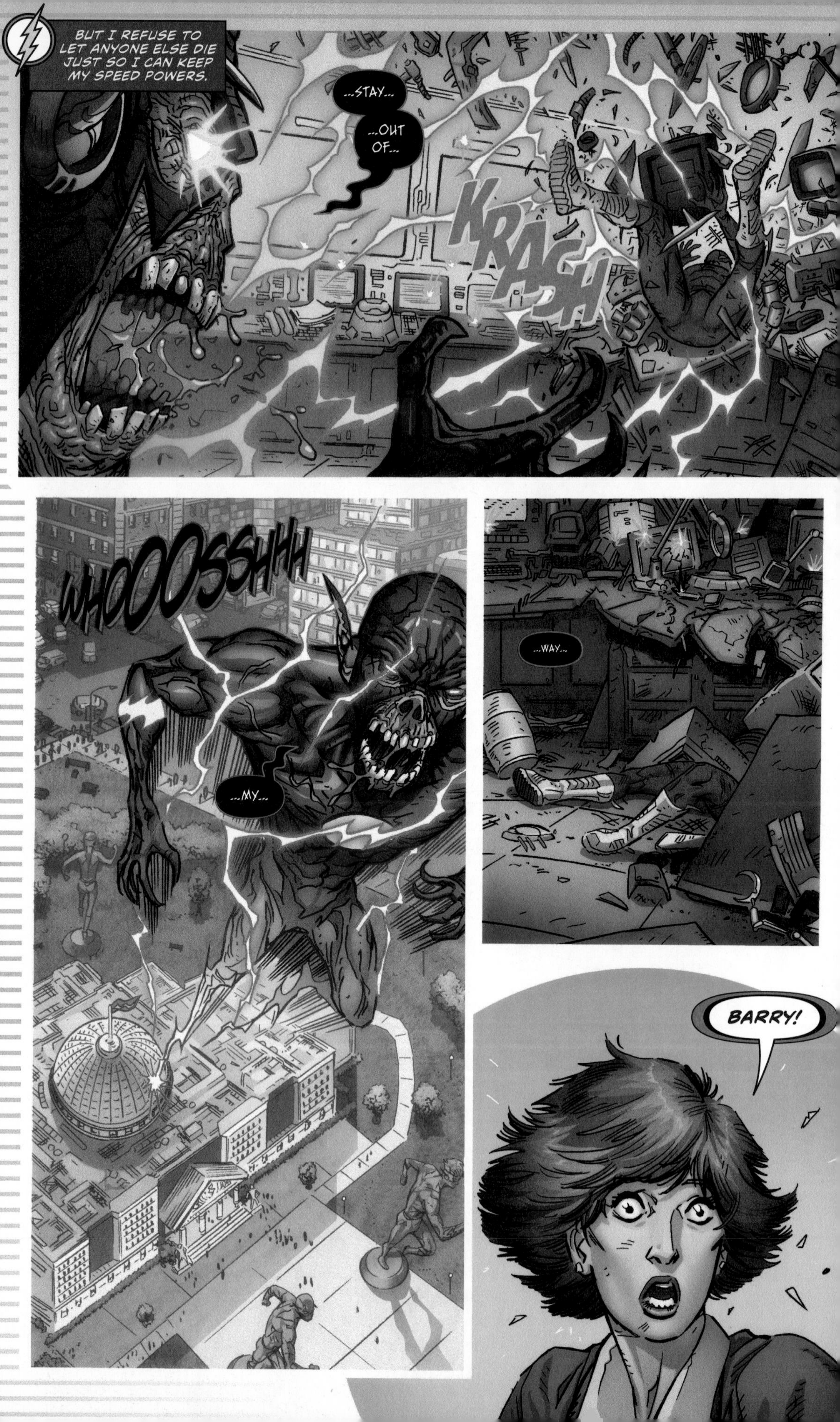
BUT I REFUSE TO LET ANYONE ELSE DIE JUST SO I CAN KEEP MY SPEED POWERS.
...STAY...
...OUT OF...
KRASH
WHOOOOSSHHH
...MY...
...WAY...
BARRY!

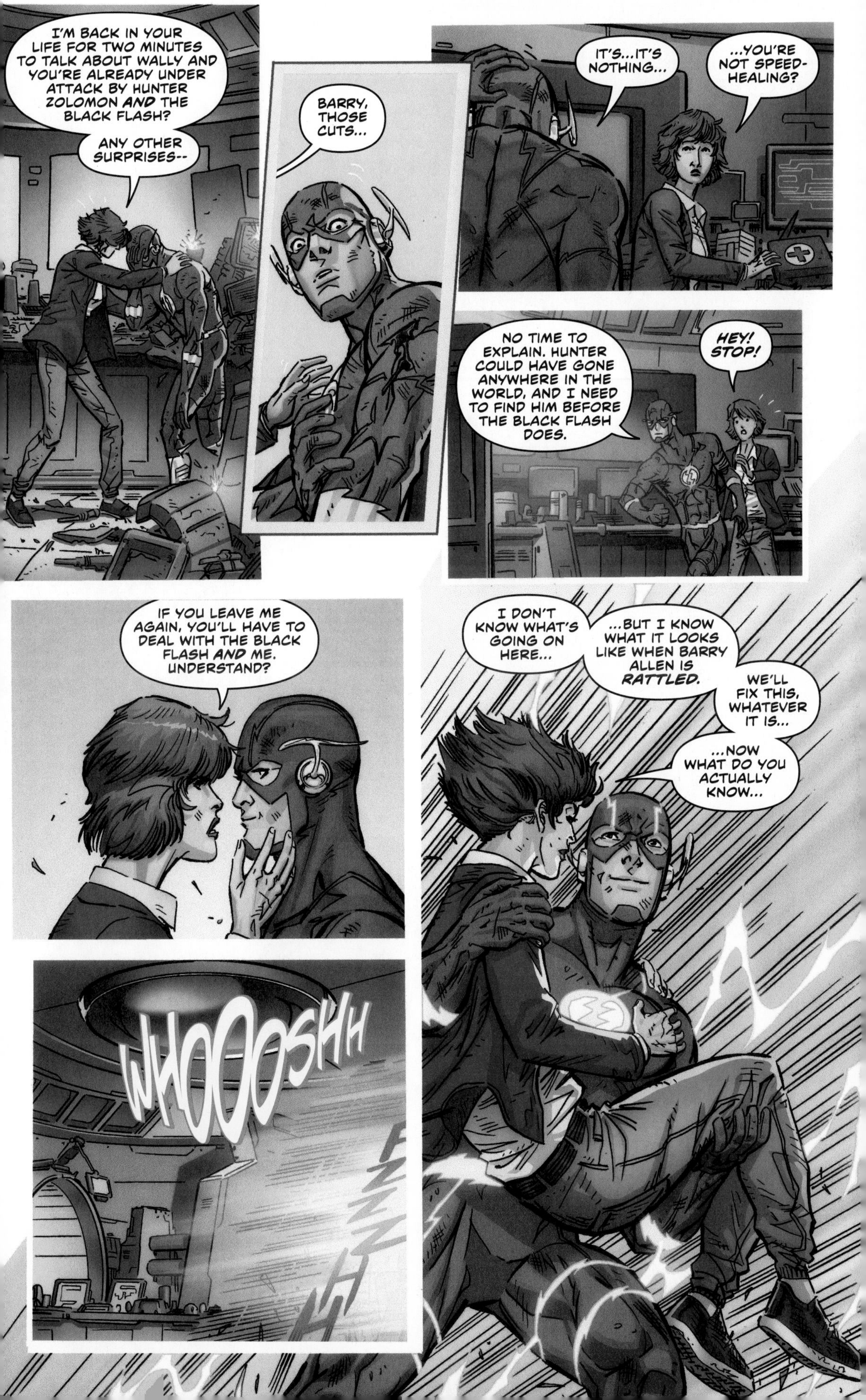

I'M BACK IN YOUR LIFE FOR TWO MINUTES TO TALK ABOUT WALLY AND YOU'RE ALREADY UNDER ATTACK BY HUNTER ZOLOMON *AND* THE BLACK FLASH?
ANY OTHER SURPRISES--
BARRY, THOSE CUTS...
IT'S...IT'S NOTHING...
...YOU'RE NOT SPEED-HEALING?
NO TIME TO EXPLAIN. HUNTER COULD HAVE GONE ANYWHERE IN THE WORLD, AND I NEED TO FIND HIM BEFORE THE BLACK FLASH DOES.
HEY! STOP!
IF YOU LEAVE ME AGAIN, YOU'LL HAVE TO DEAL WITH THE BLACK FLASH *AND* ME. UNDERSTAND?
WHOOOSHH
I DON'T KNOW WHAT'S GOING ON HERE...
...BUT I KNOW WHAT IT LOOKS LIKE WHEN BARRY ALLEN IS *RATTLED.*
WE'LL FIX THIS, WHATEVER IT IS...
...NOW WHAT DO YOU ACTUALLY KNOW...

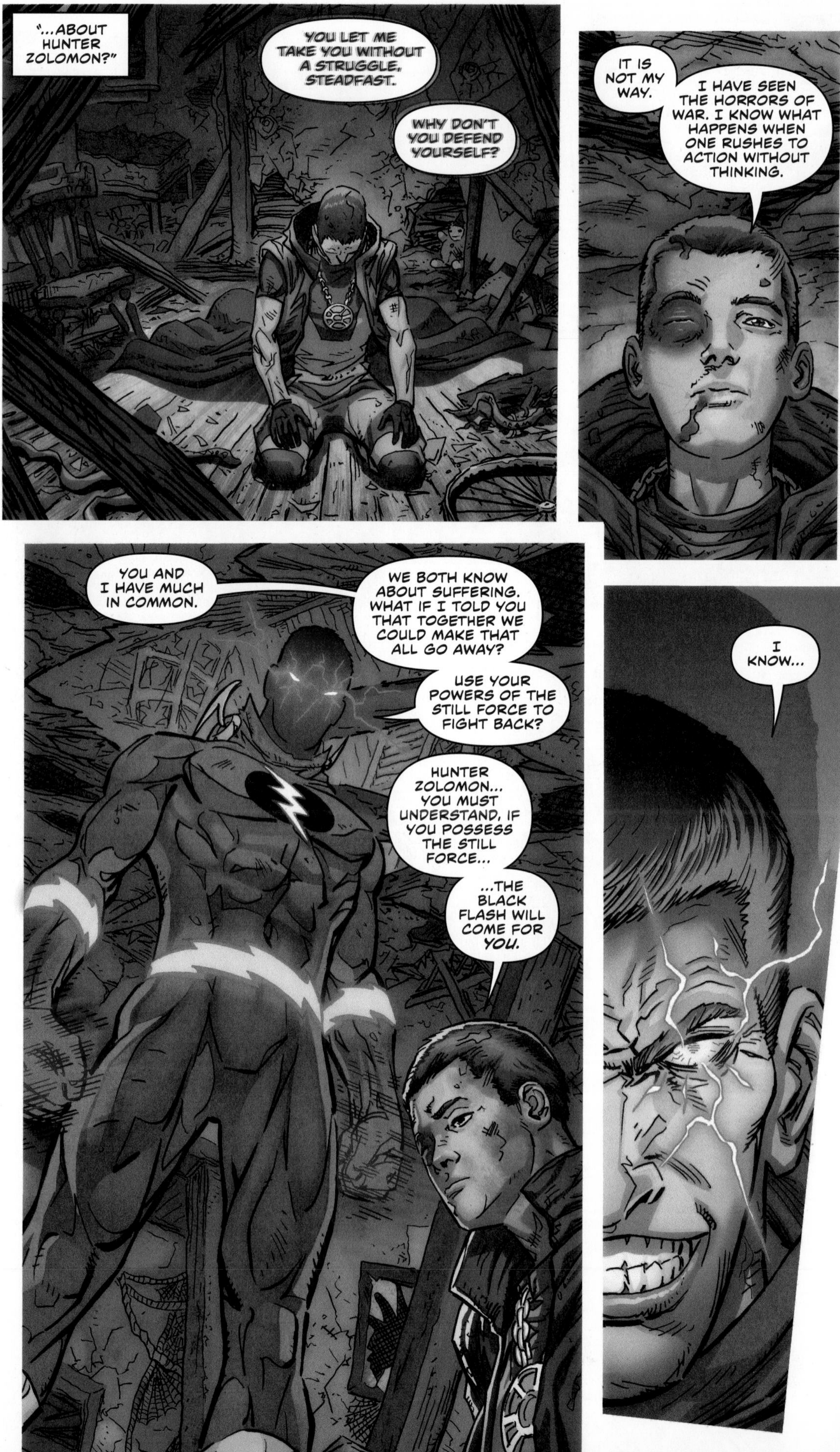
"...ABOUT HUNTER ZOLOMON?"
YOU LET ME TAKE YOU WITHOUT A STRUGGLE, STEADFAST.
WHY DON'T YOU DEFEND YOURSELF?
IT IS NOT MY WAY.
I HAVE SEEN THE HORRORS OF WAR. I KNOW WHAT HAPPENS WHEN ONE RUSHES TO ACTION WITHOUT THINKING.
YOU AND I HAVE MUCH IN COMMON.
WE BOTH KNOW ABOUT SUFFERING. WHAT IF I TOLD YOU THAT TOGETHER WE COULD MAKE THAT ALL GO AWAY?
USE YOUR POWERS OF THE STILL FORCE TO FIGHT BACK?
HUNTER ZOLOMON... YOU MUST UNDERSTAND, IF YOU POSSESS THE STILL FORCE...
...THE BLACK FLASH WILL COME FOR YOU.
I KNOW...

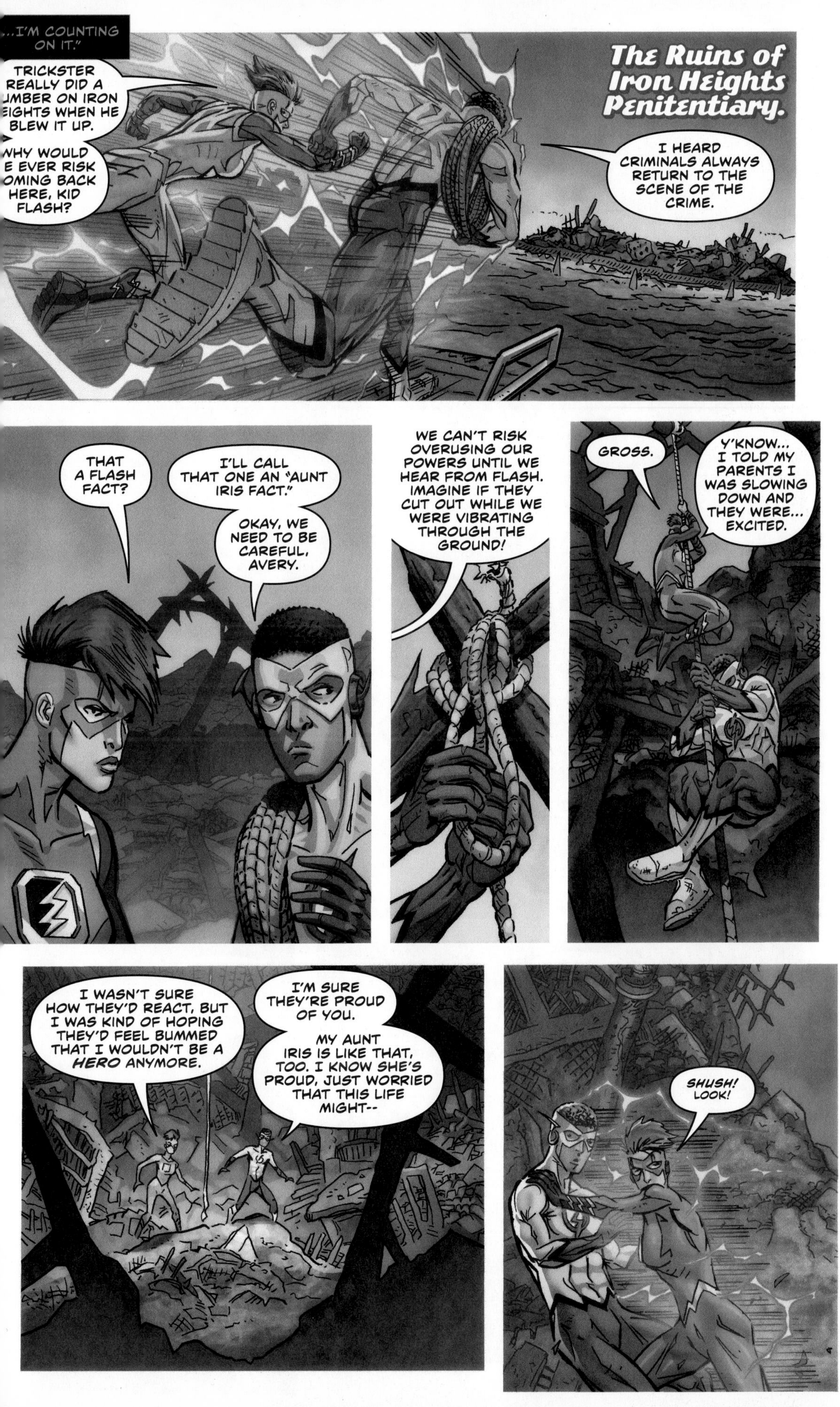
...I'M COUNTING ON IT."
TRICKSTER REALLY DID A UMBER ON IRON EIGHTS WHEN HE BLEW IT UP.
WHY WOULD E EVER RISK OMING BACK HERE, KID FLASH?
The Ruins of Iron Heights Penitentiary.
I HEARD CRIMINALS ALWAYS RETURN TO THE SCENE OF THE CRIME.
THAT A FLASH FACT?
I'LL CALL THAT ONE AN "AUNT IRIS FACT."
OKAY, WE NEED TO BE CAREFUL, AVERY.
WE CAN'T RISK OVERUSING OUR POWERS UNTIL WE HEAR FROM FLASH. IMAGINE IF THEY CUT OUT WHILE WE WERE VIBRATING THROUGH THE GROUND!
GROSS.
Y'KNOW... I TOLD MY PARENTS I WAS SLOWING DOWN AND THEY WERE... EXCITED.
I WASN'T SURE HOW THEY'D REACT, BUT I WAS KIND OF HOPING THEY'D FEEL BUMMED THAT I WOULDN'T BE A HERO ANYMORE.
I'M SURE THEY'RE PROUD OF YOU.
MY AUNT IRIS IS LIKE THAT, TOO. I KNOW SHE'S PROUD, JUST WORRIED THAT THIS LIFE MIGHT--
SHUSH! LOOK!

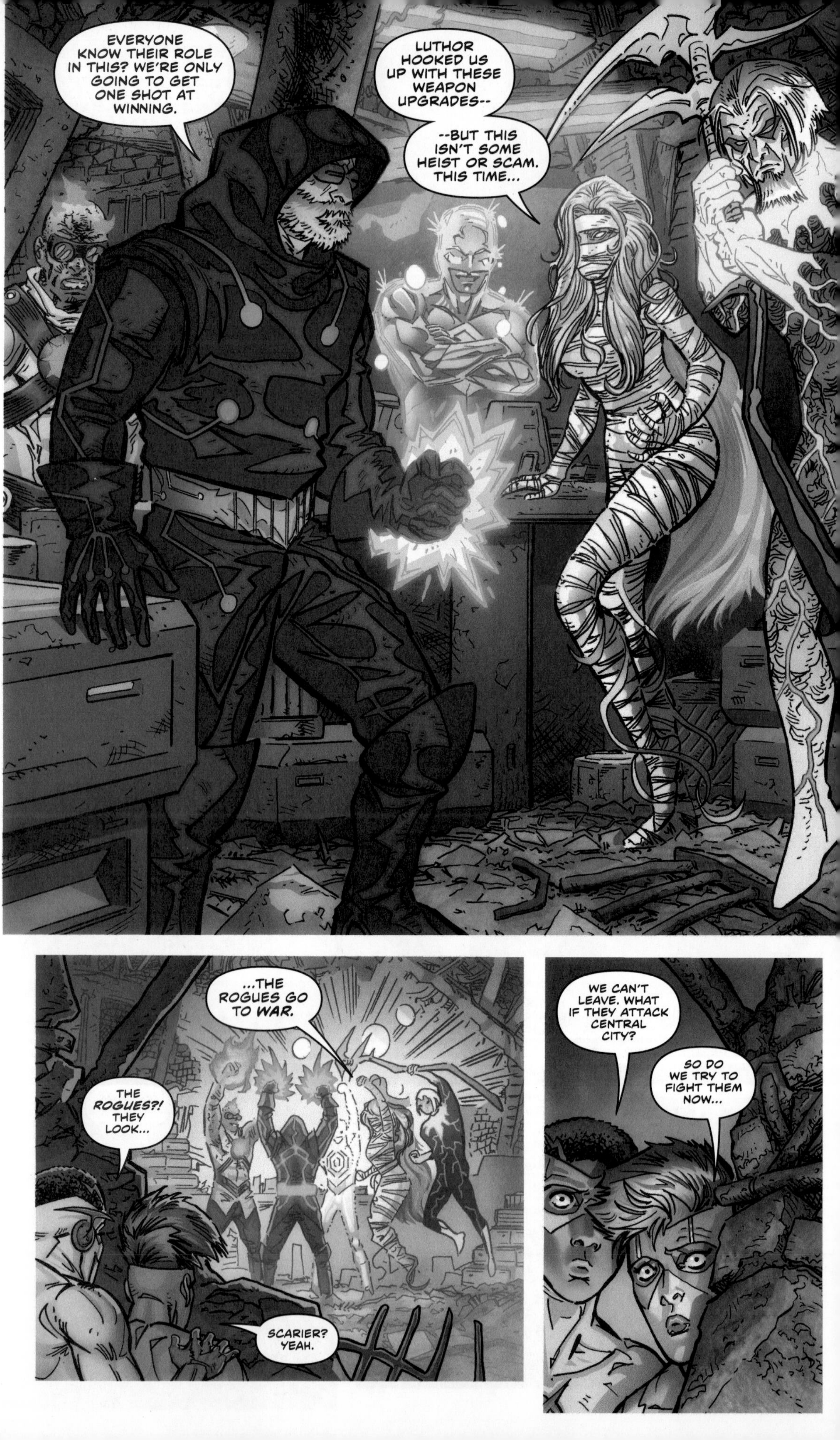
EVERYONE KNOW THEIR ROLE IN THIS? WE'RE ONLY GOING TO GET ONE SHOT AT WINNING.
LUTHOR HOOKED US UP WITH THESE WEAPON UPGRADES--
--BUT THIS ISN'T SOME HEIST OR SCAM. THIS TIME...
...THE ROGUES GO TO *WAR.*
THE *ROGUES?!* THEY LOOK...
SCARIER? YEAH.
WE CAN'T LEAVE. WHAT IF THEY ATTACK CENTRAL CITY?
SO DO WE TRY TO FIGHT THEM NOW...

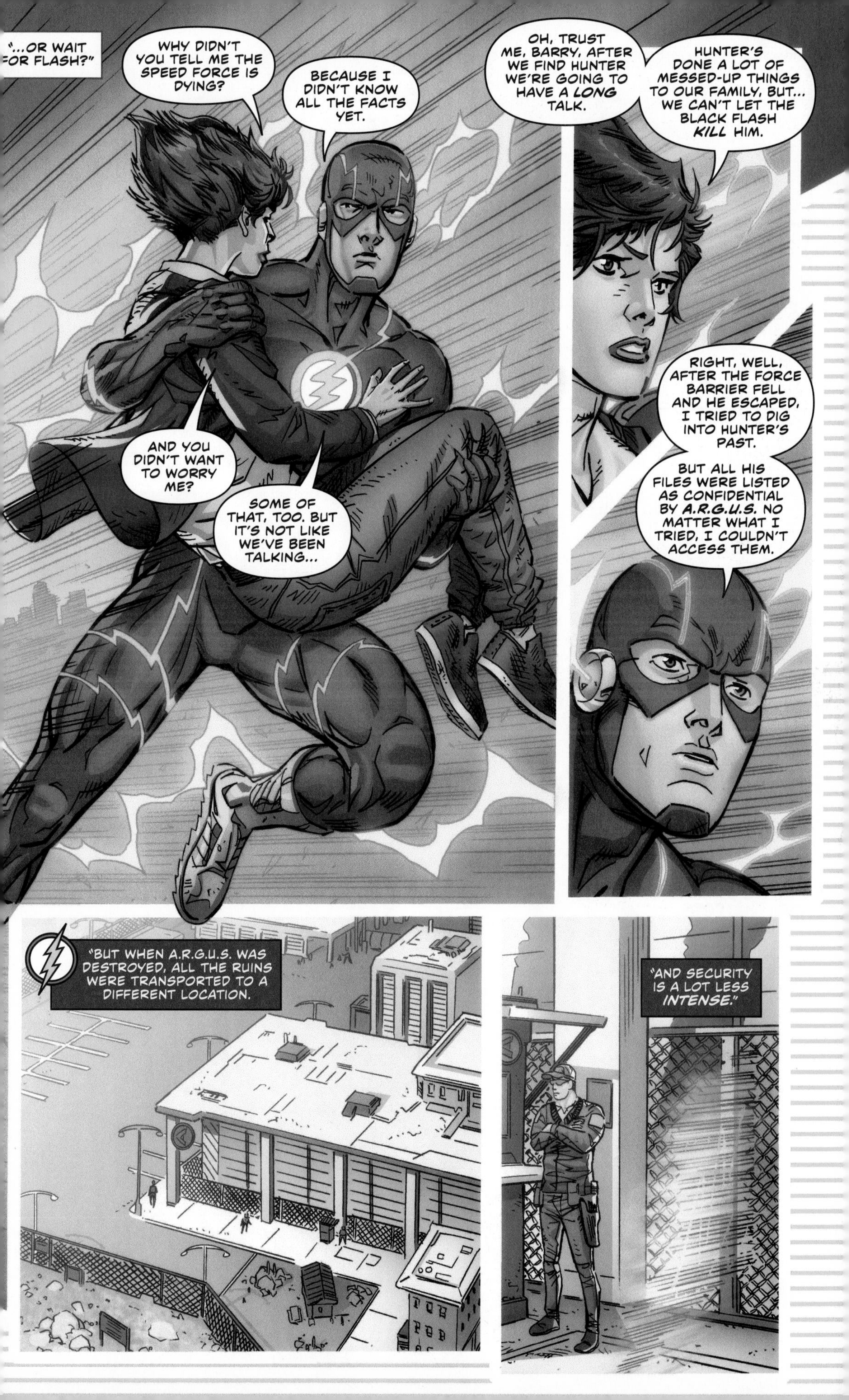
"...OR WAIT FOR FLASH?"
WHY DIDN'T YOU TELL ME THE SPEED FORCE IS DYING?
BECAUSE I DIDN'T KNOW ALL THE FACTS YET.
AND YOU DIDN'T WANT TO WORRY ME?
SOME OF THAT, TOO. BUT IT'S NOT LIKE WE'VE BEEN TALKING...
OH, TRUST ME, BARRY, AFTER WE FIND HUNTER WE'RE GOING TO HAVE A LONG TALK.
HUNTER'S DONE A LOT OF MESSED-UP THINGS TO OUR FAMILY, BUT... WE CAN'T LET THE BLACK FLASH KILL HIM.
RIGHT, WELL, AFTER THE FORCE BARRIER FELL AND HE ESCAPED, I TRIED TO DIG INTO HUNTER'S PAST.
BUT ALL HIS FILES WERE LISTED AS CONFIDENTIAL BY A.R.G.U.S. NO MATTER WHAT I TRIED, I COULDN'T ACCESS THEM.
"BUT WHEN A.R.G.U.S. WAS DESTROYED, ALL THE RUINS WERE TRANSPORTED TO A DIFFERENT LOCATION.
"AND SECURITY IS A LOT LESS INTENSE."

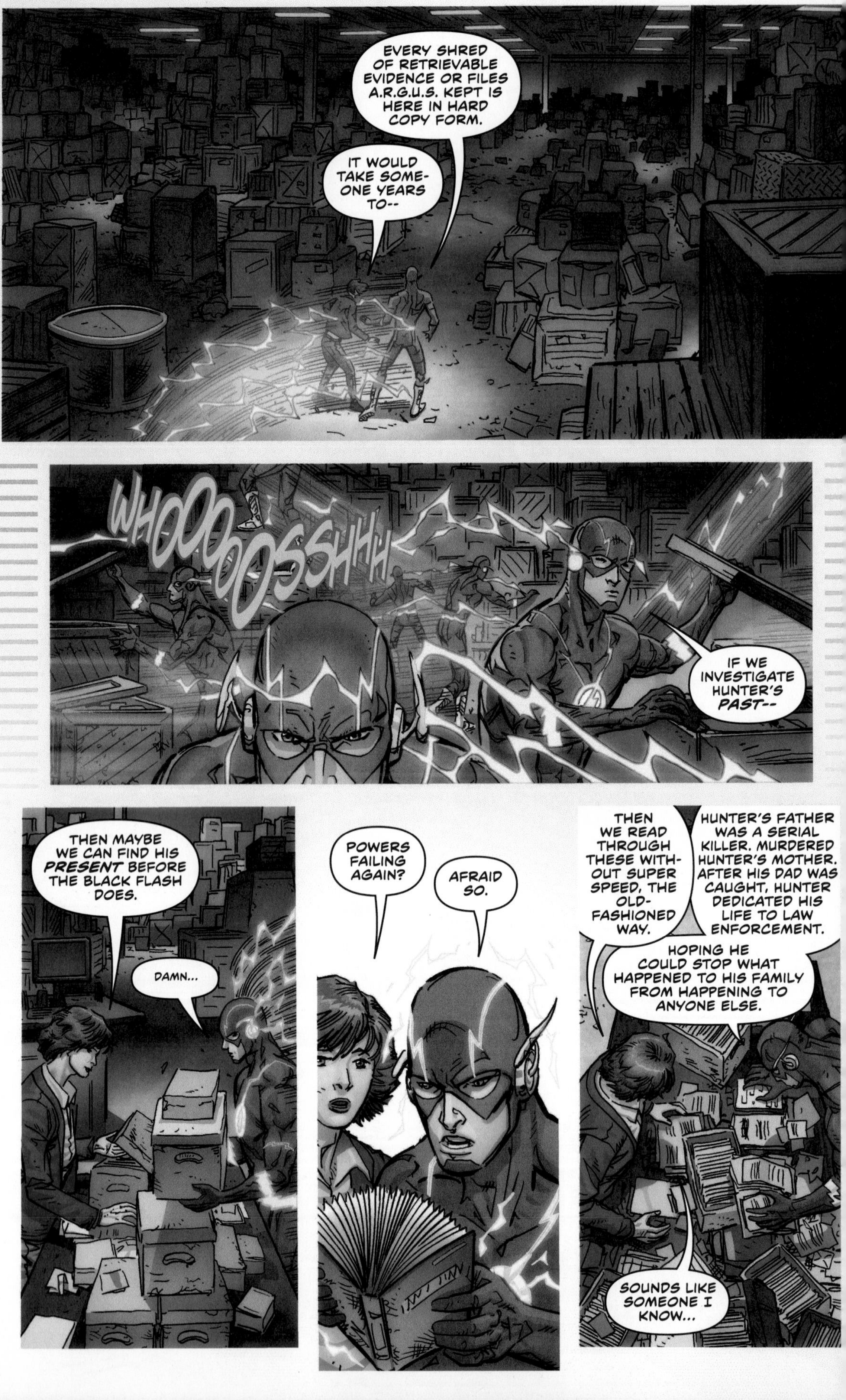
EVERY SHRED OF RETRIEVABLE EVIDENCE OR FILES A.R.G.U.S. KEPT IS HERE IN HARD COPY FORM.
IT WOULD TAKE SOME-ONE YEARS TO--
WHOOOOOOSSHHH
IF WE INVESTIGATE HUNTER'S PAST--
THEN MAYBE WE CAN FIND HIS PRESENT BEFORE THE BLACK FLASH DOES.
DAMN...
POWERS FAILING AGAIN?
AFRAID SO.
THEN WE READ THROUGH THESE WITH-OUT SUPER SPEED, THE OLD-FASHIONED WAY.
HUNTER'S FATHER WAS A SERIAL KILLER. MURDERED HUNTER'S MOTHER. AFTER HIS DAD WAS CAUGHT, HUNTER DEDICATED HIS LIFE TO LAW ENFORCEMENT.
HOPING HE COULD STOP WHAT HAPPENED TO HIS FAMILY FROM HAPPENING TO ANYONE ELSE.
SOUNDS LIKE SOMEONE I KNOW...

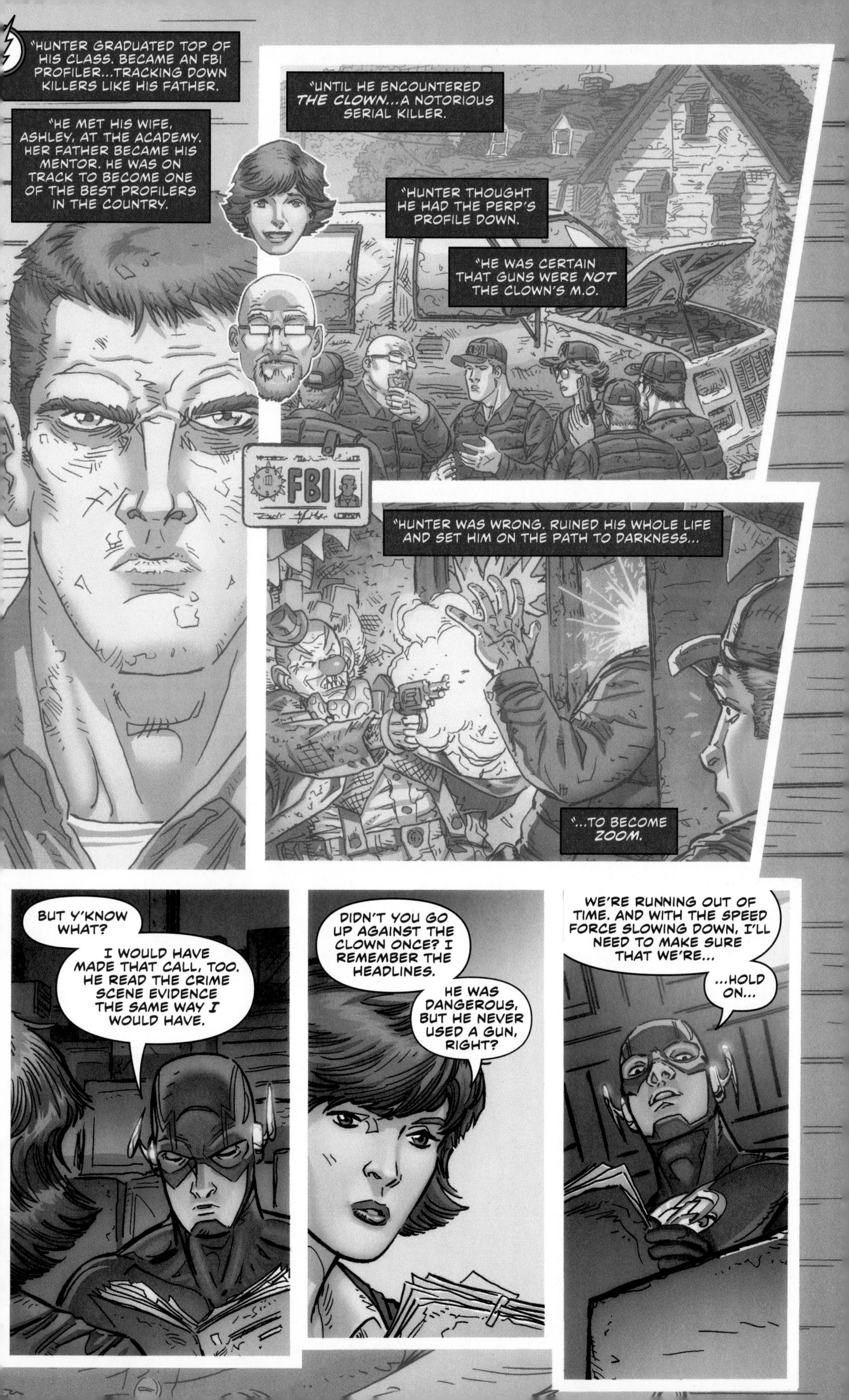
"HUNTER GRADUATED TOP OF HIS CLASS. BECAME AN FBI PROFILER...TRACKING DOWN KILLERS LIKE HIS FATHER.
"HE MET HIS WIFE, ASHLEY, AT THE ACADEMY. HER FATHER BECAME HIS MENTOR. HE WAS ON TRACK TO BECOME ONE OF THE BEST PROFILERS IN THE COUNTRY.
"UNTIL HE ENCOUNTERED *THE CLOWN*...A NOTORIOUS SERIAL KILLER.
"HUNTER THOUGHT HE HAD THE PERP'S PROFILE DOWN.
"HE WAS CERTAIN THAT GUNS WERE *NOT* THE CLOWN'S M.O.
FBI
"HUNTER WAS WRONG. RUINED HIS WHOLE LIFE AND SET HIM ON THE PATH TO DARKNESS...
"...TO BECOME *ZOOM*.
BUT Y'KNOW WHAT?
I WOULD HAVE MADE THAT CALL, TOO. HE READ THE CRIME SCENE EVIDENCE THE SAME WAY *I* WOULD HAVE.
DIDN'T YOU GO UP AGAINST THE CLOWN ONCE? I REMEMBER THE HEADLINES.
HE WAS DANGEROUS, BUT HE NEVER USED A GUN, RIGHT?
WE'RE RUNNING OUT OF TIME. AND WITH THE SPEED FORCE SLOWING DOWN, I'LL NEED TO MAKE SURE THAT WE'RE...
...HOLD ON...

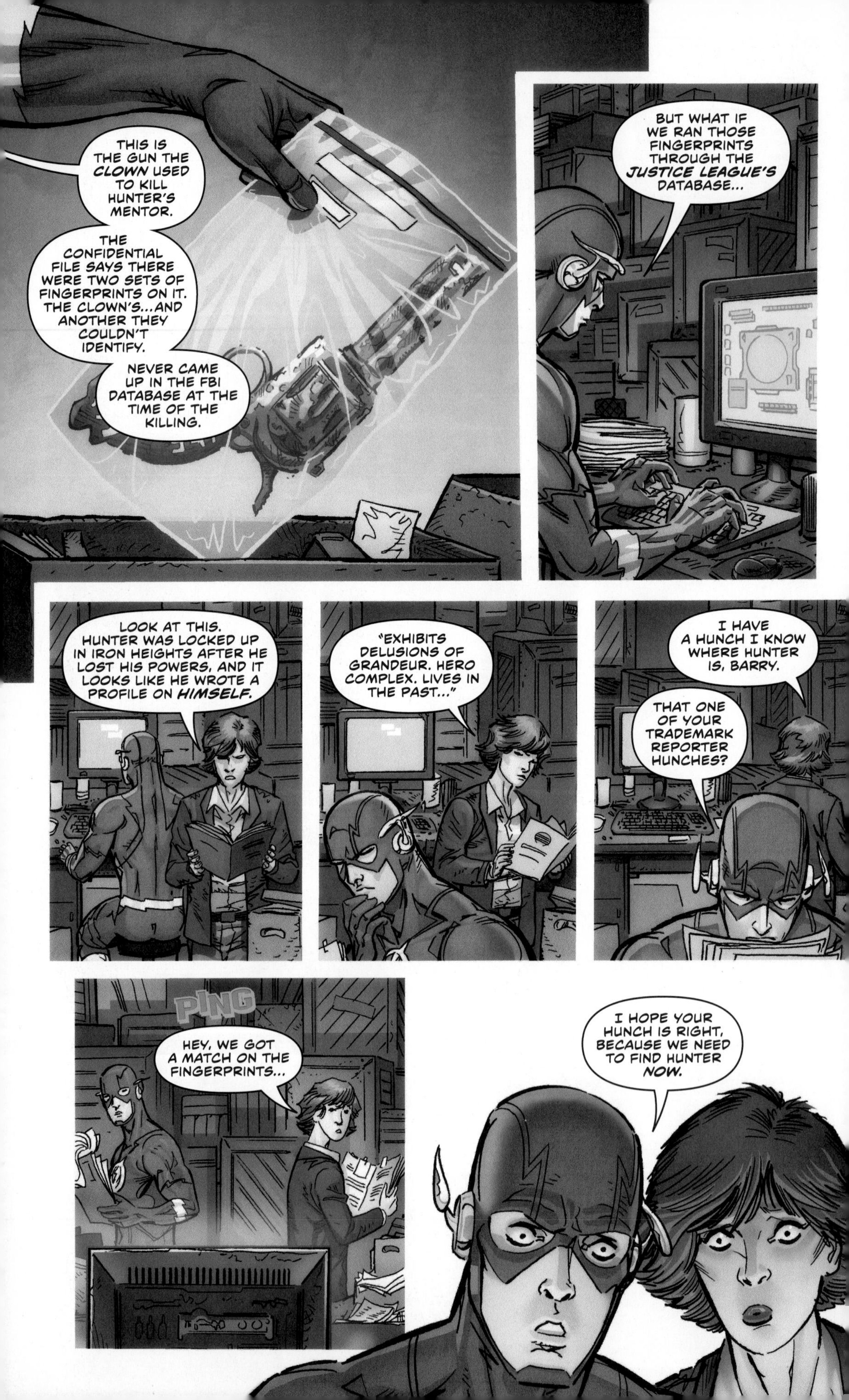
THIS IS THE GUN THE CLOWN USED TO KILL HUNTER'S MENTOR.
THE CONFIDENTIAL FILE SAYS THERE WERE TWO SETS OF FINGERPRINTS ON IT. THE CLOWN'S...AND ANOTHER THEY COULDN'T IDENTIFY.
NEVER CAME UP IN THE FBI DATABASE AT THE TIME OF THE KILLING.
BUT WHAT IF WE RAN THOSE FINGERPRINTS THROUGH THE JUSTICE LEAGUE'S DATABASE...
LOOK AT THIS. HUNTER WAS LOCKED UP IN IRON HEIGHTS AFTER HE LOST HIS POWERS, AND IT LOOKS LIKE HE WROTE A PROFILE ON HIMSELF.
"EXHIBITS DELUSIONS OF GRANDEUR. HERO COMPLEX. LIVES IN THE PAST..."
I HAVE A HUNCH I KNOW WHERE HUNTER IS, BARRY.
THAT ONE OF YOUR TRADEMARK REPORTER HUNCHES?
PING
HEY, WE GOT A MATCH ON THE FINGERPRINTS...
I HOPE YOUR HUNCH IS RIGHT, BECAUSE WE NEED TO FIND HUNTER NOW.

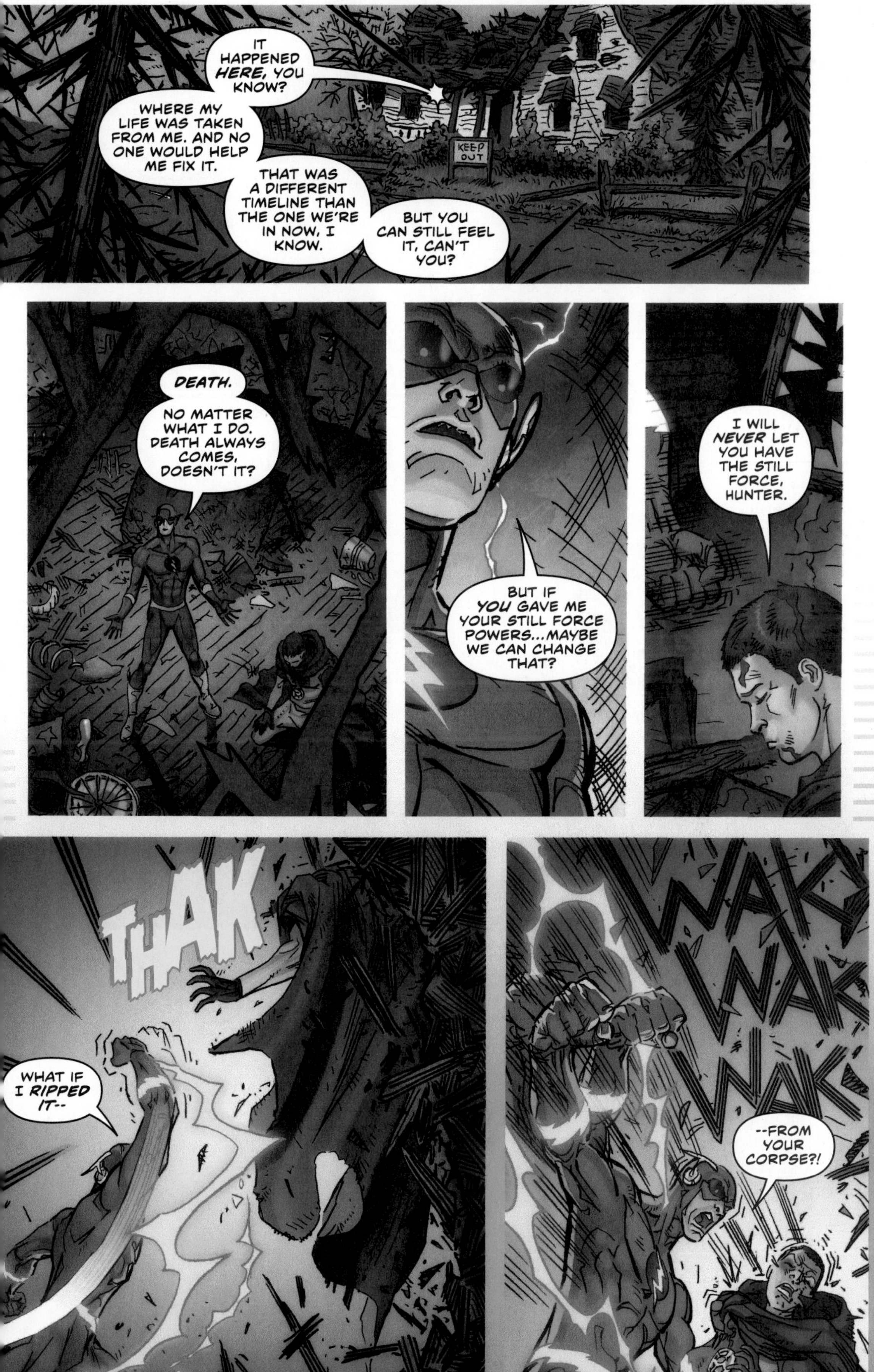
IT HAPPENED HERE, YOU KNOW?
WHERE MY LIFE WAS TAKEN FROM ME. AND NO ONE WOULD HELP ME FIX IT.
KEEP OUT
THAT WAS A DIFFERENT TIMELINE THAN THE ONE WE'RE IN NOW, I KNOW.
BUT YOU CAN STILL FEEL IT, CAN'T YOU?
DEATH.
NO MATTER WHAT I DO. DEATH ALWAYS COMES, DOESN'T IT?
BUT IF YOU GAVE ME YOUR STILL FORCE POWERS...MAYBE WE CAN CHANGE THAT?
I WILL NEVER LET YOU HAVE THE STILL FORCE, HUNTER.
THAK
WHAT IF I RIPPED IT--
WAK WAK WAK
--FROM YOUR CORPSE?!

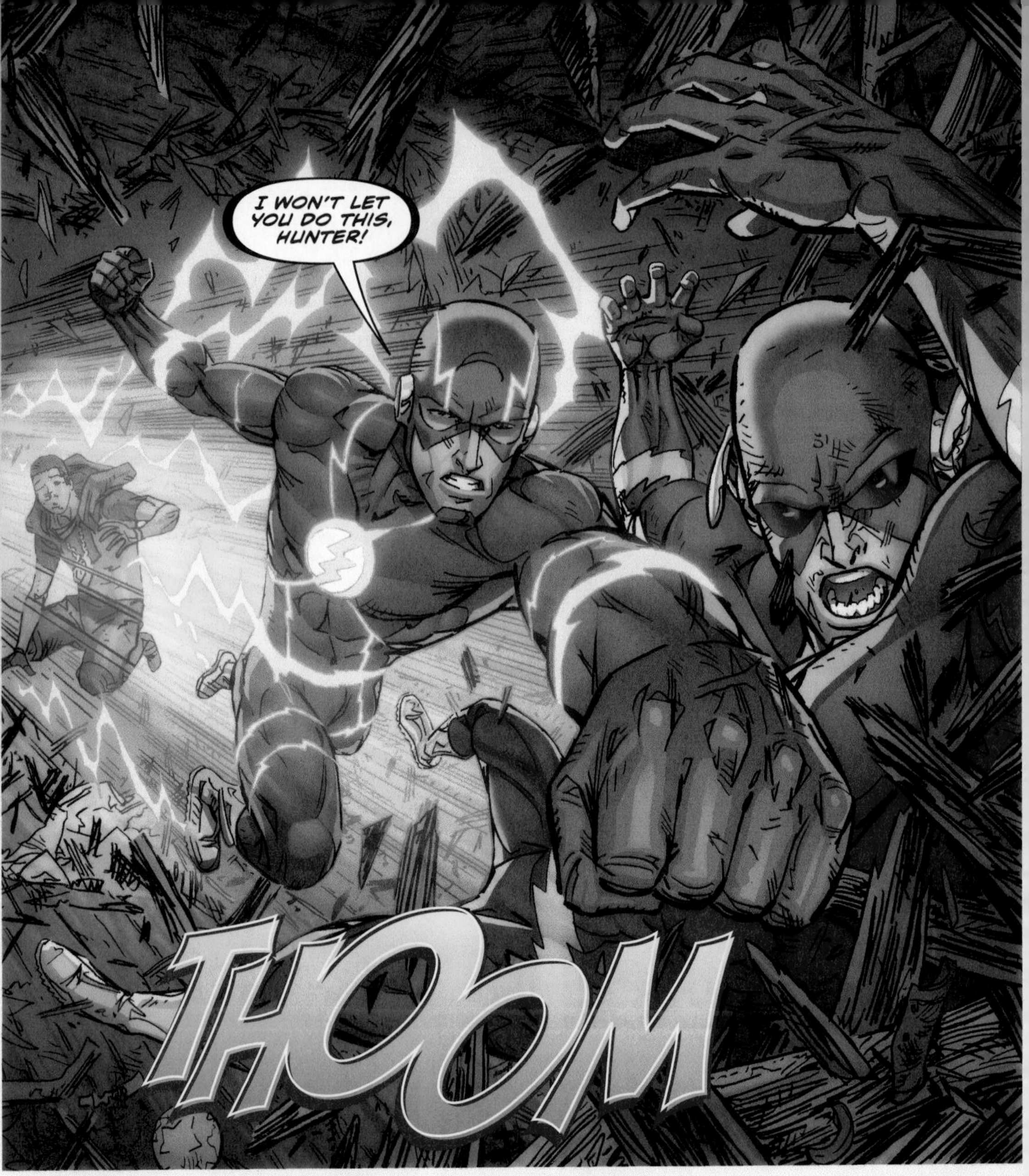
I WON'T LET YOU DO THIS, HUNTER!
THOOM

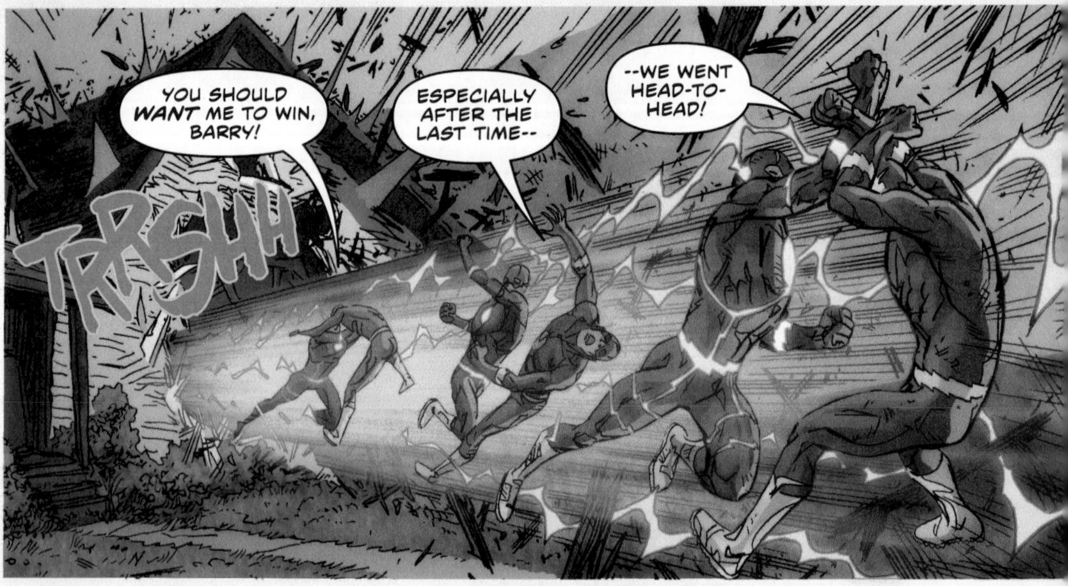
YOU SHOULD WANT ME TO WIN, BARRY!
ESPECIALLY AFTER THE LAST TIME--
--WE WENT HEAD-TO-HEAD!
TRRSHH

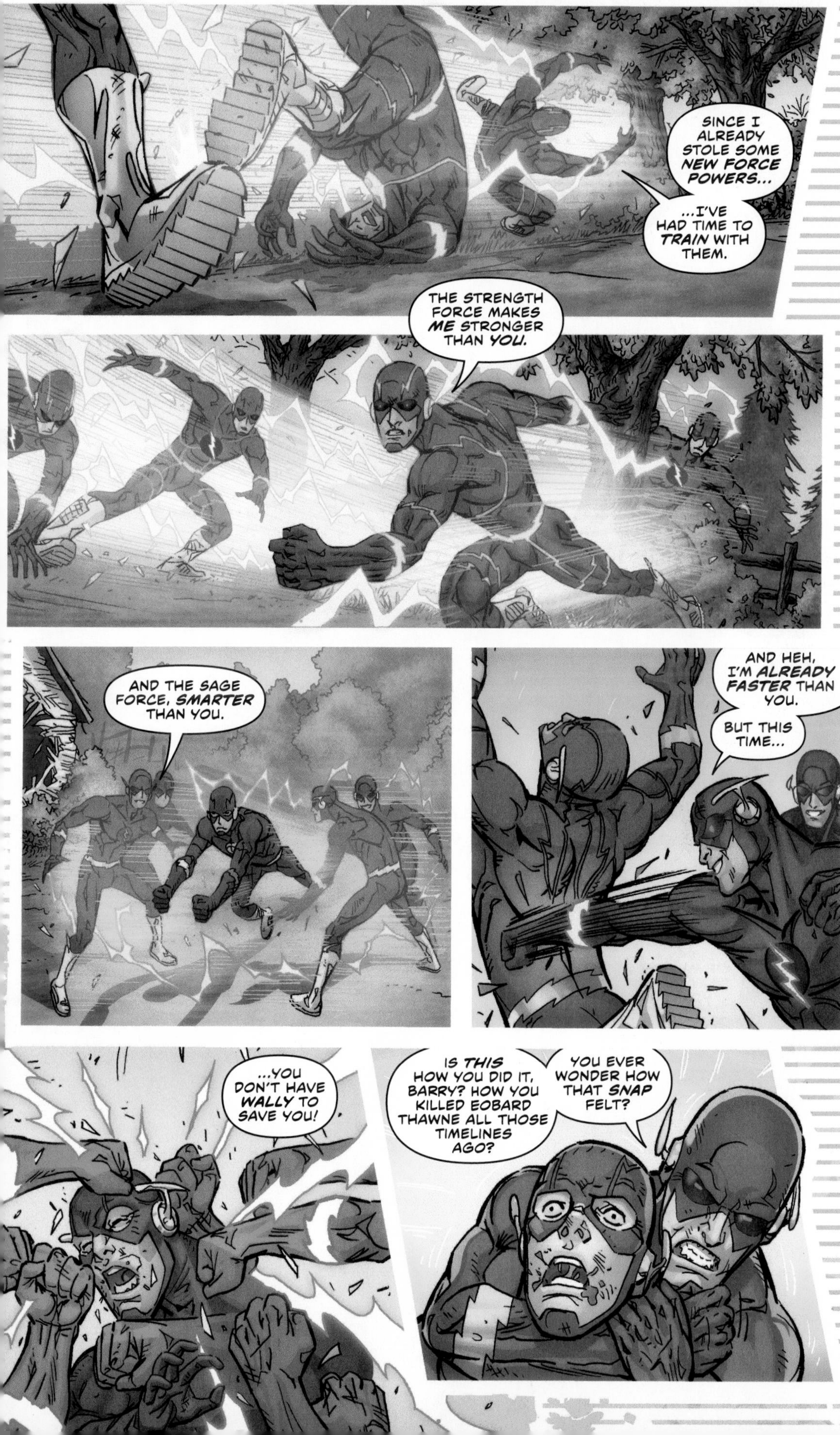

SINCE I ALREADY STOLE SOME NEW FORCE POWERS...
...I'VE HAD TIME TO TRAIN WITH THEM.
THE STRENGTH FORCE MAKES ME STRONGER THAN YOU.
AND THE SAGE FORCE, SMARTER THAN YOU.
AND HEH, I'M ALREADY FASTER THAN YOU.
BUT THIS TIME...
...YOU DON'T HAVE WALLY TO SAVE YOU!
IS THIS HOW YOU DID IT, BARRY? HOW YOU KILLED EOBARD THAWNE ALL THOSE TIMELINES AGO?
YOU EVER WONDER HOW THAT SNAP FELT?

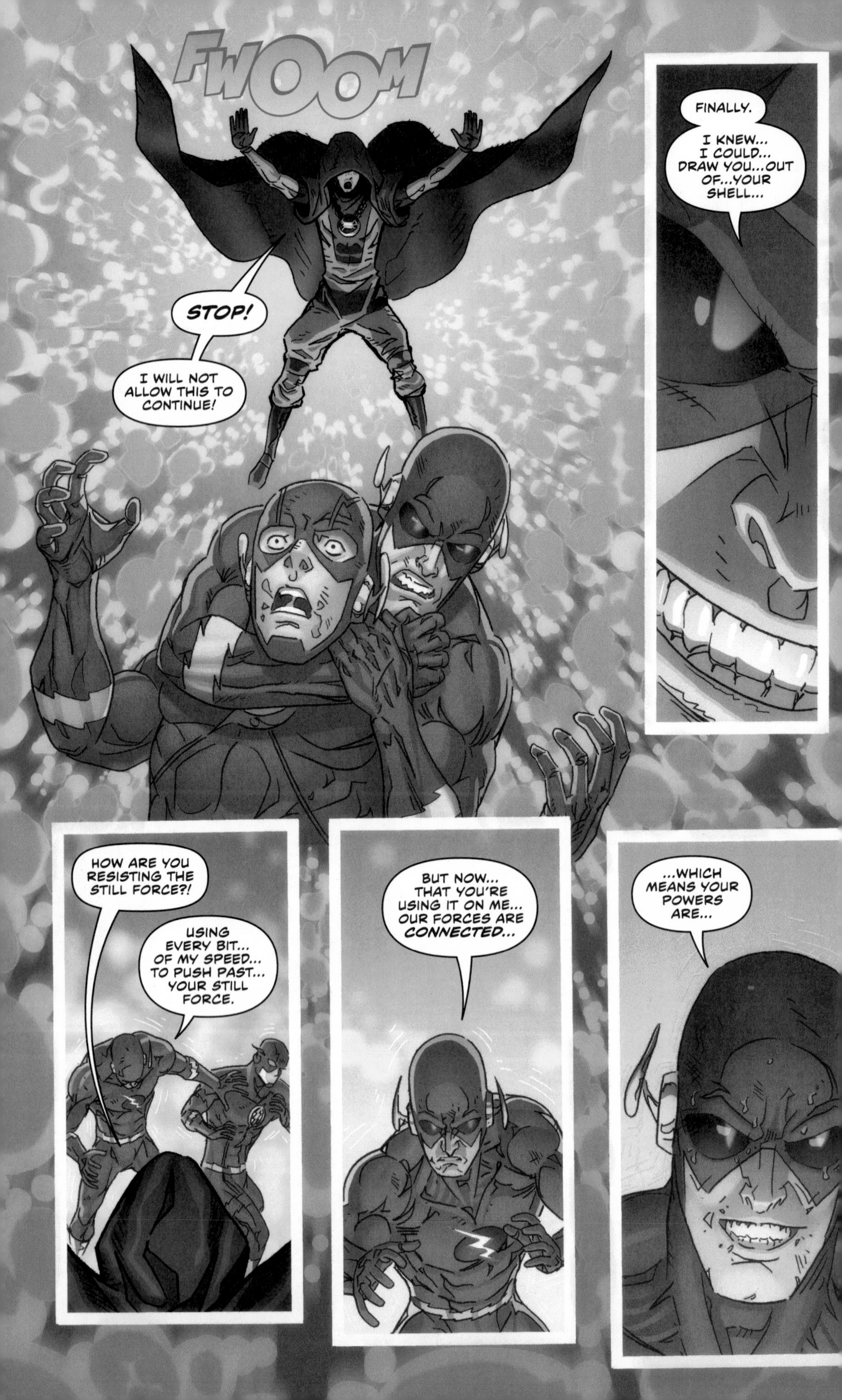
FWOOM
STOP!
I WILL NOT ALLOW THIS TO CONTINUE!
FINALLY.
I KNEW... I COULD... DRAW YOU...OUT OF...YOUR SHELL...
HOW ARE YOU RESISTING THE STILL FORCE?!
USING EVERY BIT... OF MY SPEED... TO PUSH PAST... YOUR STILL FORCE.
BUT NOW... THAT YOU'RE USING IT ON ME... OUR FORCES ARE CONNECTED...
...WHICH MEANS YOUR POWERS ARE...

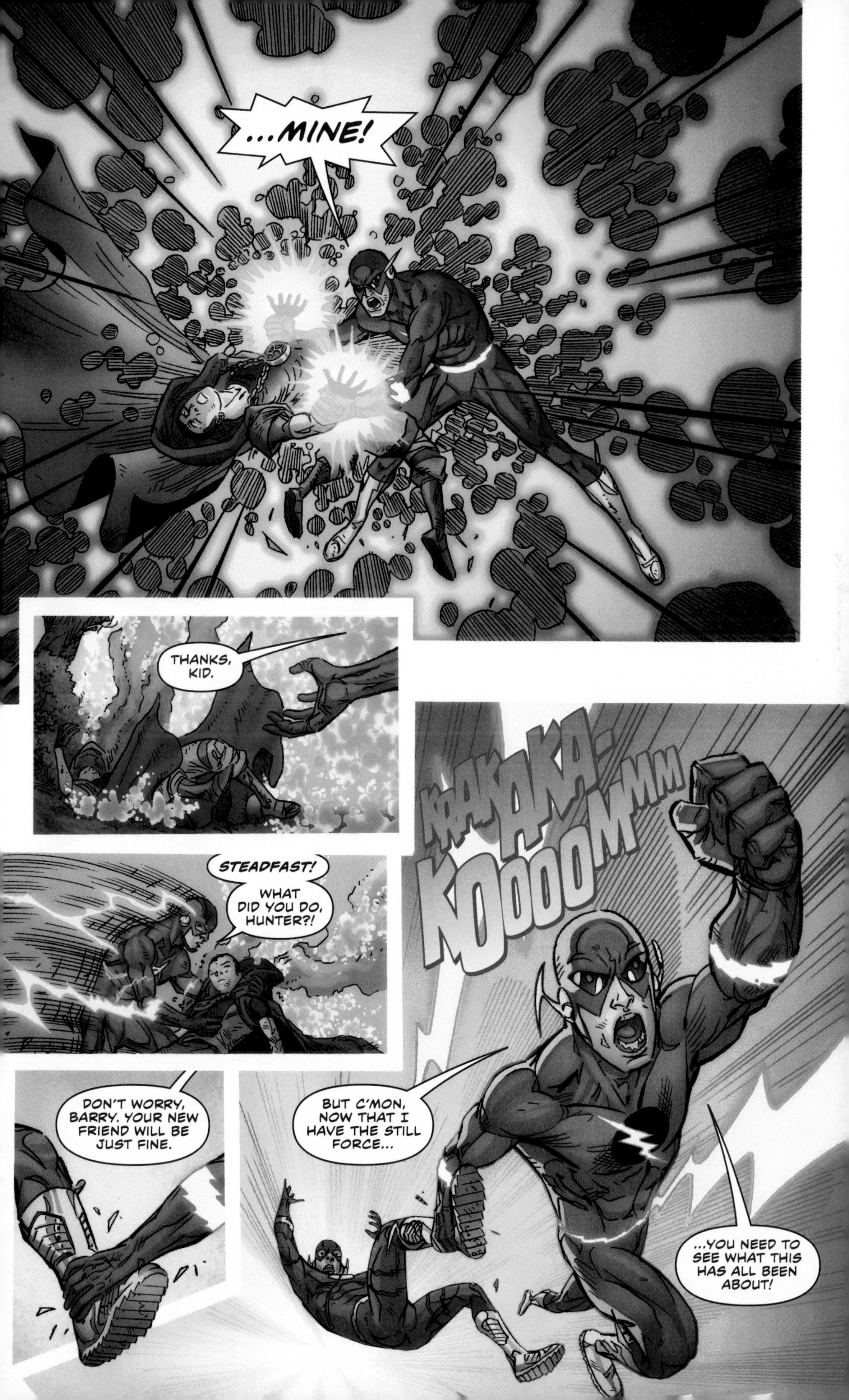
...MINE!
THANKS, KID.
STEADFAST!
WHAT DID YOU DO, HUNTER?!
KRAKAKAKA-KOOOOMMMM
DON'T WORRY, BARRY. YOUR NEW FRIEND WILL BE JUST FINE.
BUT C'MON, NOW THAT I HAVE THE STILL FORCE...
...YOU NEED TO SEE WHAT THIS HAS ALL BEEN ABOUT!

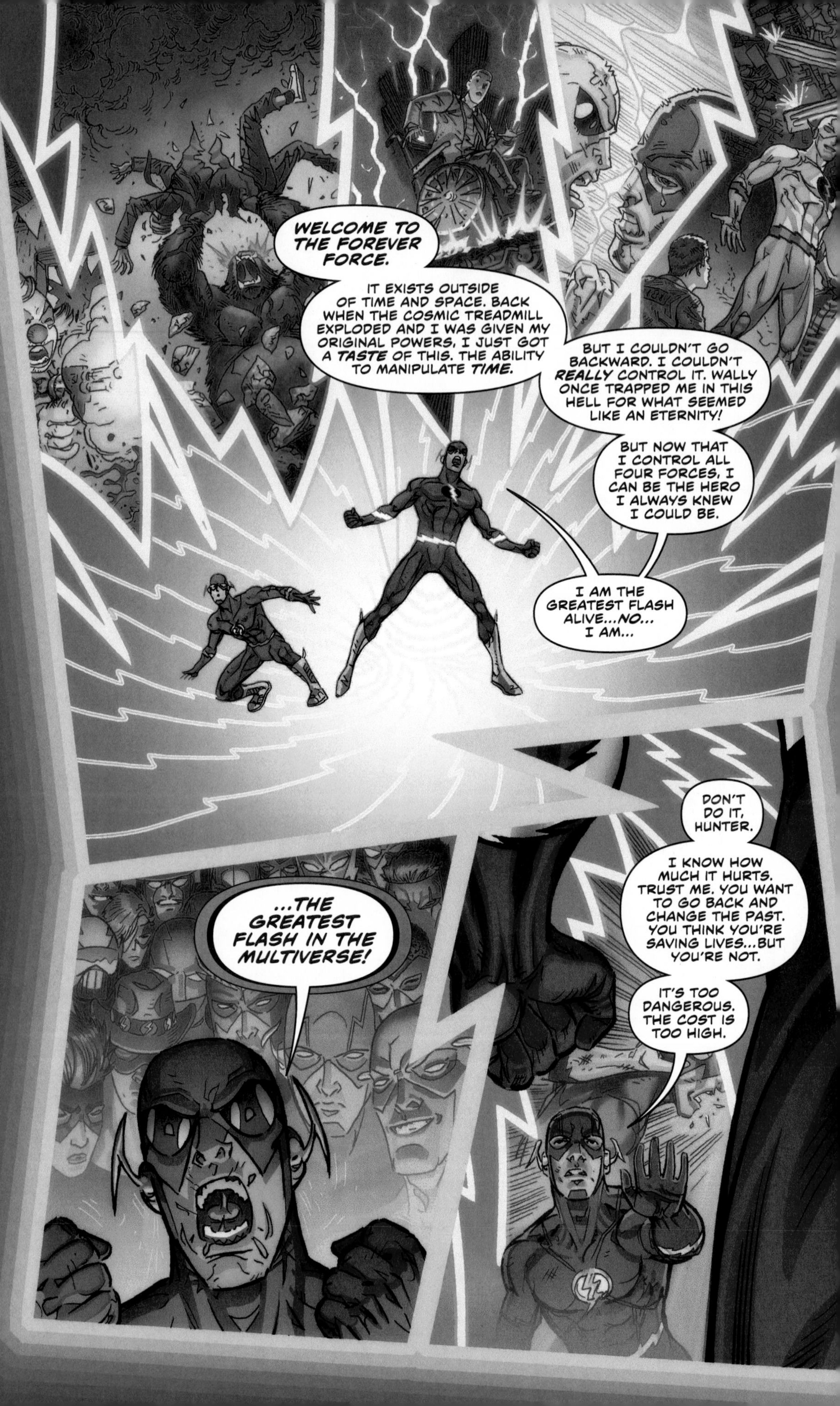
WELCOME TO THE FOREVER FORCE.
IT EXISTS OUTSIDE OF TIME AND SPACE. BACK WHEN THE COSMIC TREADMILL EXPLODED AND I WAS GIVEN MY ORIGINAL POWERS, I JUST GOT A TASTE OF THIS. THE ABILITY TO MANIPULATE TIME.
BUT I COULDN'T GO BACKWARD. I COULDN'T REALLY CONTROL IT. WALLY ONCE TRAPPED ME IN THIS HELL FOR WHAT SEEMED LIKE AN ETERNITY!
BUT NOW THAT I CONTROL ALL FOUR FORCES, I CAN BE THE HERO I ALWAYS KNEW I COULD BE.
I AM THE GREATEST FLASH ALIVE...NO... I AM...
...THE GREATEST FLASH IN THE MULTIVERSE!
DON'T DO IT, HUNTER.
I KNOW HOW MUCH IT HURTS. TRUST ME. YOU WANT TO GO BACK AND CHANGE THE PAST. YOU THINK YOU'RE SAVING LIVES...BUT YOU'RE NOT.
IT'S TOO DANGEROUS. THE COST IS TOO HIGH.

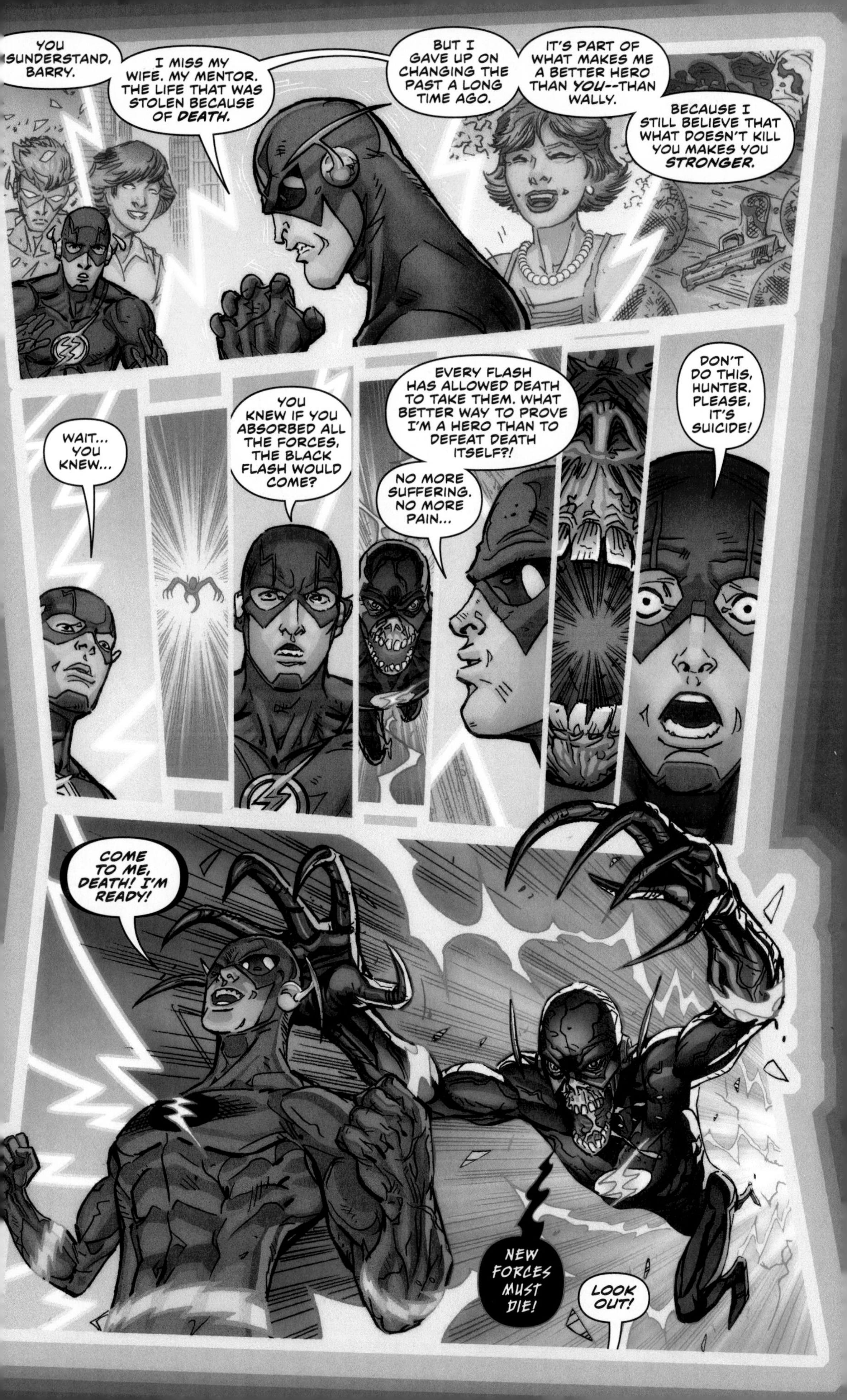
YOU SUNDERSTAND, BARRY.
I MISS MY WIFE. MY MENTOR. THE LIFE THAT WAS STOLEN BECAUSE OF DEATH.
BUT I GAVE UP ON CHANGING THE PAST A LONG TIME AGO.
IT'S PART OF WHAT MAKES ME A BETTER HERO THAN YOU--THAN WALLY.
BECAUSE I STILL BELIEVE THAT WHAT DOESN'T KILL YOU MAKES YOU STRONGER.
WAIT... YOU KNEW...
YOU KNEW IF YOU ABSORBED ALL THE FORCES, THE BLACK FLASH WOULD COME?
EVERY FLASH HAS ALLOWED DEATH TO TAKE THEM. WHAT BETTER WAY TO PROVE I'M A HERO THAN TO DEFEAT DEATH ITSELF?!
NO MORE SUFFERING. NO MORE PAIN...
DON'T DO THIS, HUNTER. PLEASE, IT'S SUICIDE!
COME TO ME, DEATH! I'M READY!
NEW FORCES MUST DIE!
LOOK OUT!

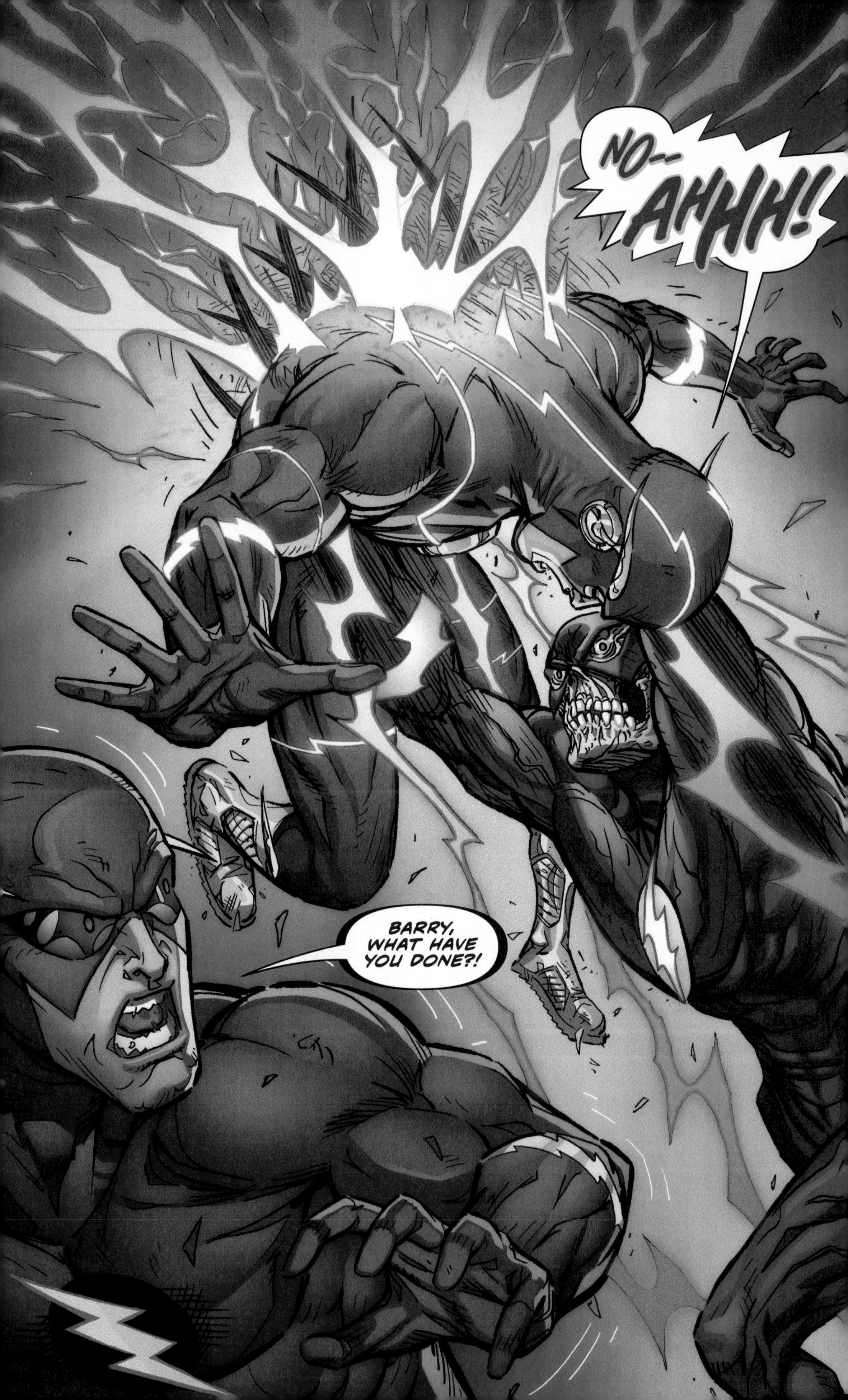
NO-- AHHH!
BARRY, WHAT HAVE YOU DONE?!

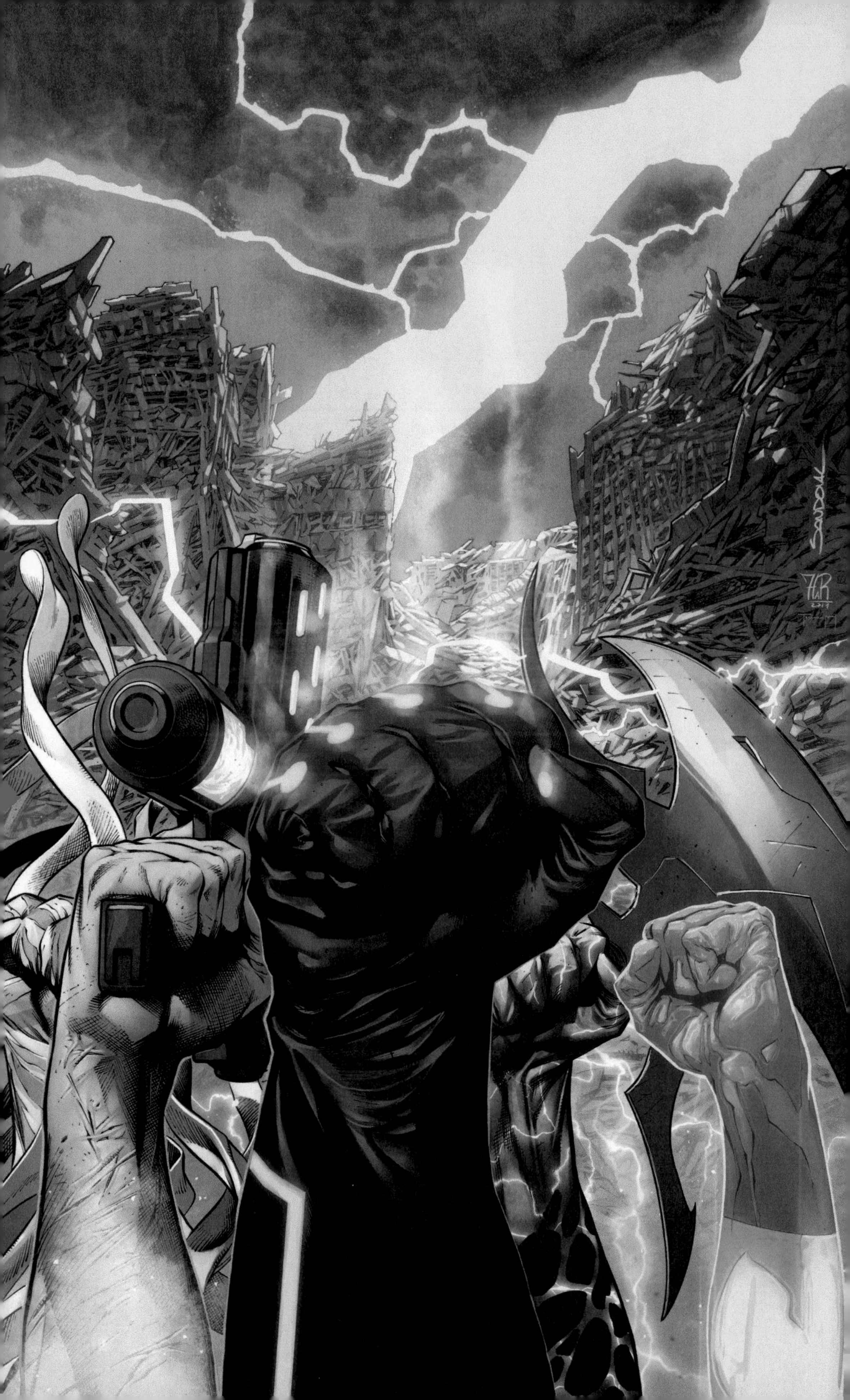

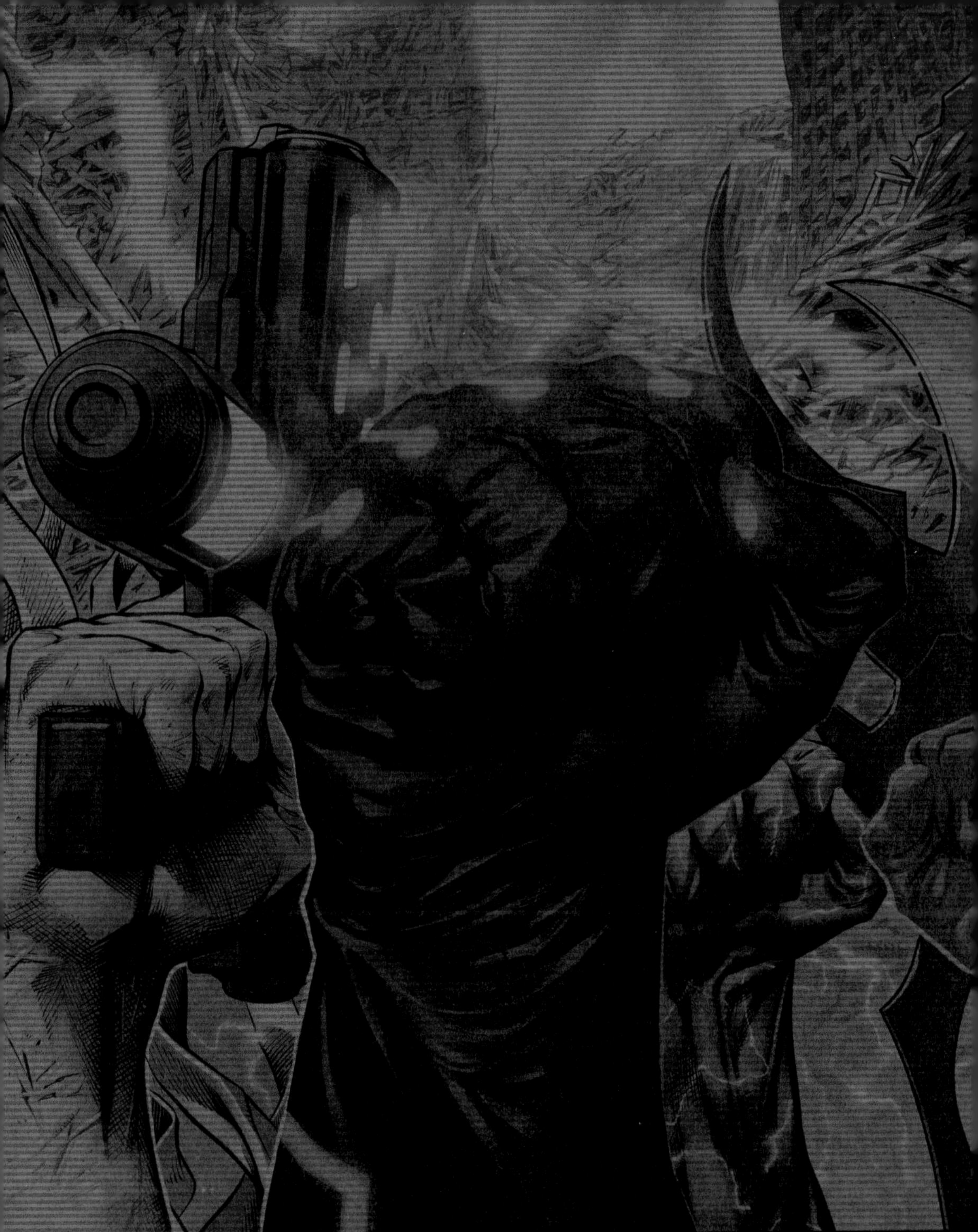

THE FLASH
#81

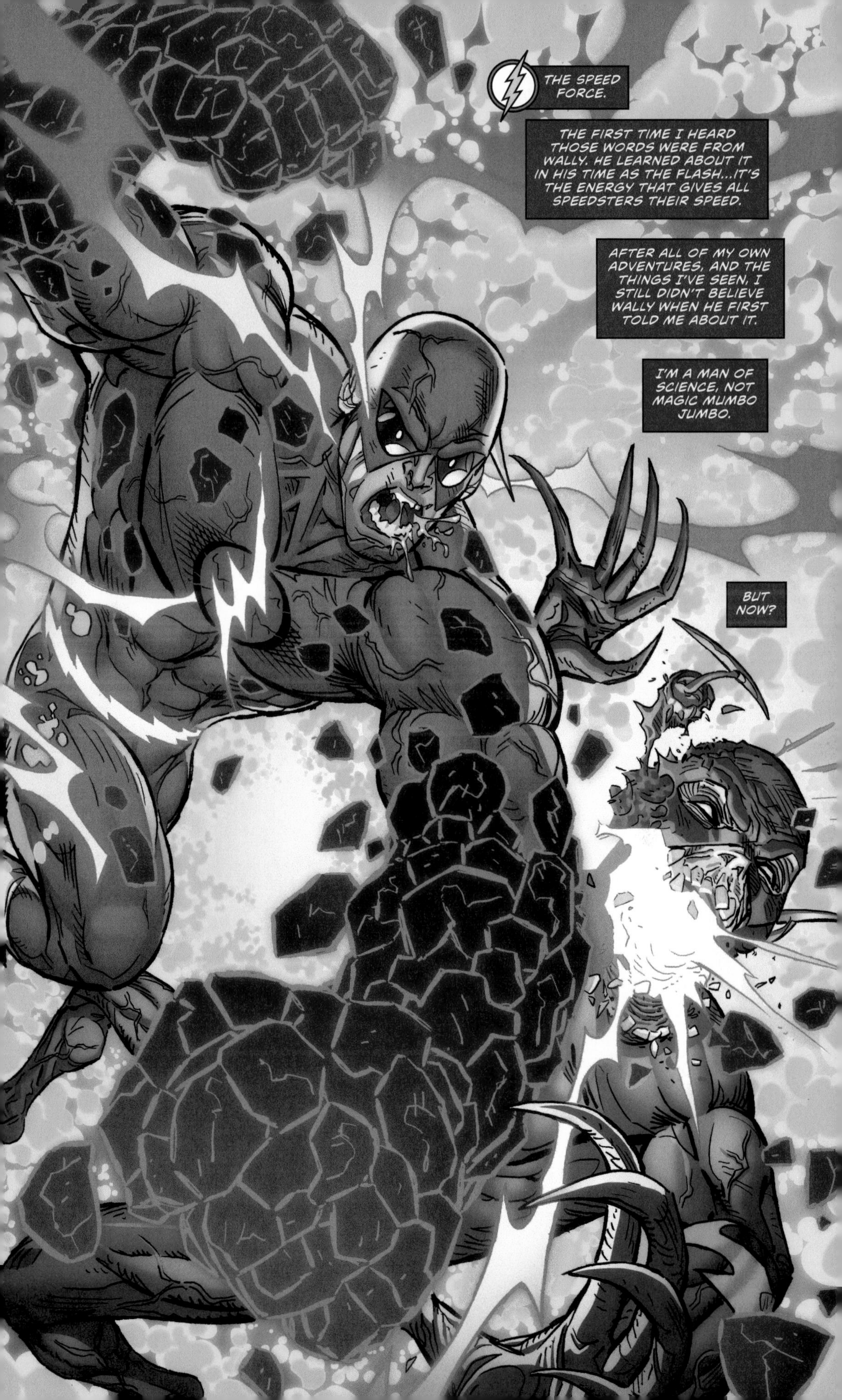
THE SPEED FORCE.
THE FIRST TIME I HEARD THOSE WORDS WERE FROM WALLY. HE LEARNED ABOUT IT IN HIS TIME AS THE FLASH...IT'S THE ENERGY THAT GIVES ALL SPEEDSTERS THEIR SPEED.
AFTER ALL OF MY OWN ADVENTURES, AND THE THINGS I'VE SEEN, I STILL DIDN'T BELIEVE WALLY WHEN HE FIRST TOLD ME ABOUT IT.
I'M A MAN OF SCIENCE, NOT MAGIC MUMBO JUMBO.
BUT NOW?

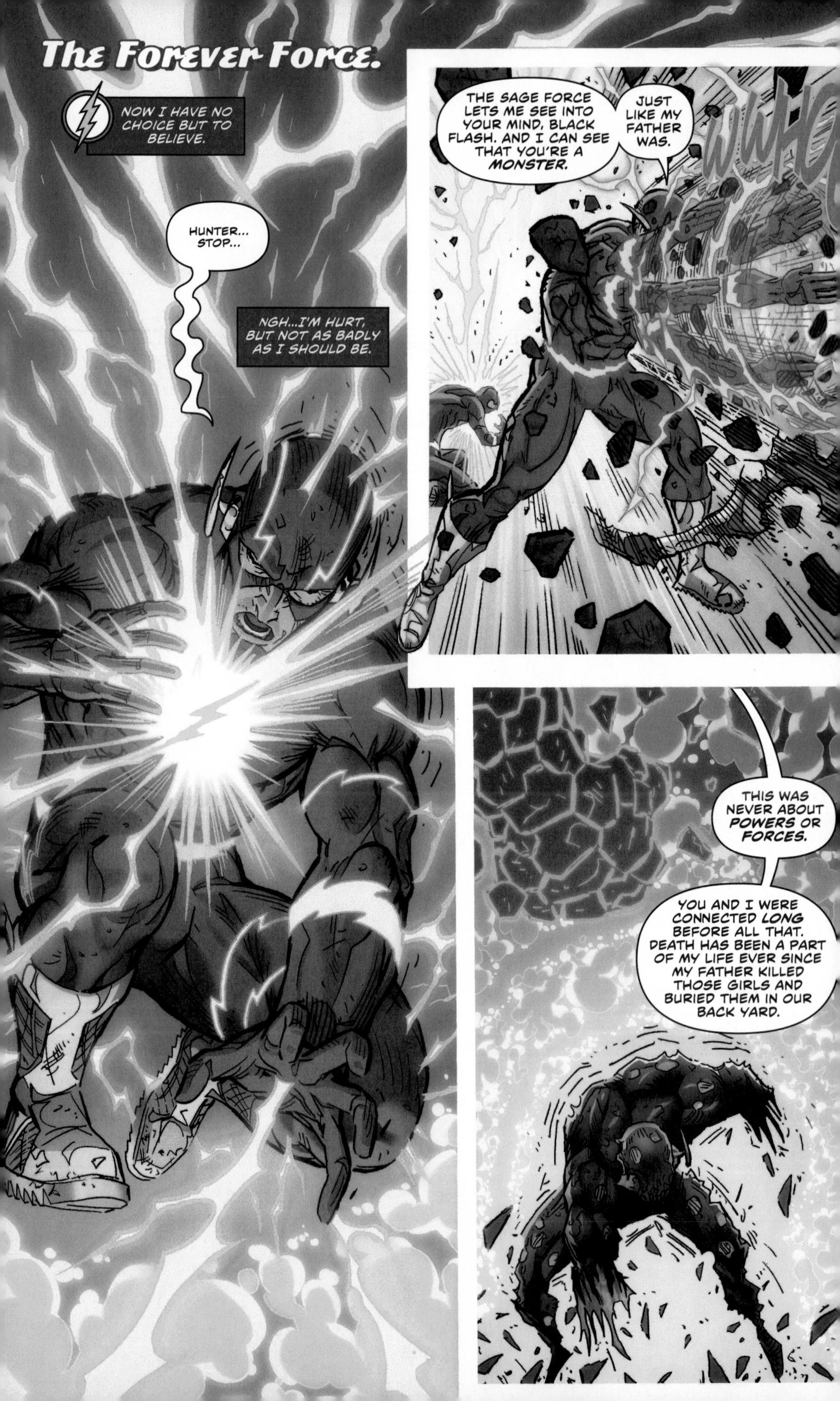
The Forever Force.
NOW I HAVE NO CHOICE BUT TO BELIEVE.
HUNTER... STOP...
NGH...I'M HURT, BUT NOT AS BADLY AS I SHOULD BE.
THE SAGE FORCE LETS ME SEE INTO YOUR MIND, BLACK FLASH. AND I CAN SEE THAT YOU'RE A MONSTER.
JUST LIKE MY FATHER WAS.
THIS WAS NEVER ABOUT POWERS OR FORCES.
YOU AND I WERE CONNECTED LONG BEFORE ALL THAT. DEATH HAS BEEN A PART OF MY LIFE EVER SINCE MY FATHER KILLED THOSE GIRLS AND BURIED THEM IN OUR BACK YARD.

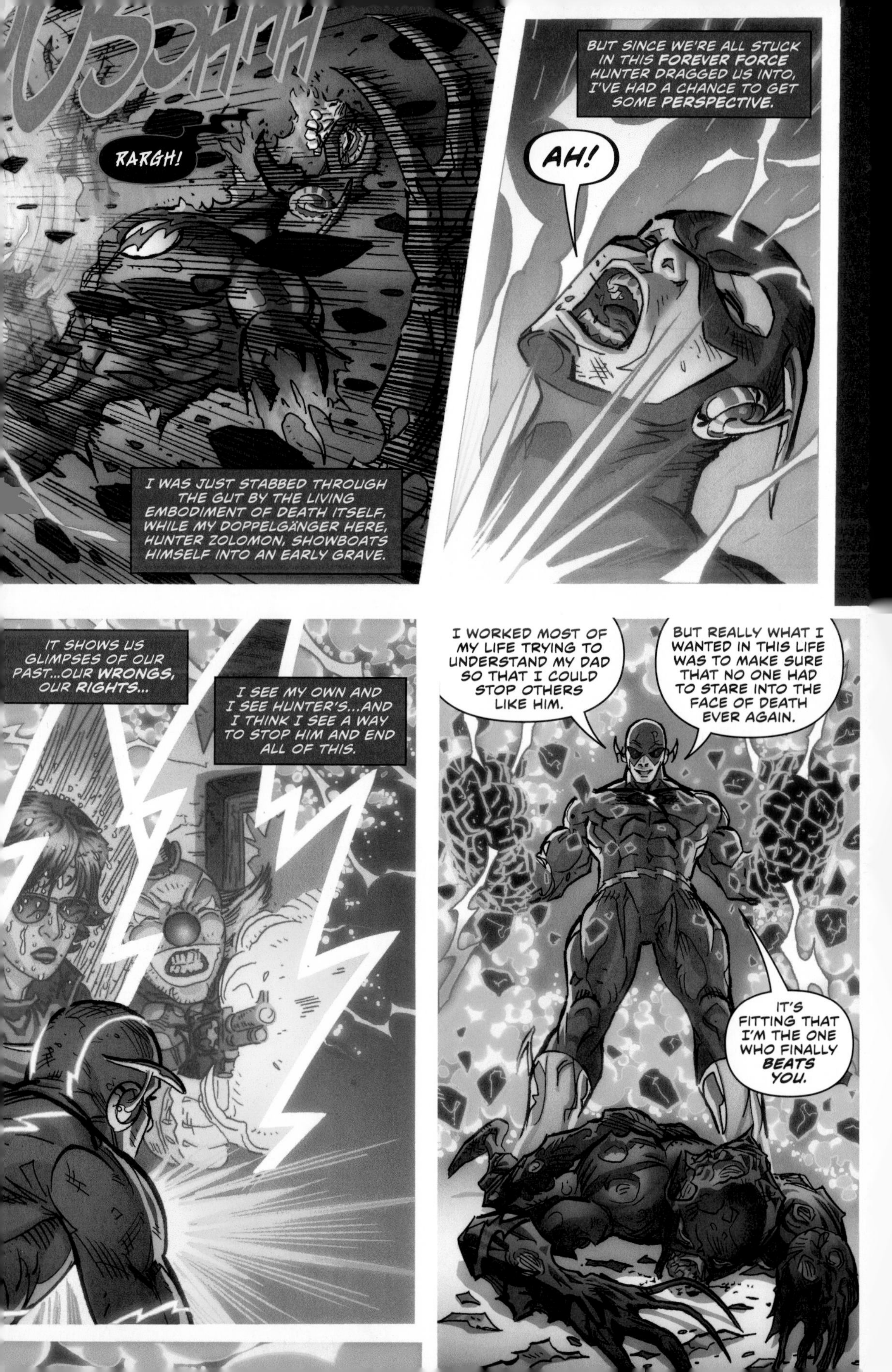
RARGH!
I WAS JUST STABBED THROUGH THE GUT BY THE LIVING EMBODIMENT OF DEATH ITSELF, WHILE MY DOPPELGÄNGER HERE, HUNTER ZOLOMON, SHOWBOATS HIMSELF INTO AN EARLY GRAVE.
BUT SINCE WE'RE ALL STUCK IN THIS FOREVER FORCE HUNTER DRAGGED US INTO, I'VE HAD A CHANCE TO GET SOME PERSPECTIVE.
AH!
IT SHOWS US GLIMPSES OF OUR PAST...OUR WRONGS, OUR RIGHTS...
I SEE MY OWN AND I SEE HUNTER'S...AND I THINK I SEE A WAY TO STOP HIM AND END ALL OF THIS.
I WORKED MOST OF MY LIFE TRYING TO UNDERSTAND MY DAD SO THAT I COULD STOP OTHERS LIKE HIM.
BUT REALLY WHAT I WANTED IN THIS LIFE WAS TO MAKE SURE THAT NO ONE HAD TO STARE INTO THE FACE OF DEATH EVER AGAIN.
IT'S FITTING THAT I'M THE ONE WHO FINALLY BEATS YOU.

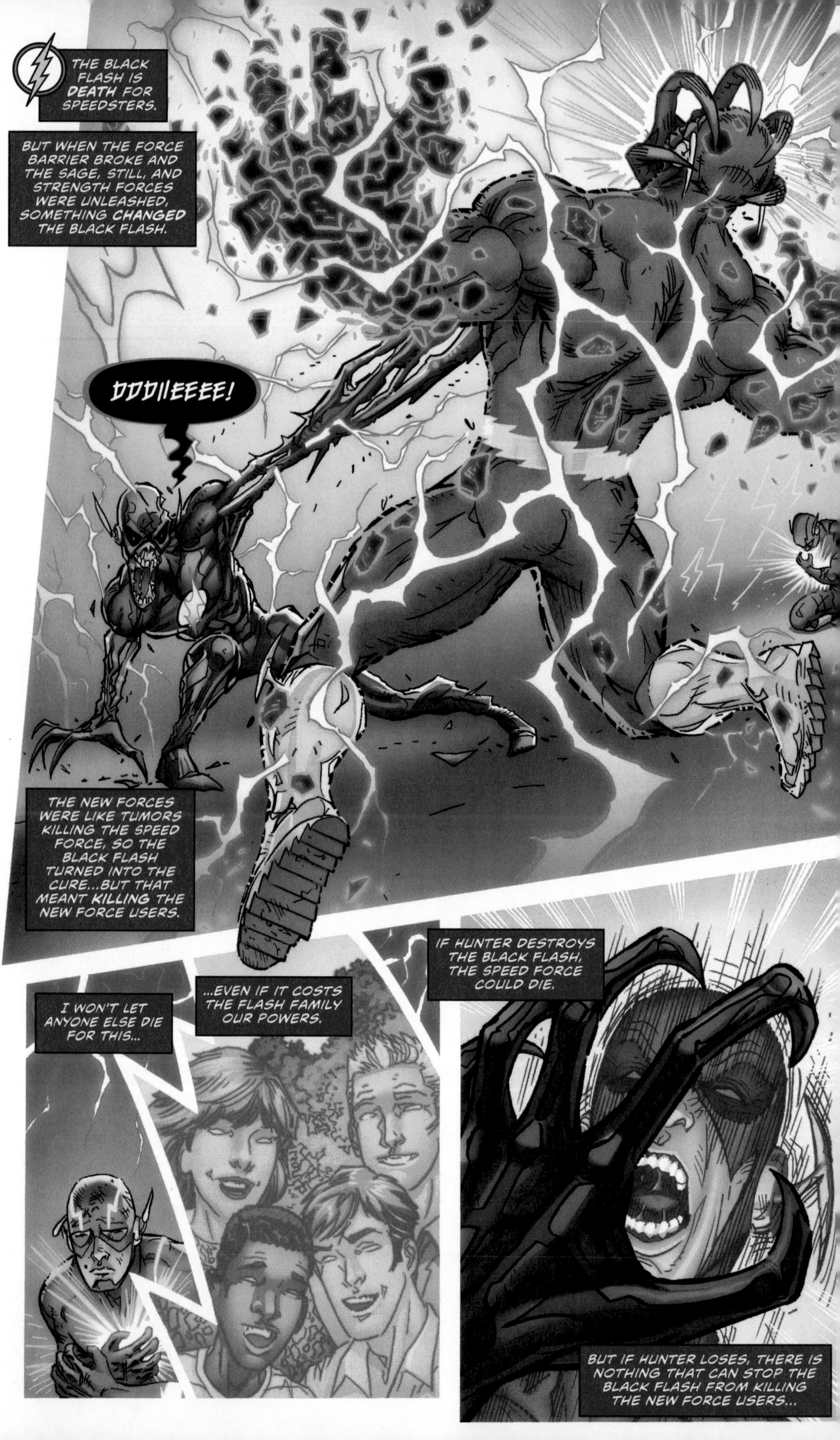
THE BLACK FLASH IS DEATH FOR SPEEDSTERS.
BUT WHEN THE FORCE BARRIER BROKE AND THE SAGE, STILL, AND STRENGTH FORCES WERE UNLEASHED, SOMETHING CHANGED THE BLACK FLASH.
DDDIIEEEE!
THE NEW FORCES WERE LIKE TUMORS KILLING THE SPEED FORCE, SO THE BLACK FLASH TURNED INTO THE CURE...BUT THAT MEANT KILLING THE NEW FORCE USERS.
I WON'T LET ANYONE ELSE DIE FOR THIS...
...EVEN IF IT COSTS THE FLASH FAMILY OUR POWERS.
IF HUNTER DESTROYS THE BLACK FLASH, THE SPEED FORCE COULD DIE.
BUT IF HUNTER LOSES, THERE IS NOTHING THAT CAN STOP THE BLACK FLASH FROM KILLING THE NEW FORCE USERS...

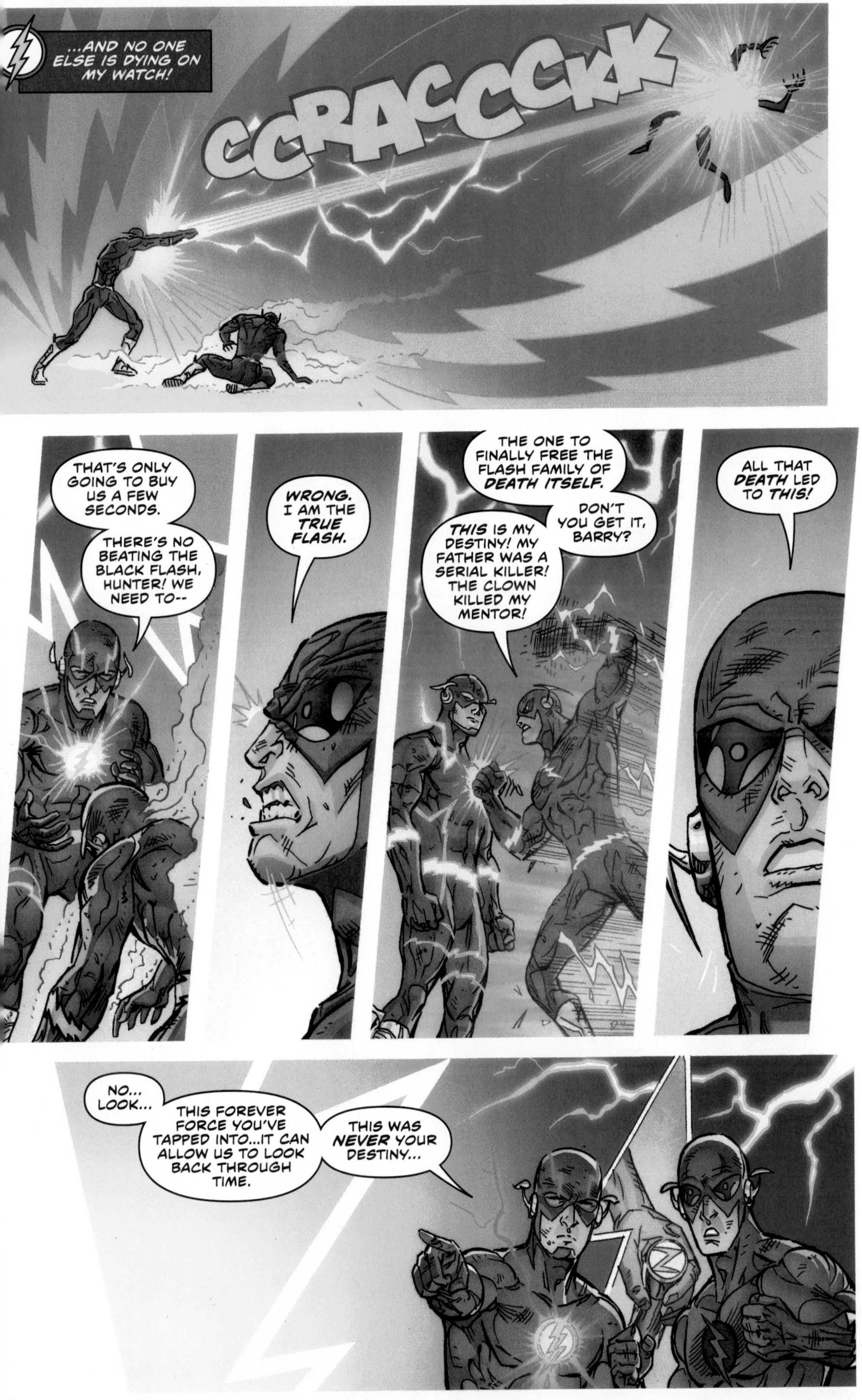

...AND NO ONE ELSE IS DYING ON MY WATCH!
CCRACCCKK
THAT'S ONLY GOING TO BUY US A FEW SECONDS.
THERE'S NO BEATING THE BLACK FLASH, HUNTER! WE NEED TO--
WRONG. I AM THE TRUE FLASH.
THE ONE TO FINALLY FREE THE FLASH FAMILY OF DEATH ITSELF.
DON'T YOU GET IT, BARRY?
THIS IS MY DESTINY! MY FATHER WAS A SERIAL KILLER! THE CLOWN KILLED MY MENTOR!
ALL THAT DEATH LED TO THIS!
NO... LOOK...
THIS FOREVER FORCE YOU'VE TAPPED INTO...IT CAN ALLOW US TO LOOK BACK THROUGH TIME.
THIS WAS NEVER YOUR DESTINY...

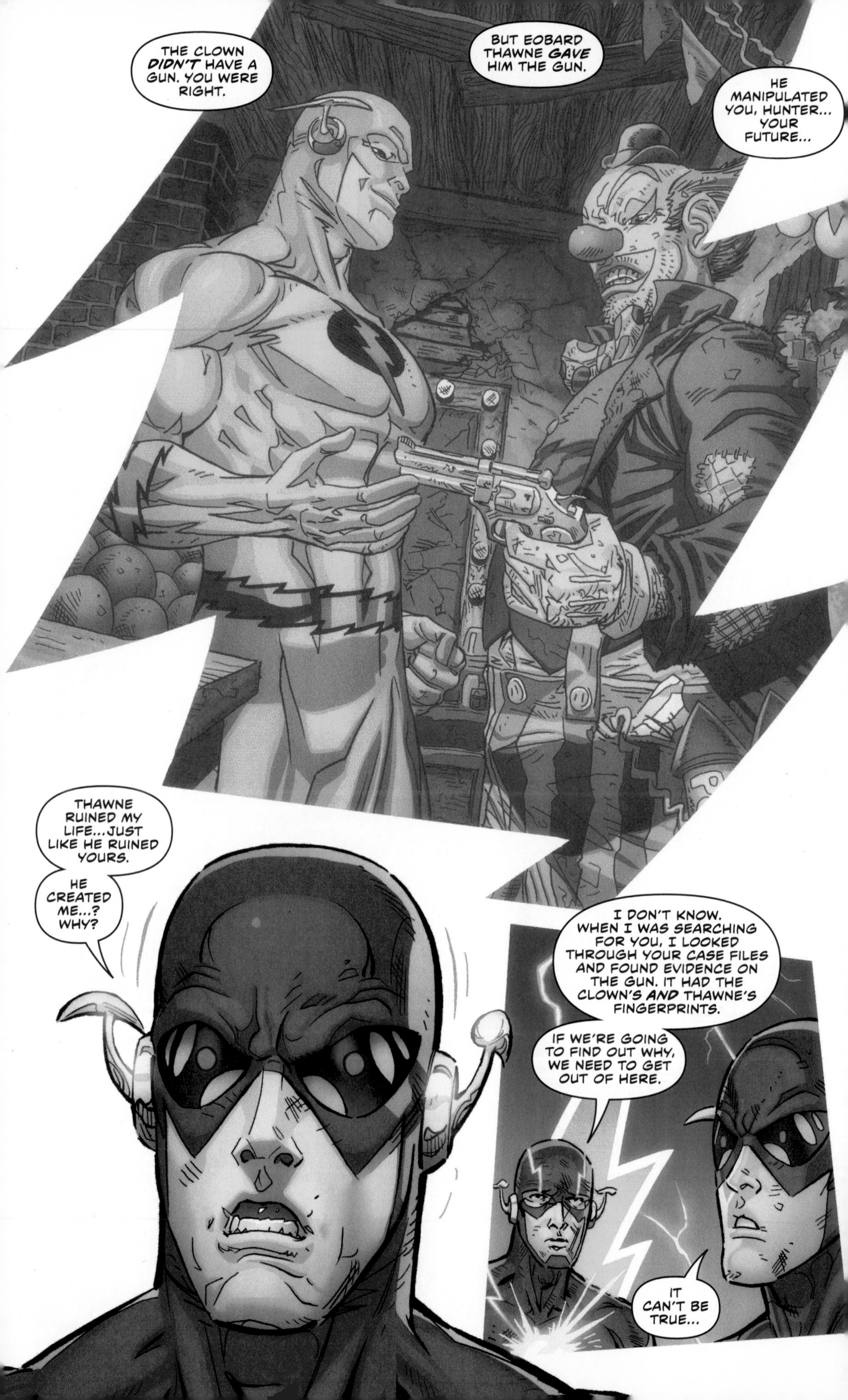

THE CLOWN DIDN'T HAVE A GUN. YOU WERE RIGHT.
BUT EOBARD THAWNE GAVE HIM THE GUN.
HE MANIPULATED YOU, HUNTER... YOUR FUTURE...
THAWNE RUINED MY LIFE...JUST LIKE HE RUINED YOURS.
HE CREATED ME...? WHY?
I DON'T KNOW. WHEN I WAS SEARCHING FOR YOU, I LOOKED THROUGH YOUR CASE FILES AND FOUND EVIDENCE ON THE GUN. IT HAD THE CLOWN'S AND THAWNE'S FINGERPRINTS.
IF WE'RE GOING TO FIND OUT WHY, WE NEED TO GET OUT OF HERE.
IT CAN'T BE TRUE...

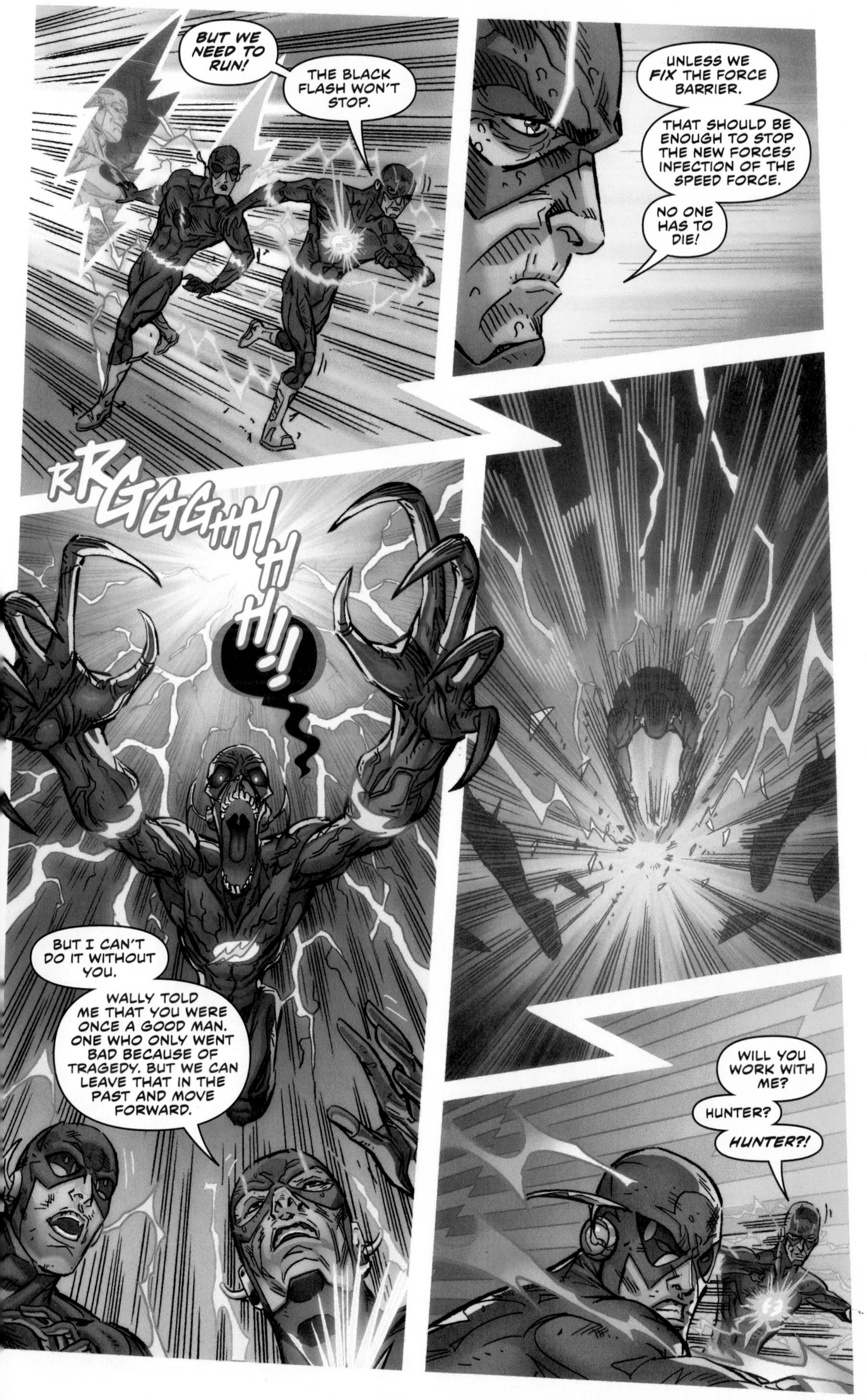

BUT WE NEED TO RUN!
THE BLACK FLASH WON'T STOP.
UNLESS WE *FIX* THE FORCE BARRIER.
THAT SHOULD BE ENOUGH TO STOP THE NEW FORCES' INFECTION OF THE SPEED FORCE.
NO ONE HAS TO DIE!
RRGGGHHHHH!!
BUT I CAN'T DO IT WITHOUT YOU.
WALLY TOLD ME THAT YOU WERE ONCE A GOOD MAN. ONE WHO ONLY WENT BAD BECAUSE OF TRAGEDY. BUT WE CAN LEAVE THAT IN THE PAST AND MOVE FORWARD.
WILL YOU WORK WITH ME?
HUNTER?
HUNTER?!

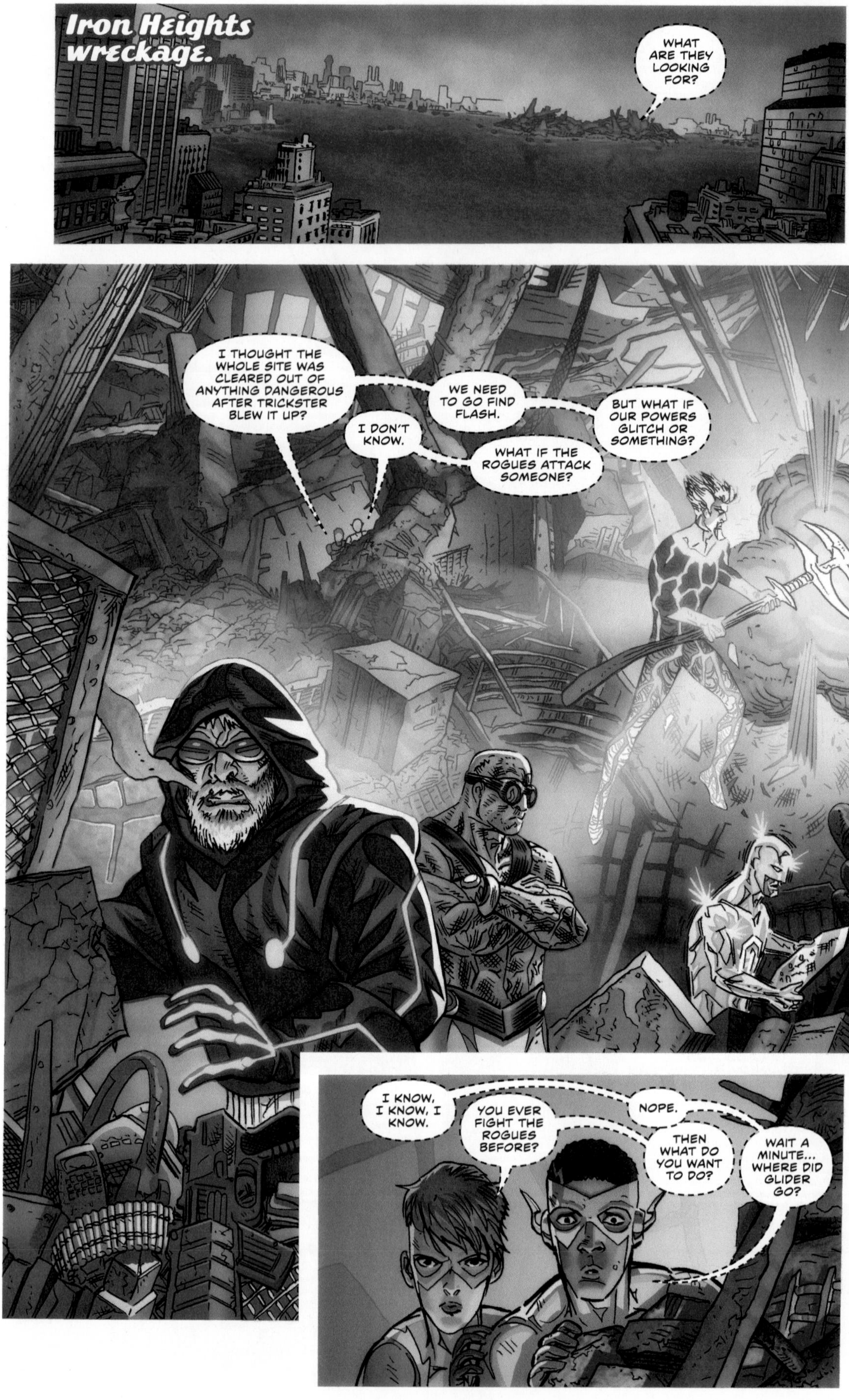
Iron Heights wreckage.
WHAT ARE THEY LOOKING FOR?
I THOUGHT THE WHOLE SITE WAS CLEARED OUT OF ANYTHING DANGEROUS AFTER TRICKSTER BLEW IT UP?
WE NEED TO GO FIND FLASH.
BUT WHAT IF OUR POWERS GLITCH OR SOMETHING?
I DON'T KNOW.
WHAT IF THE ROGUES ATTACK SOMEONE?
I KNOW, I KNOW, I KNOW.
YOU EVER FIGHT THE ROGUES BEFORE?
NOPE.
THEN WHAT DO YOU WANT TO DO?
WAIT A MINUTE... WHERE DID GLIDER GO?

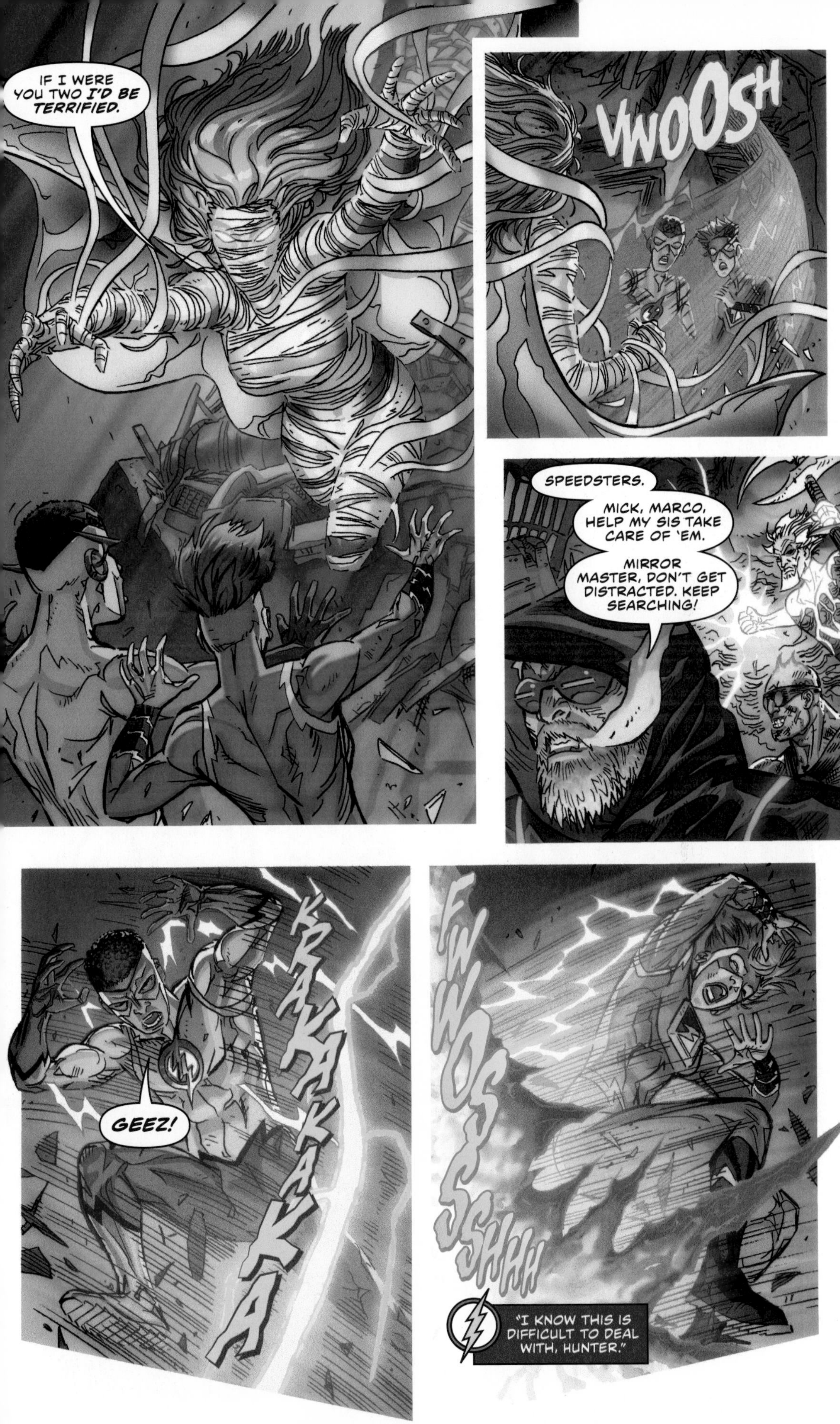
IF I WERE YOU TWO *I'D BE TERRIFIED.*
VWOOSH
SPEEDSTERS.
MICK, MARCO, HELP MY SIS TAKE CARE OF 'EM.
MIRROR MASTER, DON'T GET DISTRACTED. KEEP SEARCHING!
KRAKAKAKA
GEEZ!
FWOSSSSHHH
"I KNOW THIS IS DIFFICULT TO DEAL WITH, HUNTER."

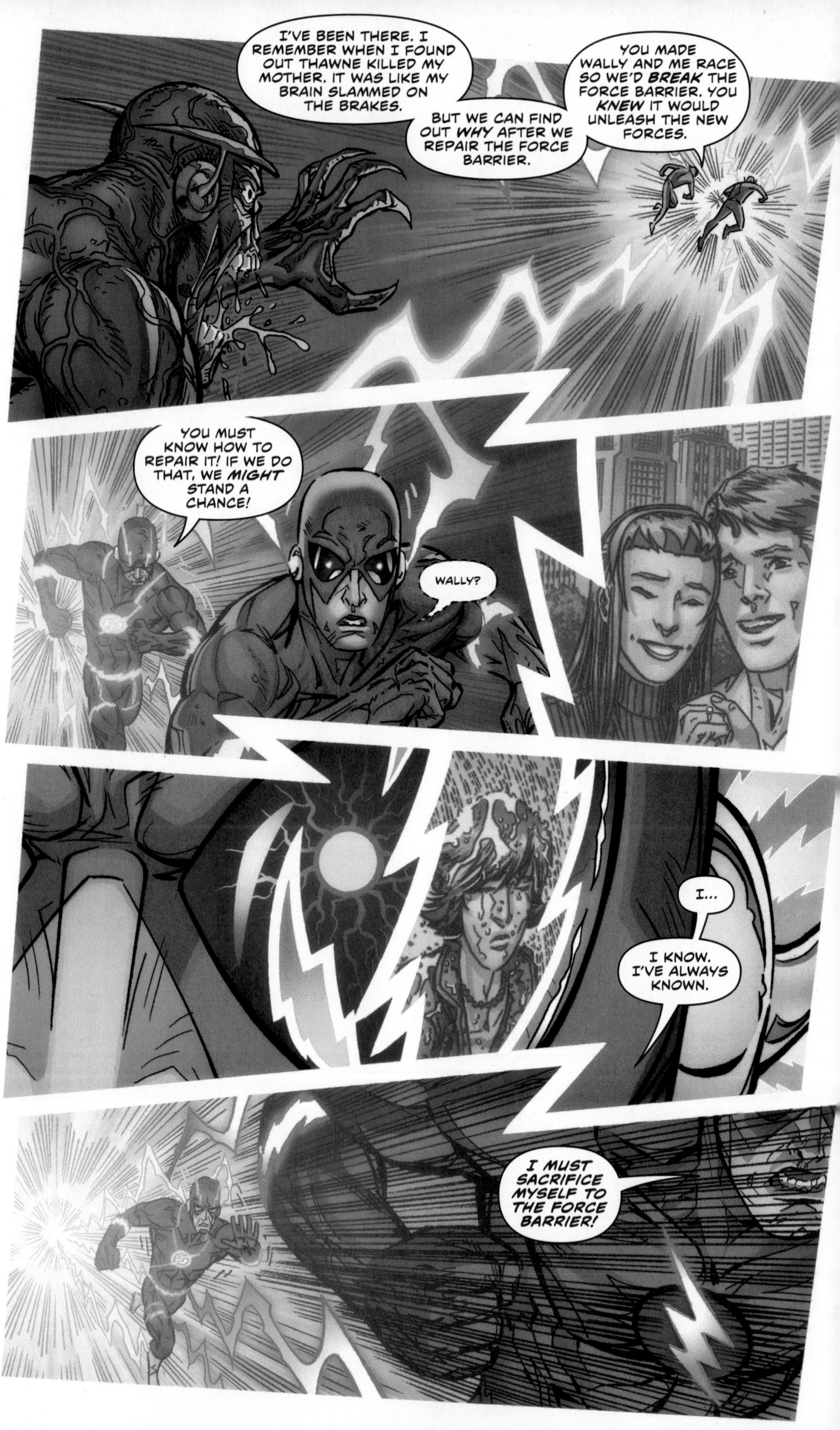
I'VE BEEN THERE. I REMEMBER WHEN I FOUND OUT THAWNE KILLED MY MOTHER. IT WAS LIKE MY BRAIN SLAMMED ON THE BRAKES.
BUT WE CAN FIND OUT WHY AFTER WE REPAIR THE FORCE BARRIER.
YOU MADE WALLY AND ME RACE SO WE'D BREAK THE FORCE BARRIER. YOU KNEW IT WOULD UNLEASH THE NEW FORCES.
YOU MUST KNOW HOW TO REPAIR IT! IF WE DO THAT, WE MIGHT STAND A CHANCE!
WALLY?
I...
I KNOW. I'VE ALWAYS KNOWN.
I MUST SACRIFICE MYSELF TO THE FORCE BARRIER!

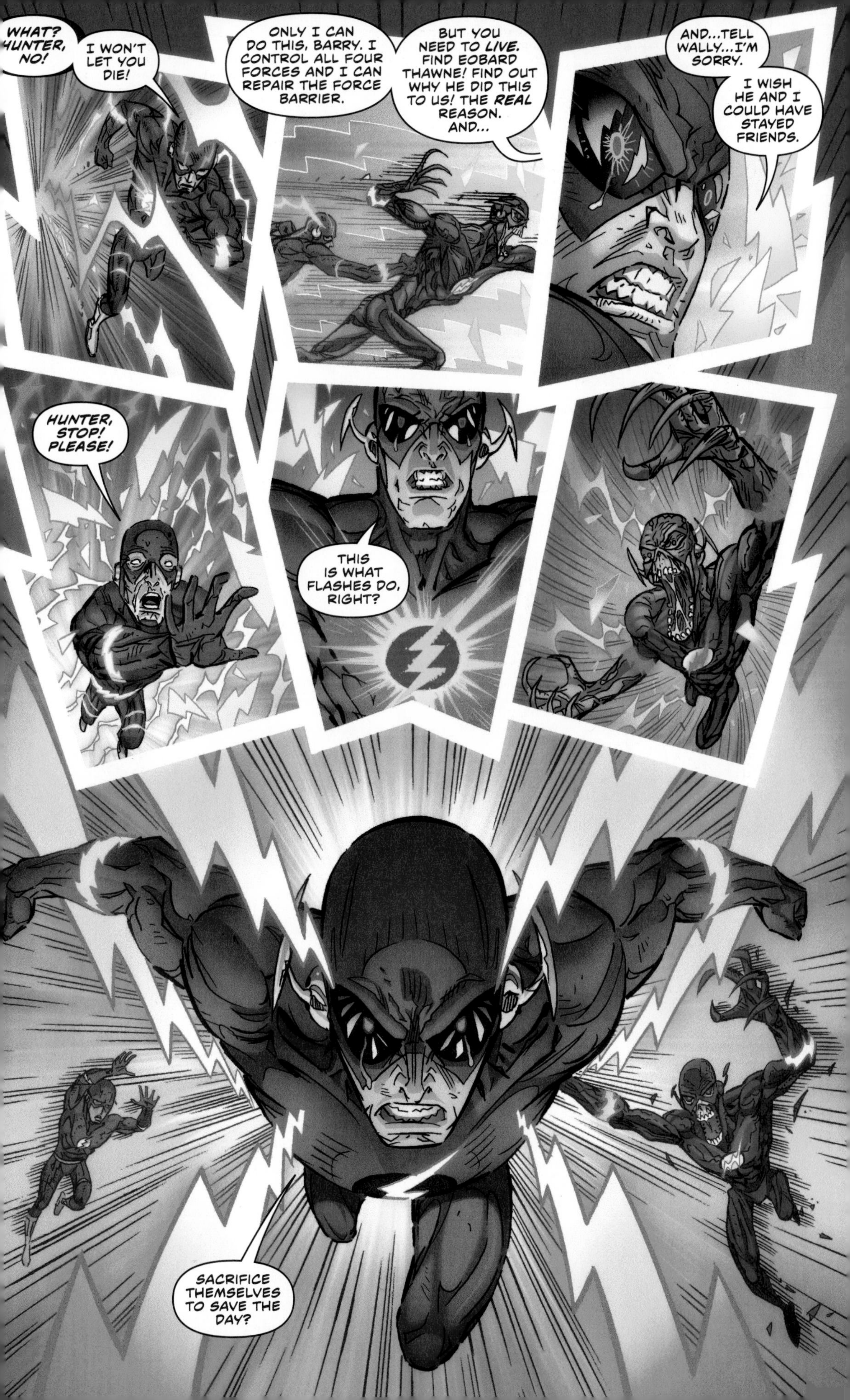
WHAT? HUNTER, NO!
I WON'T LET YOU DIE!
ONLY I CAN DO THIS, BARRY. I CONTROL ALL FOUR FORCES AND I CAN REPAIR THE FORCE BARRIER.
BUT YOU NEED TO *LIVE*. FIND EOBARD THAWNE! FIND OUT WHY HE DID THIS TO US! THE *REAL* REASON. AND...
AND...TELL WALLY...I'M SORRY.
I WISH HE AND I COULD HAVE STAYED FRIENDS.
HUNTER, STOP! PLEASE!
THIS IS WHAT FLASHES DO, RIGHT?
SACRIFICE THEMSELVES TO SAVE THE DAY?

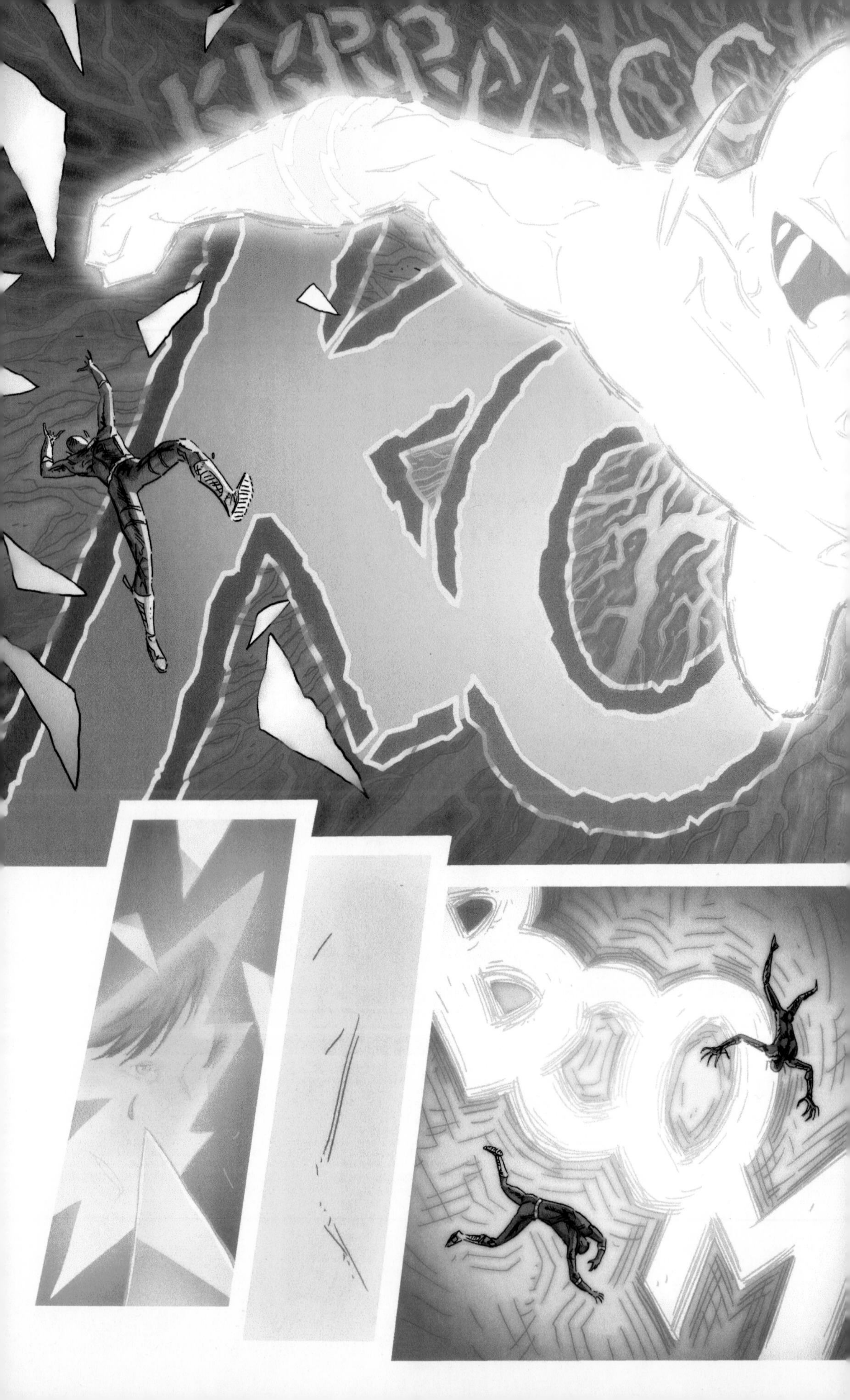
BOOM

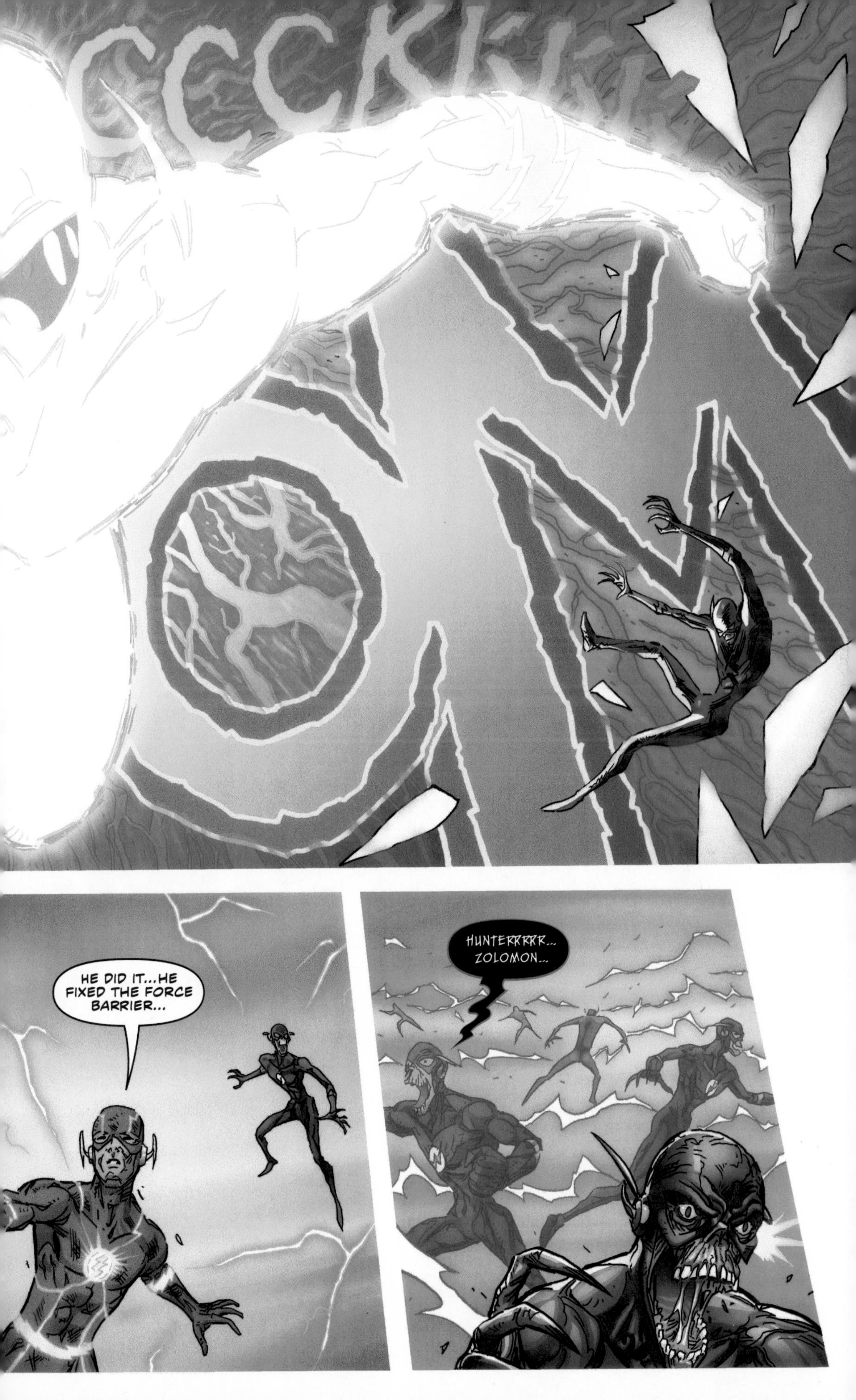
HE DID IT...HE FIXED THE FORCE BARRIER...
HUNTERRRRR... ZOLOMON...

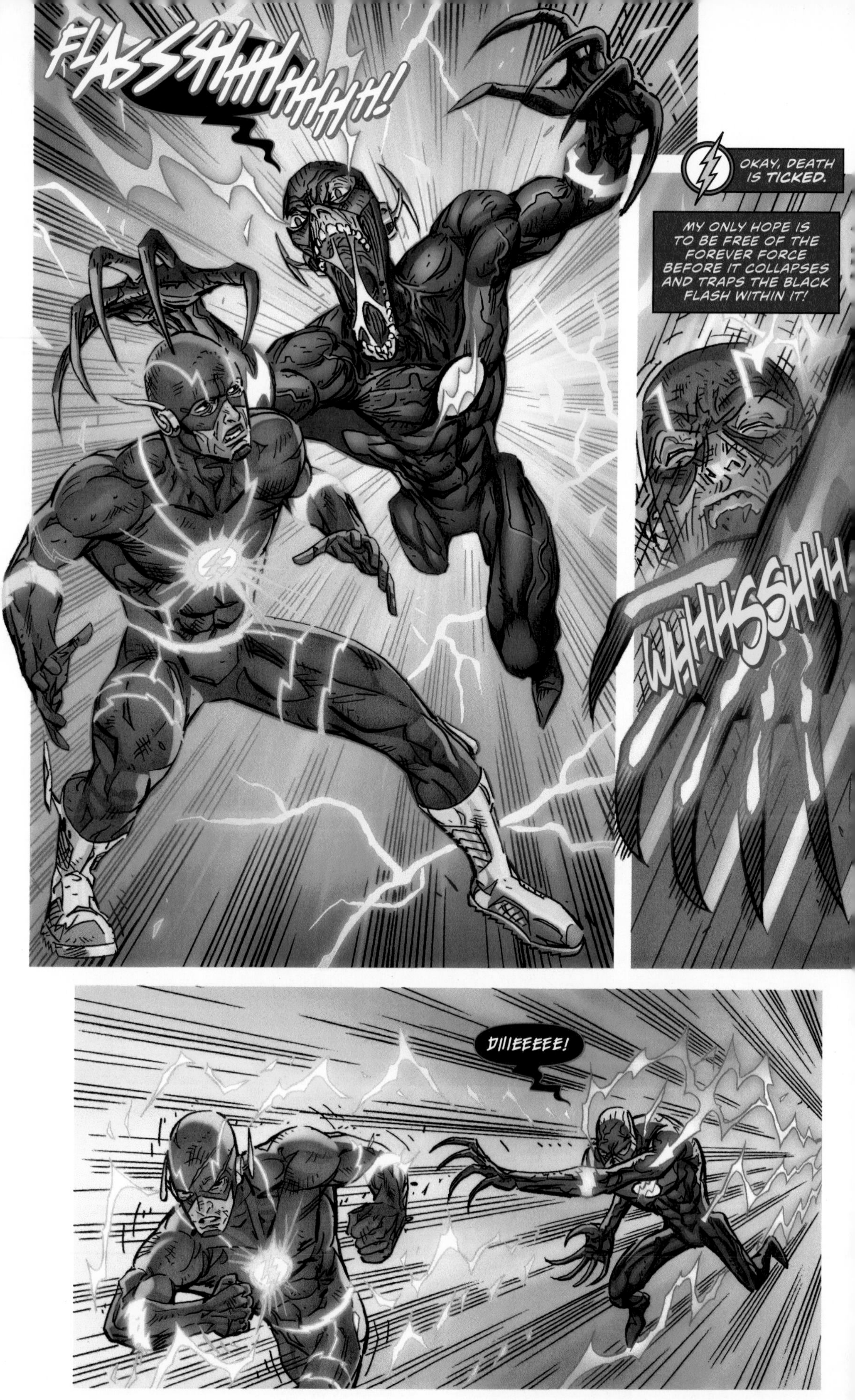
FLASSSHHHHHHHH!
OKAY, DEATH IS TICKED.
MY ONLY HOPE IS TO BE FREE OF THE FOREVER FORCE BEFORE IT COLLAPSES AND TRAPS THE BLACK FLASH WITHIN IT!
WHHSSHHH
DIIIEEEEE!

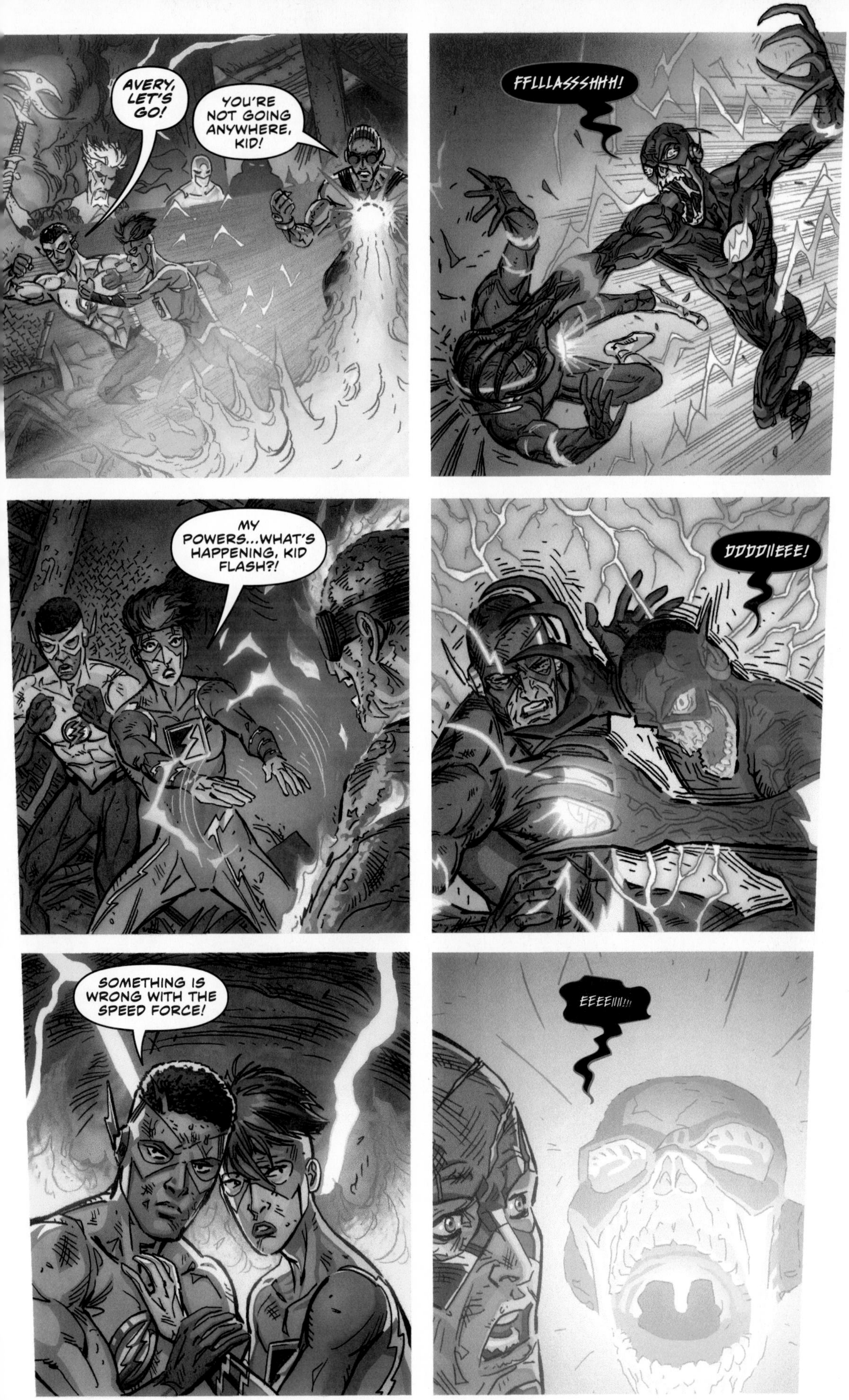
AVERY, LET'S GO!
YOU'RE NOT GOING ANYWHERE, KID!
FFLLLASSSHHH!
MY POWERS...WHAT'S HAPPENING, KID FLASH?!
DDDDIIEEE!
SOMETHING IS WRONG WITH THE SPEED FORCE!
EEEEIIII!!!

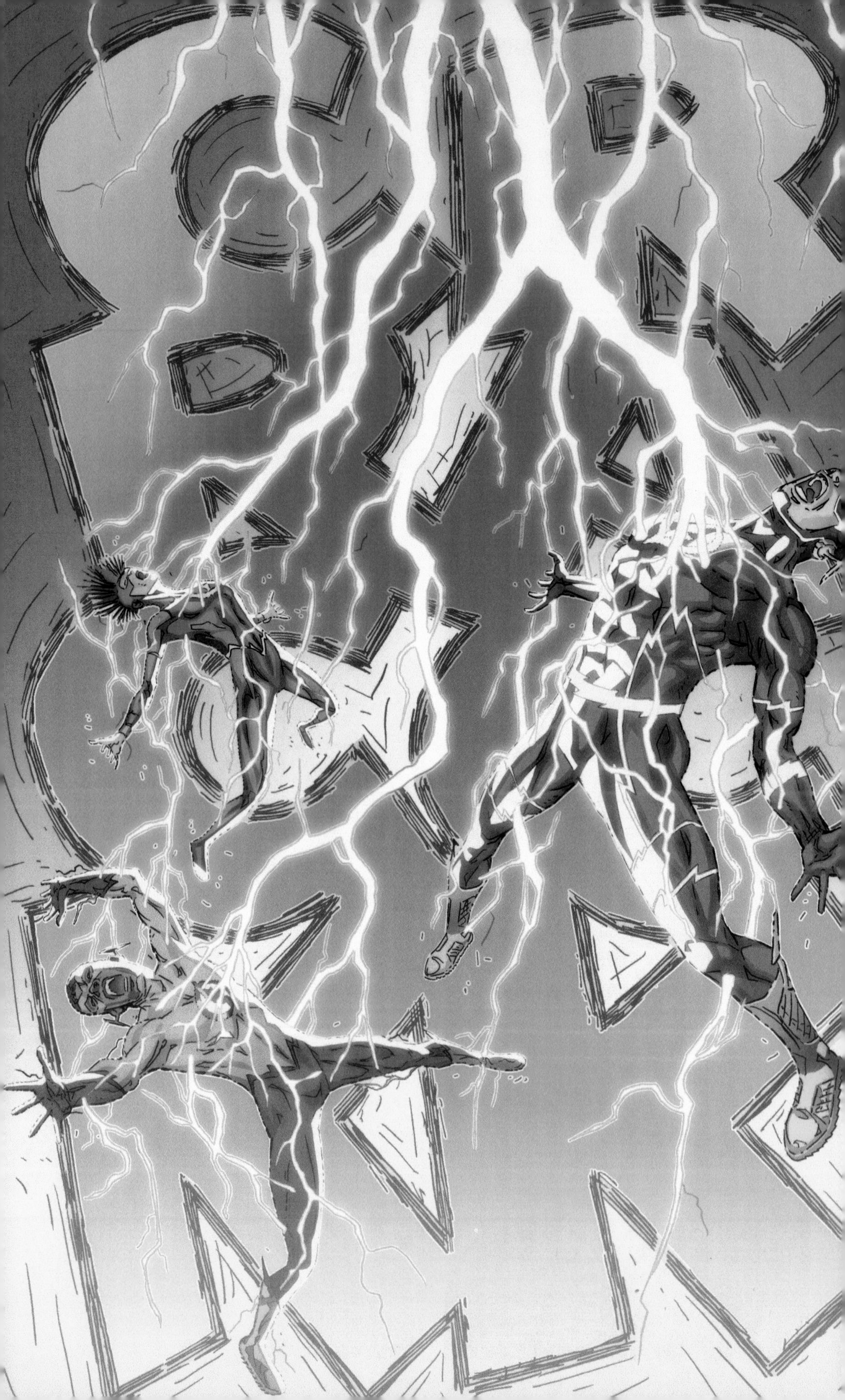

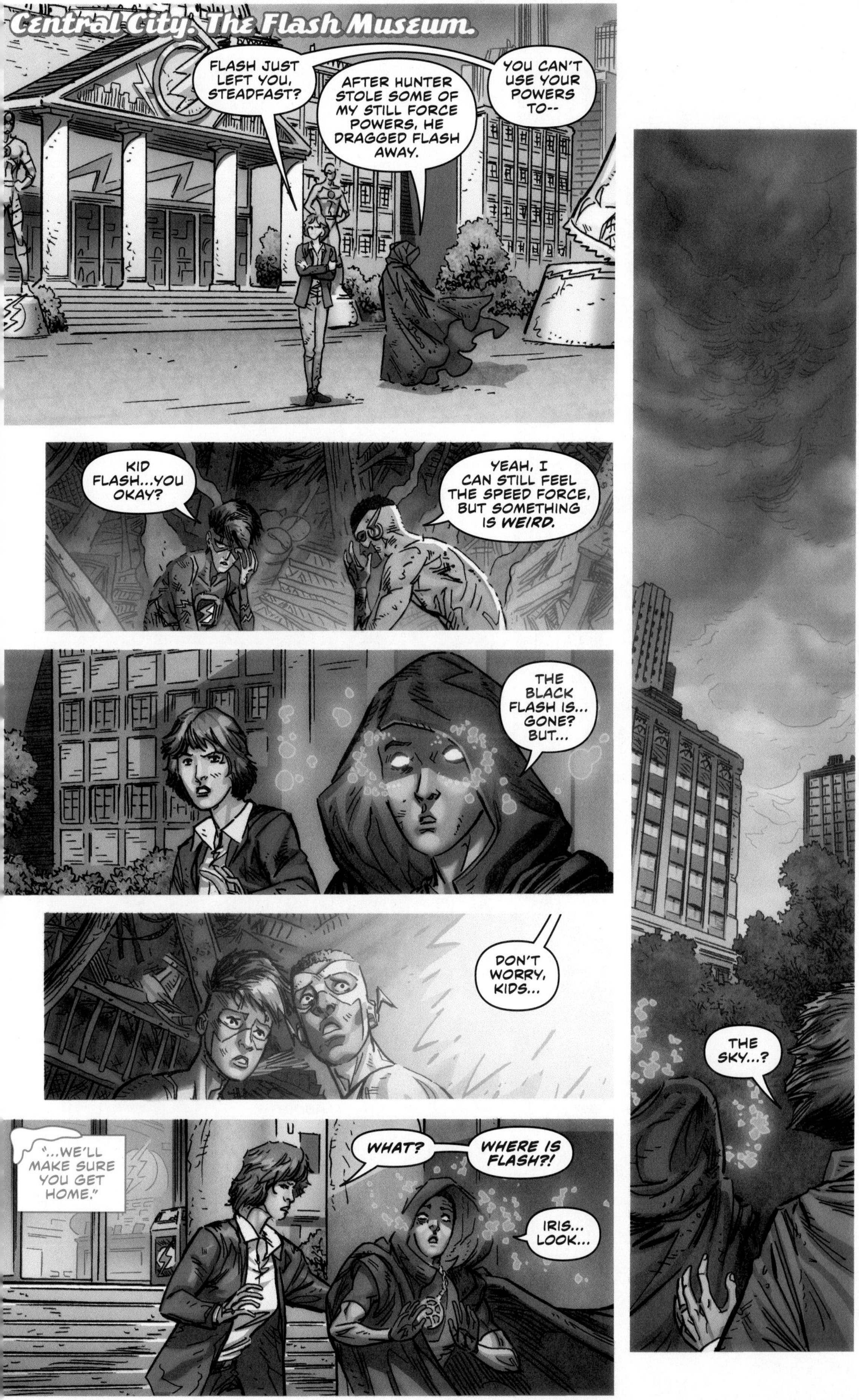

Central City. The Flash Museum.
FLASH JUST LEFT YOU, STEADFAST?
AFTER HUNTER STOLE SOME OF MY STILL FORCE POWERS, HE DRAGGED FLASH AWAY.
YOU CAN'T USE YOUR POWERS TO--
KID FLASH...YOU OKAY?
YEAH, I CAN STILL FEEL THE SPEED FORCE, BUT SOMETHING IS WEIRD.
THE BLACK FLASH IS... GONE? BUT...
DON'T WORRY, KIDS...
"...WE'LL MAKE SURE YOU GET HOME."
WHAT?
WHERE IS FLASH?!
IRIS... LOOK...
THE SKY...?

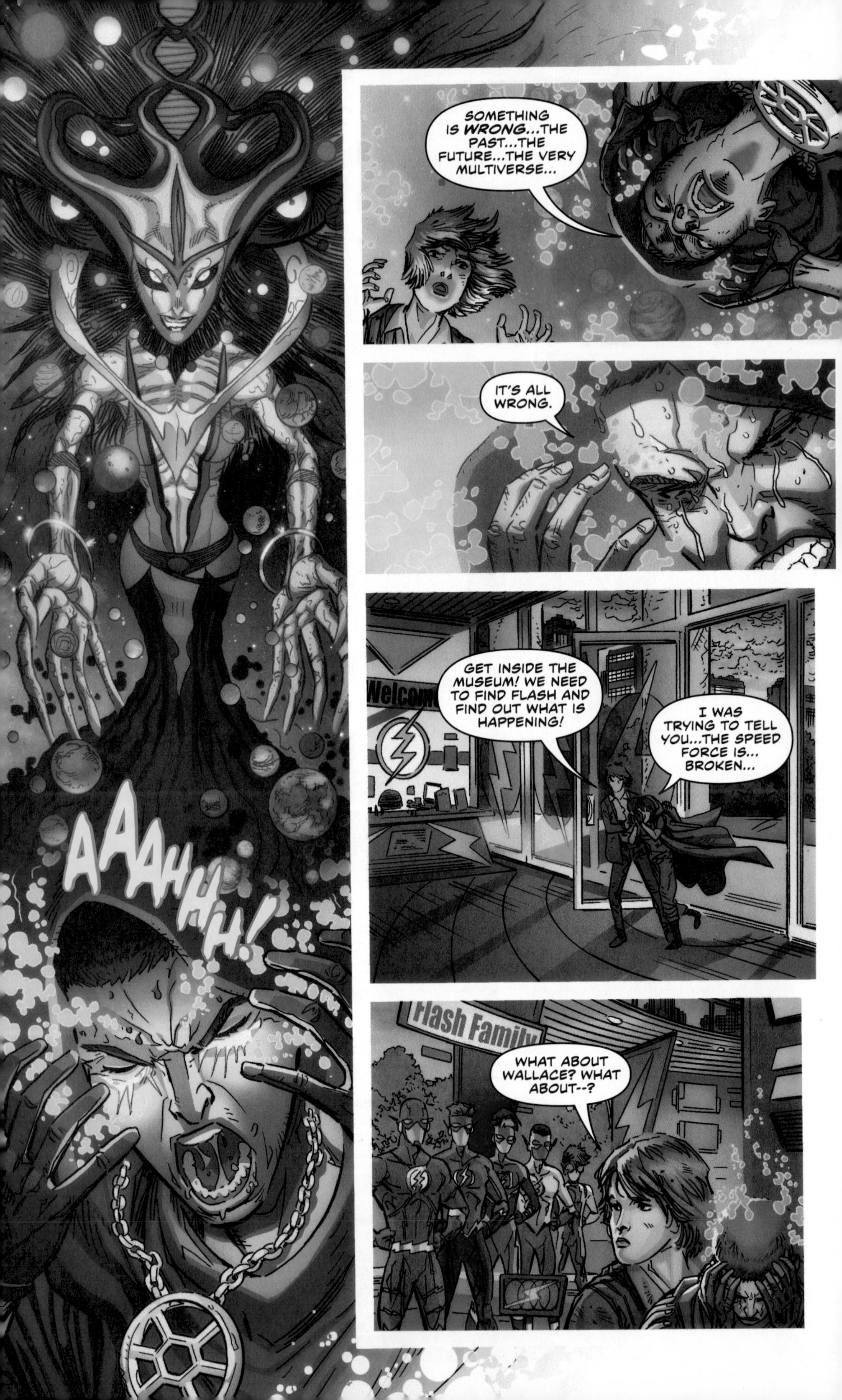
AAAHHHH!
SOMETHING IS WRONG...THE PAST...THE FUTURE...THE VERY MULTIVERSE...
IT'S ALL WRONG.
Welcome
GET INSIDE THE MUSEUM! WE NEED TO FIND FLASH AND FIND OUT WHAT IS HAPPENING!
I WAS TRYING TO TELL YOU...THE SPEED FORCE IS... BROKEN...
Flash Family
WHAT ABOUT WALLACE? WHAT ABOUT--?

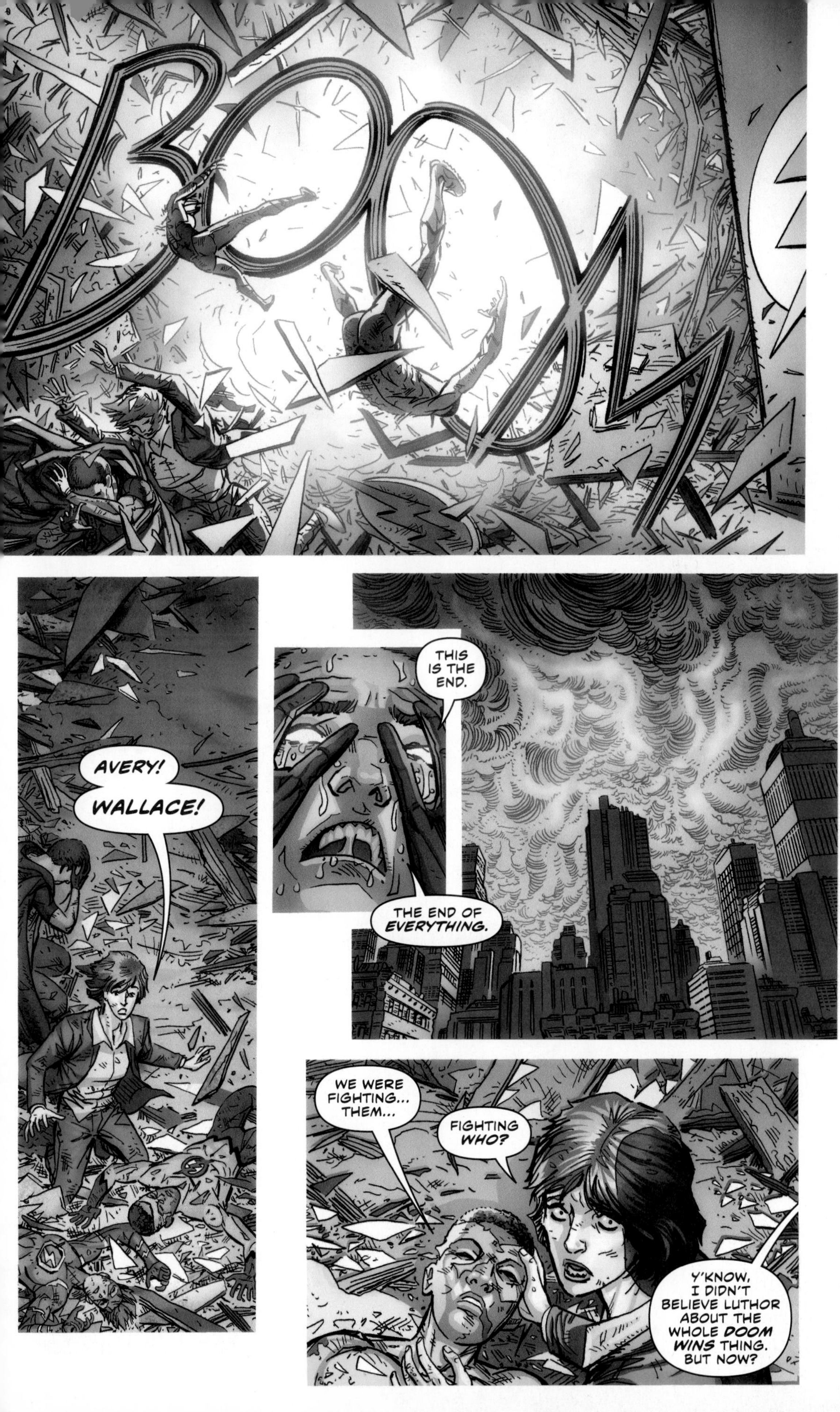
BOOM
AVERY!
WALLACE!
THIS IS THE END.
THE END OF EVERYTHING.
WE WERE FIGHTING... THEM...
FIGHTING WHO?
Y'KNOW, I DIDN'T BELIEVE LUTHOR ABOUT THE WHOLE DOOM WINS THING. BUT NOW?

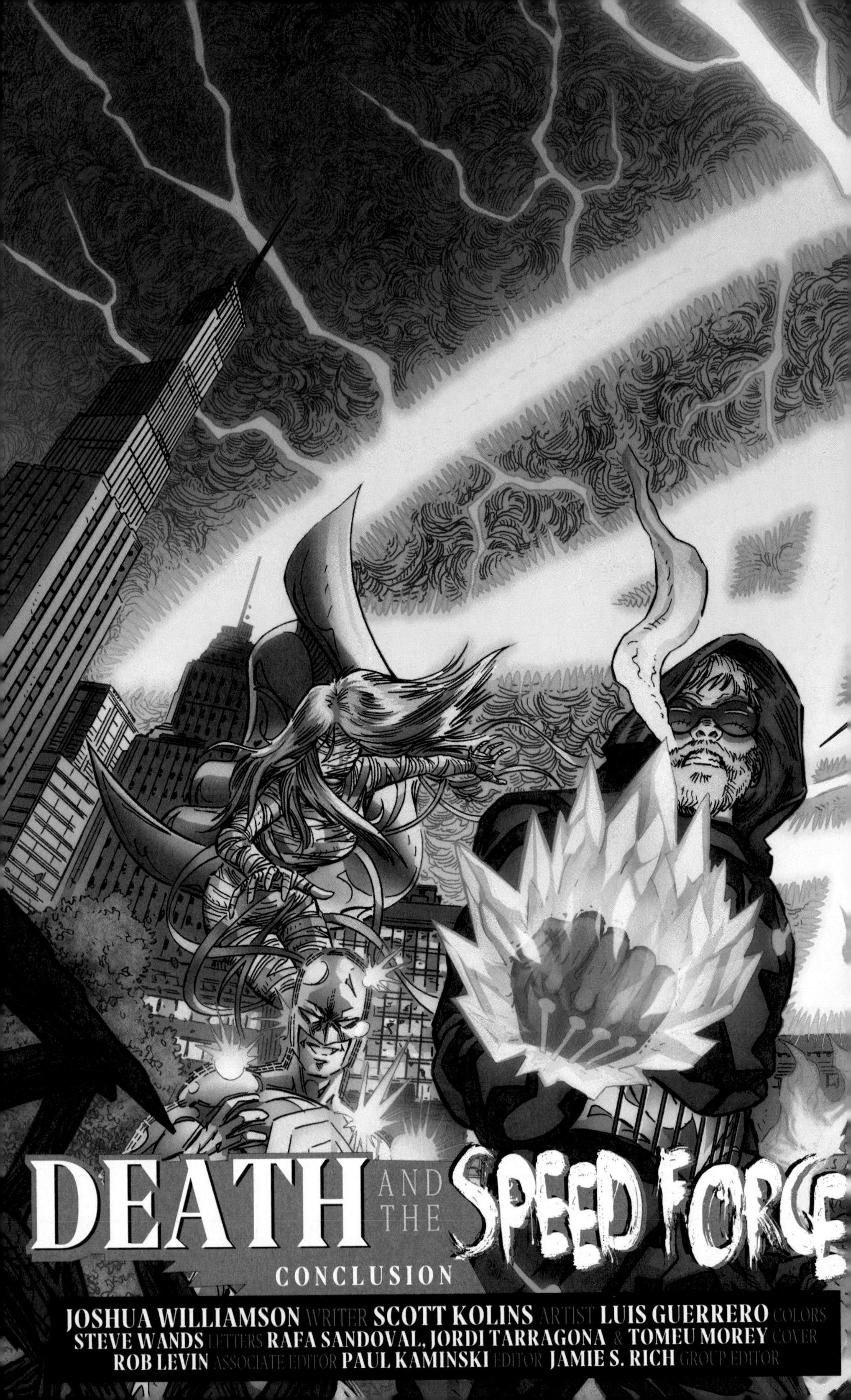
DEATH AND THE SPEED FORCE
CONCLUSION
JOSHUA WILLIAMSON WRITER SCOTT KOLINS ARTIST LUIS GUERRERO COLORS
STEVE WANDS LETTERS RAFA SANDOVAL, JORDI TARRAGONA & TOMEU MOREY COVER
ROB LEVIN ASSOCIATE EDITOR PAUL KAMINSKI EDITOR JAMIE S. RICH GROUP EDITOR

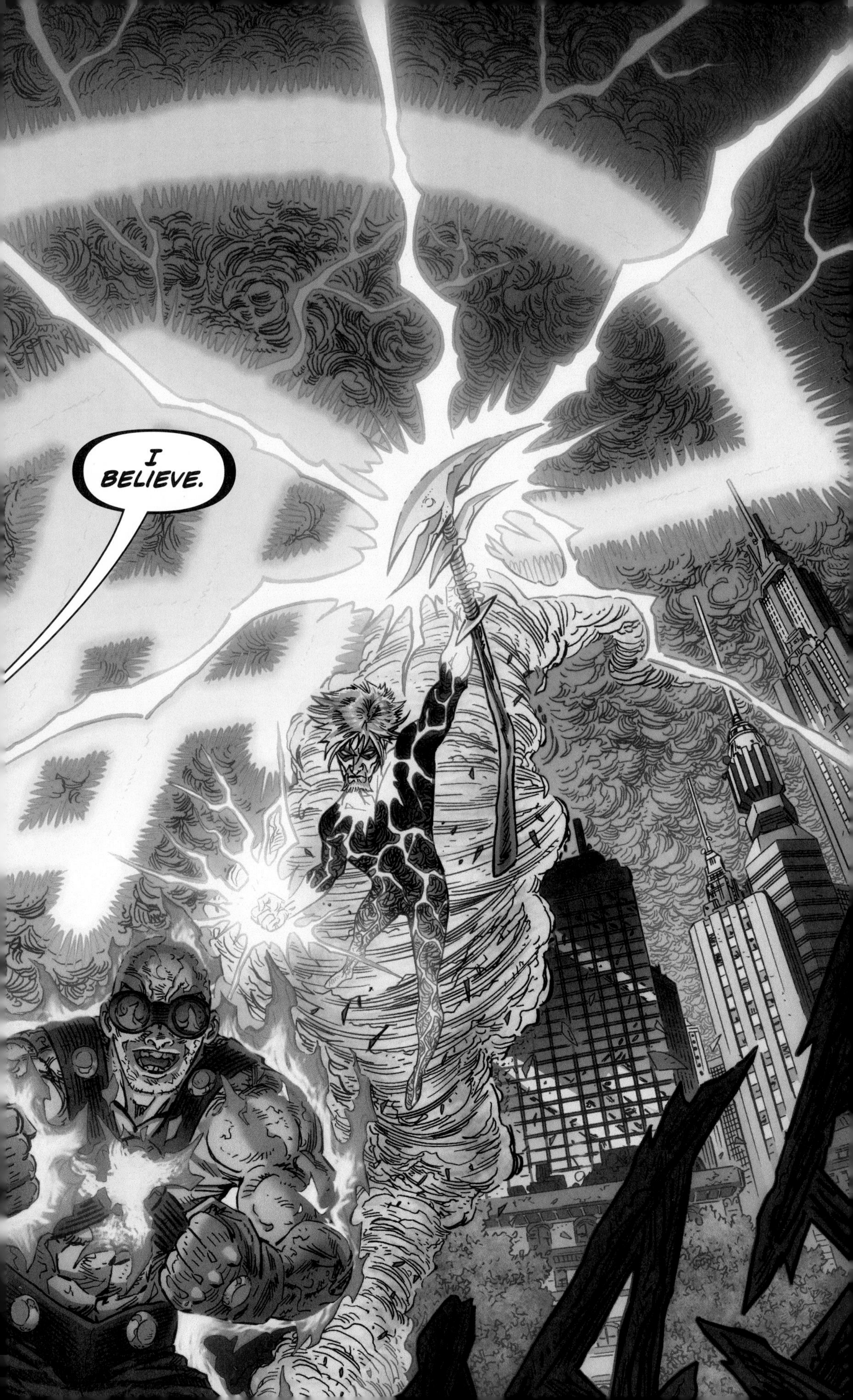
I BELIEVE.

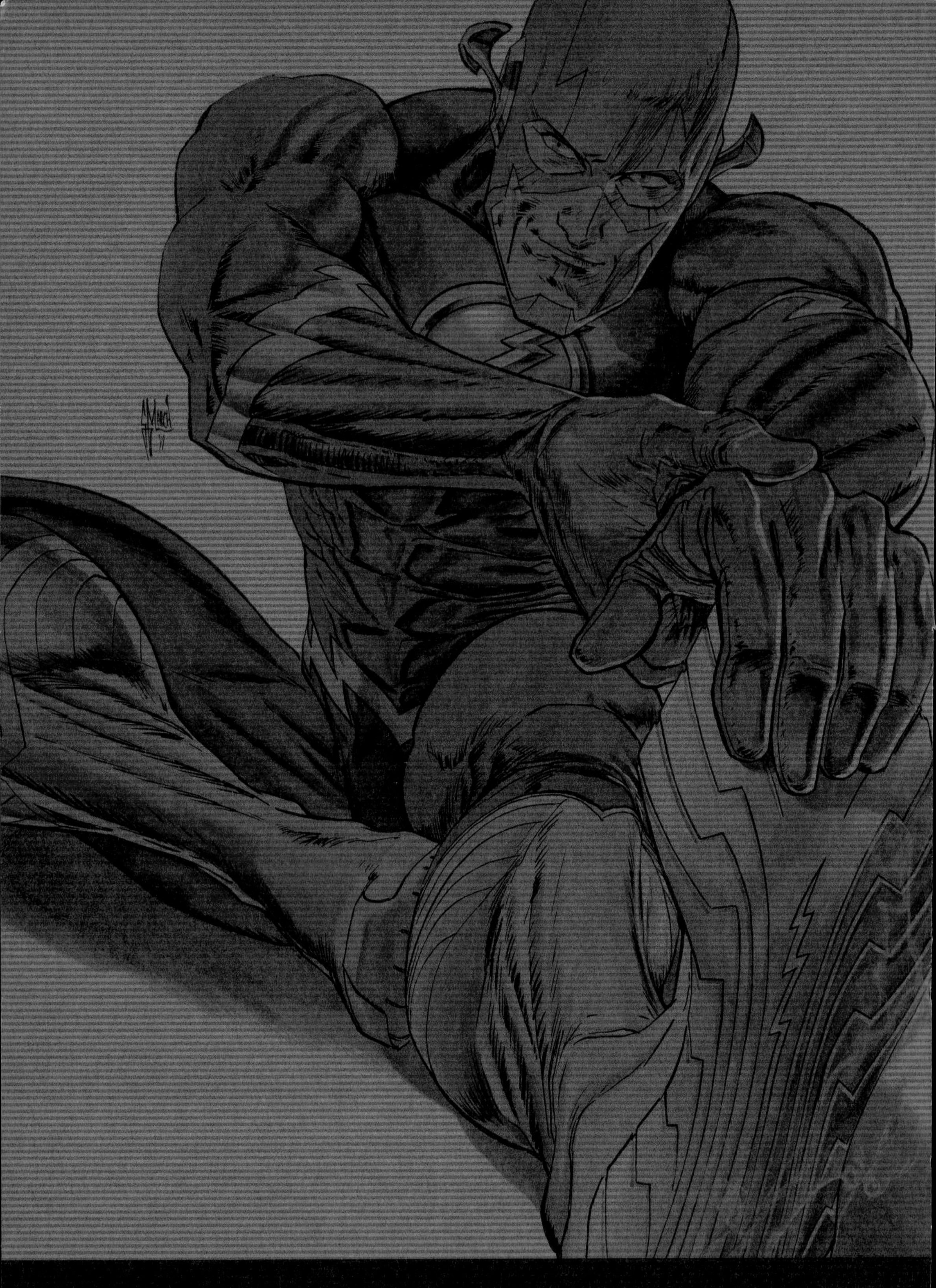

VARIANT COVER GALLERY

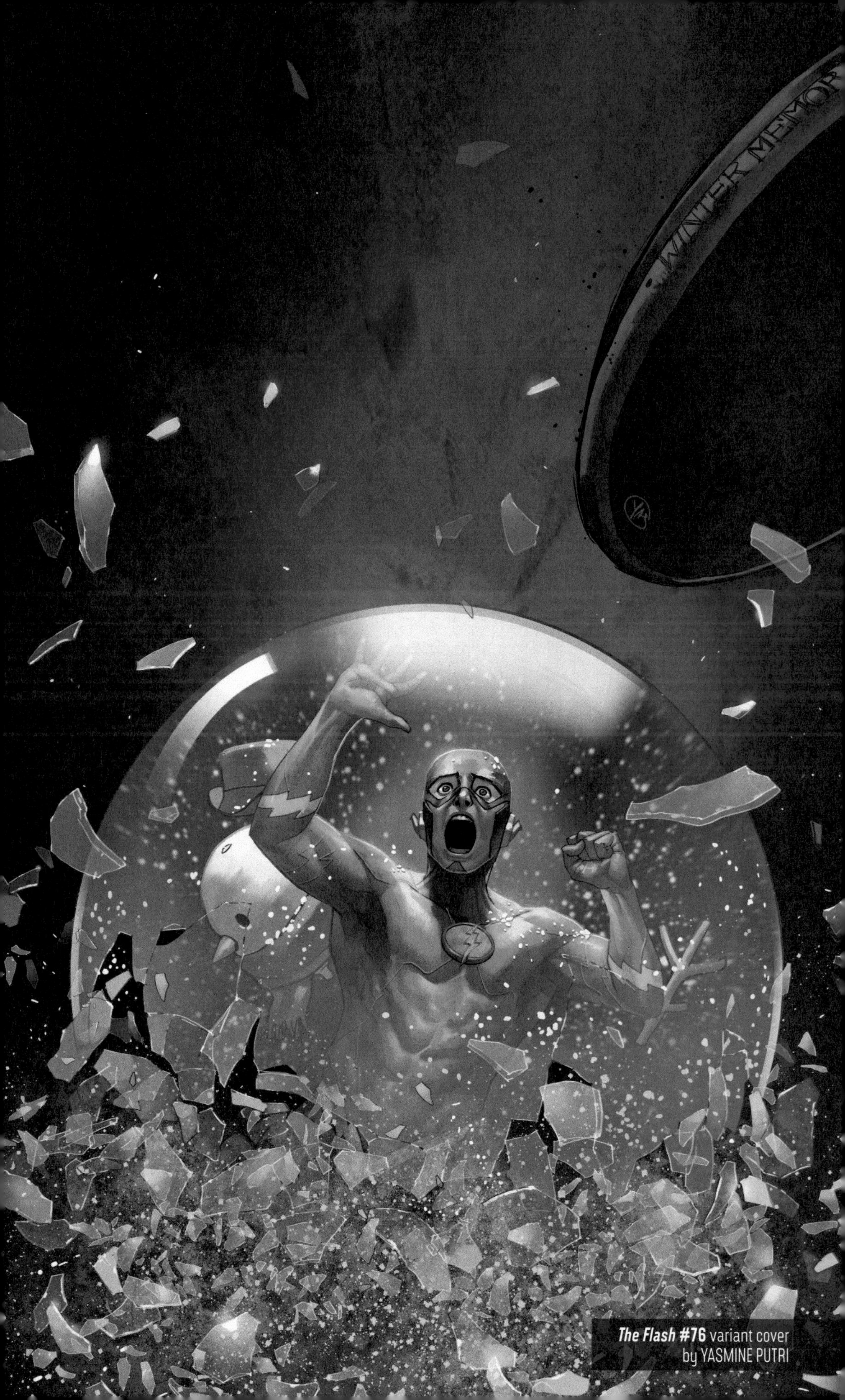
WINTER MEMOR

The Flash **#76** variant cover
by YASMINE PUTRI

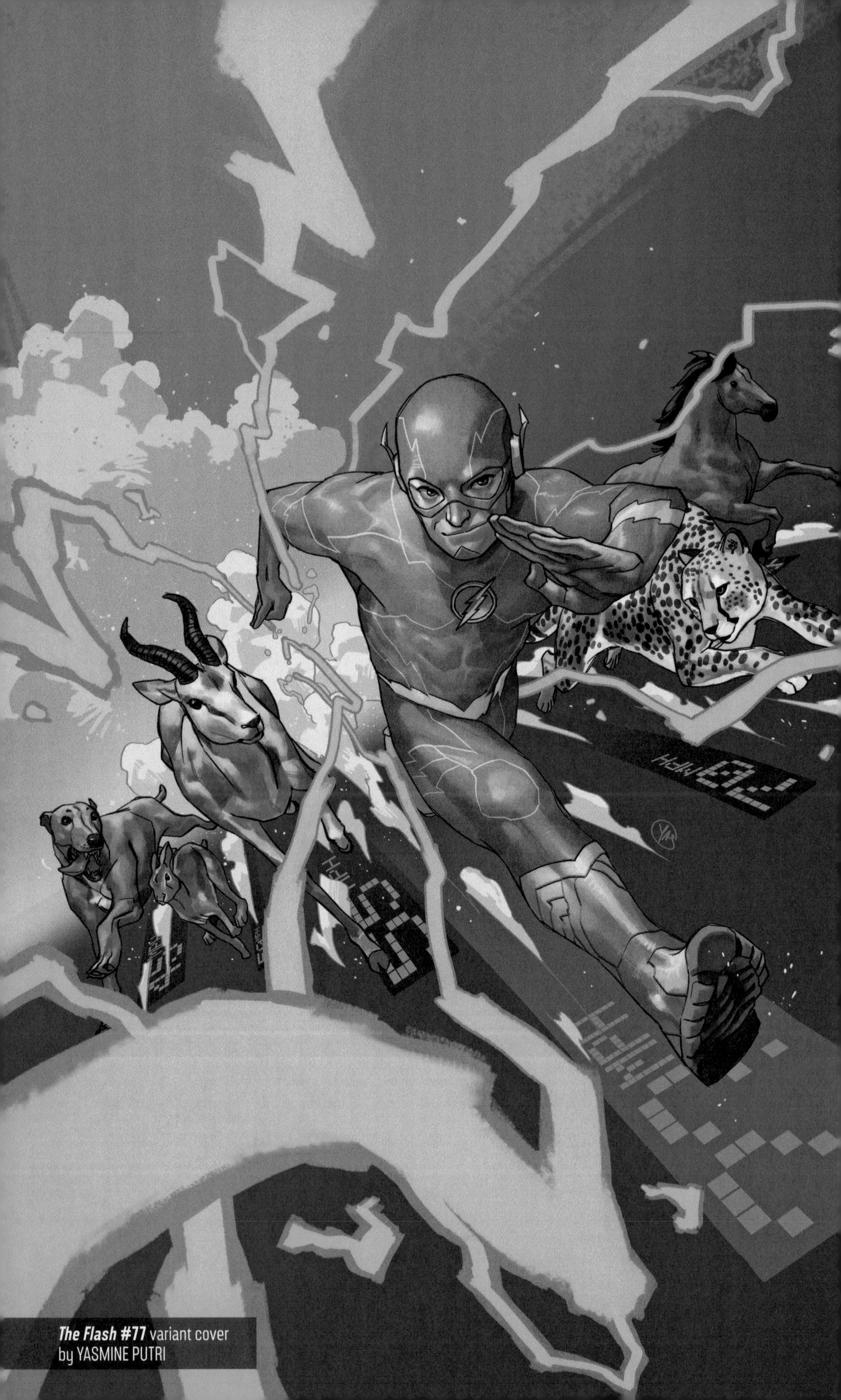

***The Flash* #77** variant cover
by YASMINE PUTRI

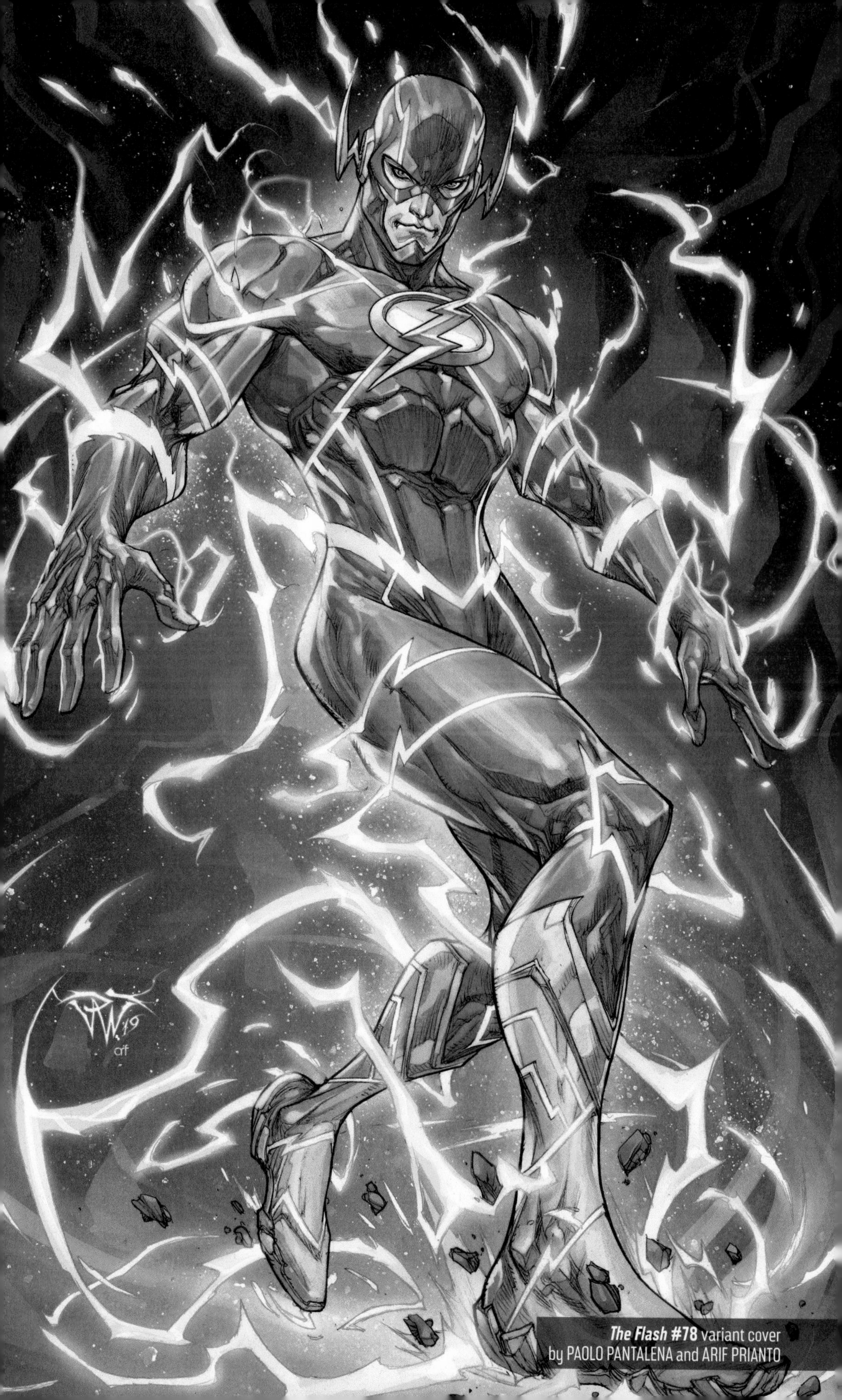

***The Flash* #78** variant cover
by PAOLO PANTALENA and ARIF PRIANTO

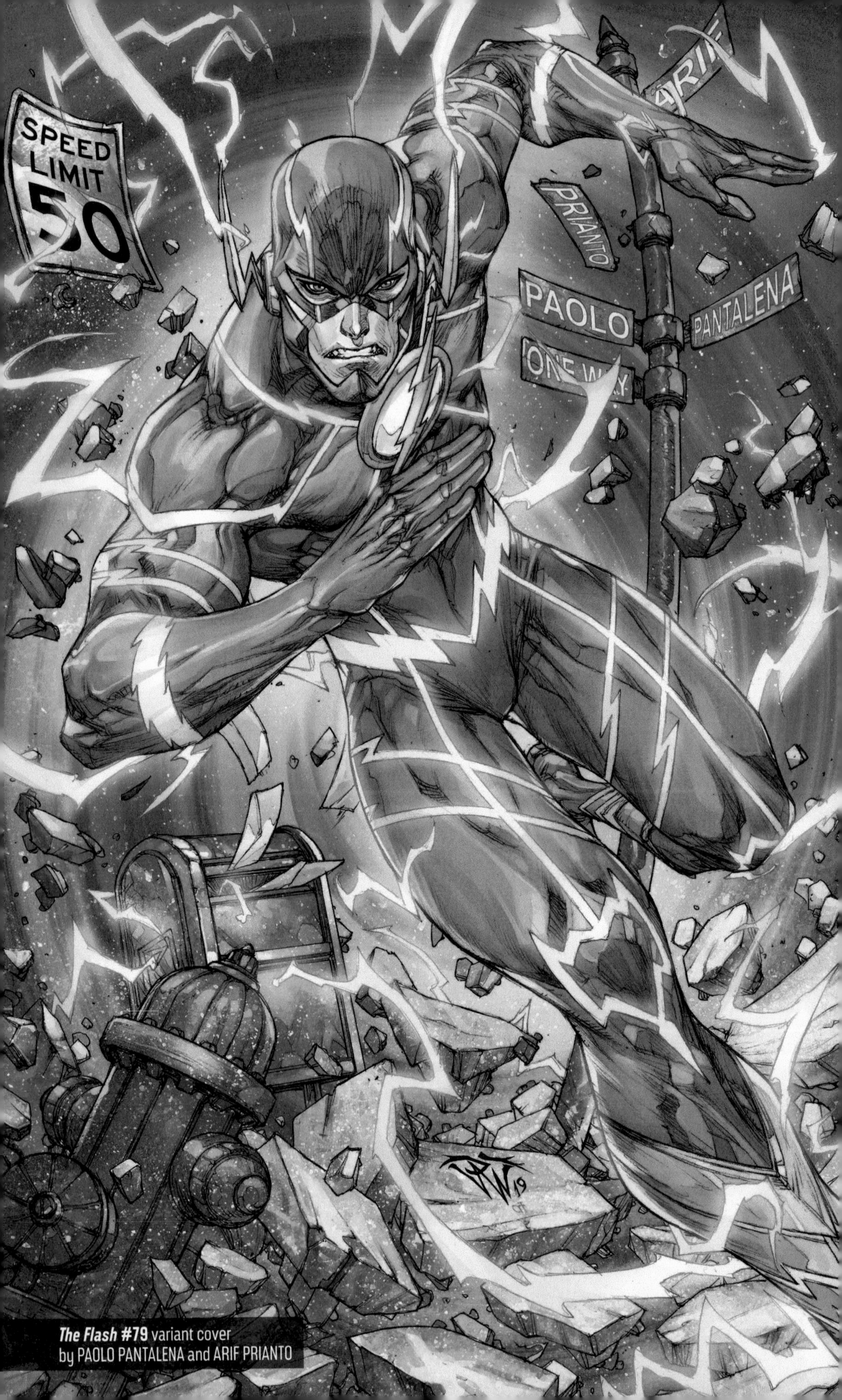

SPEED
LIMIT
50
PRIANTO
PAOLO
PANTALENA
ONE WAY

The Flash **#79** variant cover
by PAOLO PANTALENA and ARIF PRIANTO

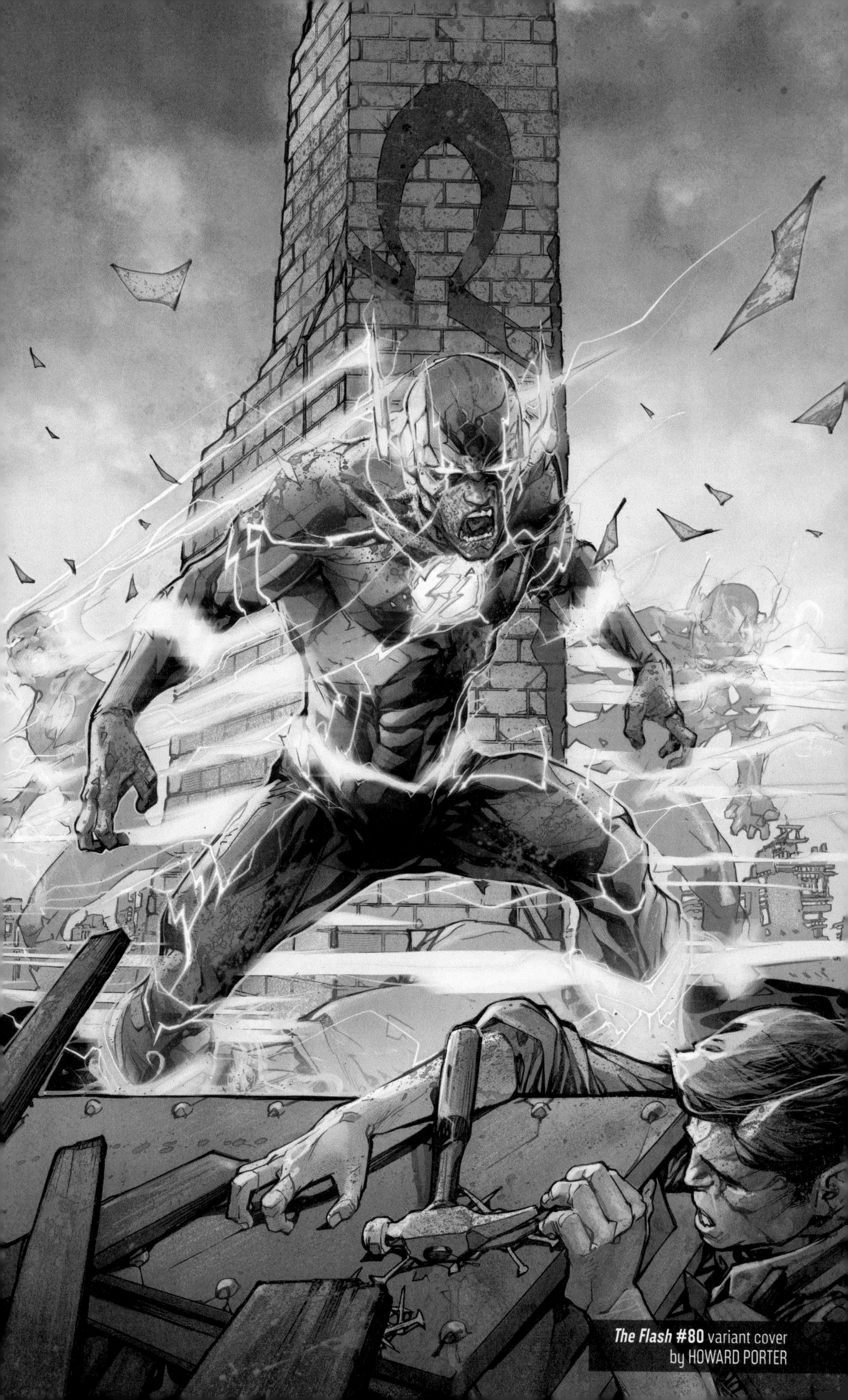

The Flash **#80** variant cover
by HOWARD PORTER

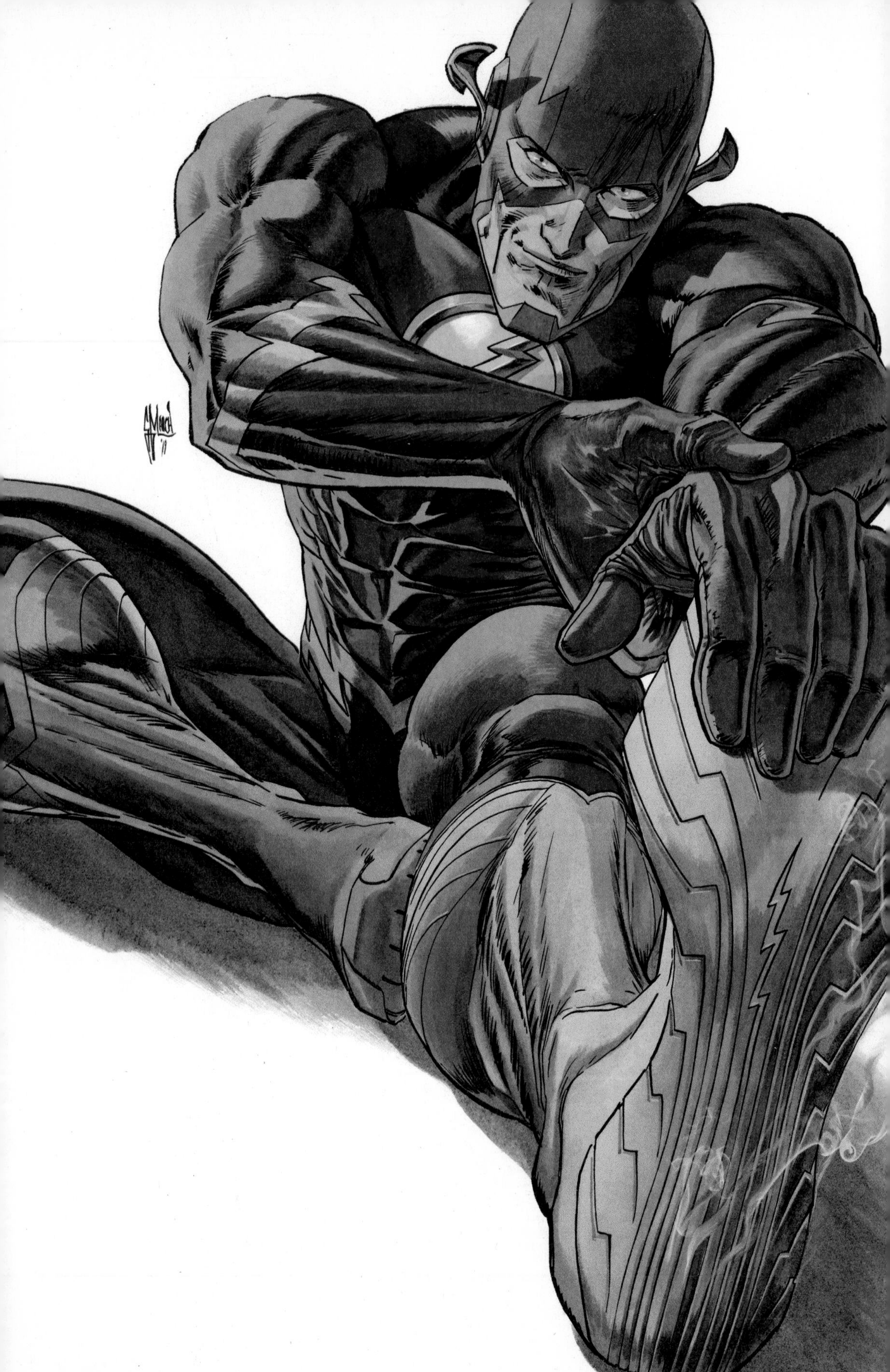

***The Flash* #81** variant cover
by GUILLEM MARCH